Milton's Cambridge Latin

Performing in the Genres 1625–1632

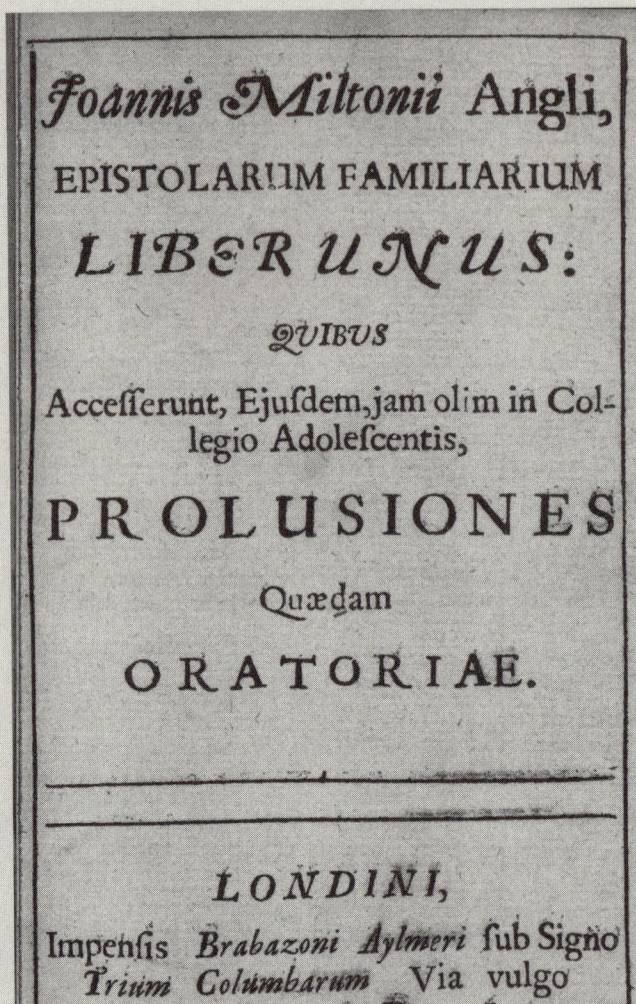

Title-page of first edition of Milton's Cambridge speeches (the University exercises which it terms Prolusions). The seven prolusions were added to the 1674 volume of his private letters when the intended accompaniment, his state letters, was vetoed by the licenser. Translation: "John Milton Englishman's / Familiar Letters / One Book / to which / have been added from the same writer when long / since a / young man at College / certain / oratorical / Prolusions / London, / at the expense of Brabazon Aylmer at the Sign / of the Three Pigeons on the Street vernacularly / called Cornhill, in the year of our Lord 1674." Reproduced by kind permission of the Alexander Turnbull Library, Wellington, New Zealand.

Milton's Cambridge Latin

Performing in the Genres 1625–1632

by

John K. Hale

Arizona Center for Medieval and Renaissance Studies
Tempe, Arizona

© Copyright 2005

Arizona Board of Regents for Arizona State University

Library of Congress Cataloging-in-Publication Data

Hale, John K.
  Milton's Cambridge Latin : performing in the genres, 1625–1632 / by John K. Hale.
    p. cm. — (Medieval and Renaissance text and studies ; v. 289)
    Includes bibliographical references.

  ISBN-13: 978-0-86698-332-7 (alk. paper)
  1. Milton, John, 1608–1674—Knowledge—Rome. 2. Milton, John, 1608–1674—Knowledge—Language and languages. 3. Milton, John, 1608–1674—Homes and haunts—England—Cambridge. 4. Latin philology—Study and teaching—England—Cambridge—History—17th century. 5. Cambridge (England)—Intellectual life—17th century. 6. English literature—Roman influences. I. Title. II. Series.

PR3592.R65H35 2005
821'.4—dc22

2005021090

∞
This book is made to last.
It is set in Adobe OpenType WarnockPro
on acid-free paper to library specifications.

Printed in the United States of America

Medieval and Renaissance Texts and Studies

Volume 289

Contents

Illustrations
Abbreviations
Preface
Introduction ... 1

PART ONE: Milton and the University Exercises ... 13
  1. Disputations ... 15
  2. Milton's Philosophic Verses and the Cambridge Act Verses ... 33
  3. Declamations ... 67
  4. Milton's Last Declamation, Prolusion VII: (In Sacrario habita pro Arte. Oratio.Beatiores reddit Homines Ars quam Ignorantia.) ... 91
  5. The Cambridge Exercises and the *Defence of the English People* ... 107

PART TWO: Voluntaries ... 123
  6. Praising Dead Worthies, 1626 ... 127
  7. The University Anthologies ... 147
  8. *In Quintum Novembris* and the other Gunpowder Poems ... 163

PART THREE: For the College Community ... 185
  9. Milton Plays the Fool: Prolusion VI and "At a Vacation Exercise" ... 195
  10. Further Perspectives ... 221

PART FOUR: *Milton's Salting* (editio princeps) ... 237
Text and Translation
  Milton's Salting: Text History and Problems of the Texts ... 239
  Oratio ... 243
  Prolusio ... 269

Bibliography ... 295
Index ... 301

Illustrations

Title-page of first edition of Milton's *Prolusiones Oratoriae*, 1674   ii

A disputation in the Divinity School, Oxford, by Ackermann   14

Act verses in MS by Alexander Bolde   42–43

Beginning of Milton's declamation, Prolusion I   78

Beginning of Milton's salting text, Prolusion VI: Oratio   243

Close of the salting Oratio   266

Beginning of second piece of Milton's salting text: Prolusio   269

Transition between second and third pieces of salting   288

End of extant, third piece of Milton's salting   293

Alexander Bolde's act verses in manuscript are reproduced by permission of the Master and Fellows of St John's College, Cambridge.

Ackermann's picture of a disputation, and the pages and passages from Milton's 1674 Prolusions *and from his* Poems 1673, *are reproduced by kind permission of the Alexander Turnbull Library, Wellington, New Zealand.*

Front cover caricature by Murray Webb.
The young John Milton, toga-clad and laurel-wreathed, is based on the "Onslow" portrait. He is orating in Latin in the University Schools. The combination of Romanized behaviour with Scholastic and Gothic forms typifies the Cambridge of 1625-1632.

Back cover photograph of the author by Bill Murphy, October 2004.

Abbreviations

BLN	*John Milton. Latin Writings. A Selection*, ed. and trans. John K. Hale. Bibliotheca Latinitatis Novae. Assen: van Gorcum and Tempe: MRTS, 1998.
Bush, Variorum	Douglas Bush, ed., *A Variorum Commentary on the Poems of John Milton*, vol. 1. New York: Columbia University Press, 1970.
Carey	John Carey, ed., *John Milton. Complete Shorter Poems*, 2nd ed. London: Longman, 1997.
ColWks	*The Works of John Milton*, gen. ed. Frank Allen Patterson. The Columbia Edition. 18 vols. + 2 index vols. New York: Columbia University Press, 1931-1940.
French *LR*	*The Life Records of John Milton*, ed. J. Milton French. 5 vols. New Brunswick, NJ: Rutgers University Press, 1949-1958.
LS	*A Latin Dictionary*, ed. Charlton T. Lewis and Charles Short. First pub. 1879: 1962 impression from Oxford: Clarendon Press, 1962.
ML	John K. Hale, *Milton's Languages. The Impact of Multilingualism on Style*. Cambridge: Cambridge University Press, 1997.
Parker	William Riley Parker, *Milton. A Biography*, rev. by Gordon Campbell. 2 vols. Oxford: Clarendon Press, 1996.
R.E.E.D.	Alan H. Nelson, ed. *Records of Early English Drama. Cambridge.* 2 vols. Toronto: University of Toronto Press, 1989.
Tillyards	Phyllis B. and E. M. W. Tillyard, *Milton. Private Correspondence and Academic Exercises.* Cambridge: Cambridge University Press, 1932.
YPW	Don M. Wolfe et al., eds. *Complete Prose Works of John Milton*. 8 vols. New Haven: Yale University Press, 1953-1982.

Preface

This study takes in new directions some parts of my monograph *Milton's Languages* (1997) and of my selection *John Milton: Latin Writings* (1998). It thinks about what Latin meant for Milton by examining on their own terms the student writings which were only touched on in the monograph. Similarly, though my view of his Cambridge life is foreshadowed in the selection, and developed in essays which underlie the present study, I am now bringing together their scattered analyses and hints. The intention is to see Milton's compositions from the inside, hence again with full respect for their original tongue, but now equally for the conditions of understanding set by their genres. The intention is to see them not solely as compositions, either, but as performances. The oral dimension of most of these writings is vital for understanding the tone and the relations of performer to audience.

I use the Latin texts, Milton's own and extant congeneric ones, to investigate what it was like to be Milton at his Cambridge compositions and performances. We often hear the performances deprecated as mere exercises, or (to push the blame from Milton onto the Cambridge curriculum) as merely "the University at its Exercises." By reading the texts in close conjunction with their conditions of understanding, however, these being historical and anthropological as well as linguistic and literary, we shall know Milton better, at a formative time.

Through case-studies of the Latin, then, I seek to recover a distinctive phase of his life. Milton is presented in considerable depth, in a study of his imagination at work in the Latin which was second nature to him, and was the first language of Cambridge itself.

I gratefully acknowledge help received for this undertaking, from scholars and friends, libraries, audiences, and journals.

Scholars who helped by answering questions or listening to me include these: Michael Black, Greg Dening, Peter Gathercole, Pierre Gorman, Jonathan Hall, Yasmin Haskell, Felicity Henderson, Elisabeth Leedham-Green, the late Jeremy Maule, David Money, John Morrill, Alan Nelson, Joseph Saunders, Peter Searby, Beverley Sherry, and Jan

Waszink. I am grateful to Katherine Liddy and Katharine Hale for help with proof-reading; to Paul Sorrell with transcriptions as well, although the mistakes which remain are all my own work; and to Irene Sutton with the manuscript.

Libraries which helped with manuscript material relating to the Cambridge exercises and rituals in Milton's epoch include Caius College, Christ's College, Pembroke College, Queens' College, St John's College, Trinity College, and the University Library, all in Cambridge. Further libraries which provided access to relevant books and journals include the Alexander Turnbull Library (Wellington), the Baillieu Library (Melbourne University), the Library of the Harvard Divinity School, and the Widener Library (Harvard), the University of Leiden Library, and the University of Otago Library.

Audiences who heard early versions of parts or aspects of the work and helped by suggestions or questions include the Cambridge Society for Neo-Latin Studies, the Leiden Early-Modern Seminar, and at Otago the departmental seminars of Anthropology, Classics, and English.

Portions of the work have appeared as essays in journals, to whose editors I am grateful: *Classical and Modern Literature*, for much of Chapter 9; *Humanistica Lovaniensia*, for part of Chapter 2 and for Chapter 8; and the *University of Melbourne Library Journal*, for which I wrote an early overview. Portions of the text and translation of Milton's salting have appeared in *John Milton. Latin Writings. A Selection* (Assen: van Gorcum, 1998), a volume of their series Bibliotheca Latinitatis Novae, shared with MRTS. Similarly with my version of *De Idea Platonica*. My thanks to both publishers and to the series editor, Jan Waszink.

Finally, I thank the University of Otago and the Department of English for help with publication costs; and the readers and staff of MRTS for their vigilant and acute help.

The dedication records a longer-standing debt, to Darwin College, Cambridge. Darwin has been my sabbatical home since 1981. It has been my best counterpart to those Italian academies which Milton so admired on his own 1638-1639 sabbatical. It has been the model of a generous, enlightened intellectual community.

—Dunedin, September, 2005

The work is dedicated to

Darwin College

Cambridge

Introduction

The Cambridge Latin Genres

When Milton went up to Cambridge University in 1625, Latin ruled supreme in large areas of its life. Across Europe and into the Americas Latin enabled international exchange, both intellectual and diplomatic. In England at large it provided the agreed language of memorial, and conferred intellectual credibility on many a public occasion. Where royalty travelled, Latin would be heard alongside the mother tongue; indeed, if anything, the succession of the Scottish dynasty in 1603—the advent of the intellectually aspiring James VI and I—gave Latin a greater prominence.

Certainly this was true of Cambridge, which he loved to visit, customarily after a day of his obsessive hunting nearby at Newmarket. Latin debates, and speeches and Latin plays, would follow his arrival, "as the night the day." These oral Latin performances would sometimes involve Latin verses.

All this Latin vociferation for royalty represented no departure from Cambridge normality, for Cambridge believed in Latin speech-acts for more everyday purposes too. The speeches and debates and verses which could fascinate the intellectual monarch on his visits were also the staple expression of the University's public face, its training and routine and curriculum—in fact its selfhood in so far as a large institution can have one. Like the universities across Europe, Cambridge measured itself by the quality of its Latin expression, and turned on its best Latin for kings and ambassadors. These high personages, indeed, could join in the debating if they wished. James, famously, did.

As for students, it was through regular Latin tasks that they were being trained by the University in logic or oratory, and more optional skills like verse. The logic and oratory tasks were of a set kind, regulated by the University and its constituent colleges alike. Although tutors at the colleges, including Milton's, taught their pupils other subjects and could use the mother tongue to do so, and although there is testimony to dislike of the established Latin performances on the part of many (including many of the ablest, such as Bacon and Milton himself), there is a countervailing body of evidence that the Latin was enjoyed by many others. Late in the seventeenth century a Latin disputation drew an Oxford audience of *thousands* to the Sheldonian Theatre. Latin disputation was thought to improve one's reasoning and eristic powers.[1]

Milton in his time did all the required tasks. He throve at some. He did many of the more voluntary ones, and throve at these even more. He kept his scripts, he printed them in later life, and in short he perpetuated by eventual print the fine reputation which he had won at Cambridge by his Latin. As the anonymous biographer puts it:

> At about eighteen yeers of age hee went to Christs College in Cambridge; where for his diligent study, his performance of public exercises, and for choice Verses, written on the occasions usually solemniz'd by the Universities,[2] as well as for his virtuous and sober life, hee was in high esteem with the best of his time.[3]

It is important here to note that Milton was engaged in "performance" of some of his Latin scripts, out loud. A study of the Latin offers the best available way of recovering such performance aspects as Milton's interactions with his audiences, and his reception by them.

The present work, accordingly, undertakes to examine these unfamiliar texts, and not so much in translation (though translation is of course provided) but in and through their Latinity. The work is a series of case-studies, taking the relevant Cambridge genres one by one to show what each gave to Milton, composing and performing in them. It seeks to recover what he then made the given genres mean, what songs he made them sing. It probes, so far as evidence and legitimate inference allow, his manipulation of audiences and his impact upon them.

---

[1] See for examples (Aubrey and Clarendon) Mordechai Feingold, "The Humanities," Chap. 5 of *The History of the University of Oxford*, vol. 4, *Seventeenth-Century Oxford*, ed. Nicholas Tyacke (Oxford: Clarendon Press, 1997), 301-2.

[2] The plural entails that exercises and verses alike prevailed at Oxford too, and beyond. It will be necessary at appropriate times, as in Chap. 9 for example, to differentiate Cambridge practices from general Oxbridge or European ones.

[3] The Anonymous Life of Milton (by Cyriack Skinner?) is quoted from the *Riverside Milton*, ed. Roy Flannagan (Boston: Houghton Mifflin, 1998), 6.

All of this is undertaken in order to uncover the meaning of these Latin doings for himself. Arcane as they may seem nowadays, they represent Milton's working life for more than five formative years.

The method of the investigation is first and foremost philological, philological in two senses. Its philology is linguistic in the English sense of "philology," and it embarks on *Philologie*, in the German sense of examining Latin words to penetrate to *Altertumswissenschaft*, the knowledge of antiquity.[4] It seeks to recover the relevant, generic conditions of understanding. It is a "pre-criticism," passing over into criticism proper.[5] Thereby, the neglected texts—a large and significant body of work for understanding the young Milton—can be understood on their own terms; and even, I hope, enjoyed.

The Cambridge Genres

A survey of the Cambridge Latin genres will be useful at this point, together with an indication of which ones required or attracted Milton's participation. Although the case-studies will show more exactly what he did with each generic subject or medium, the reader needs a prior sense of the whole within which Milton might compete for reputation. Such a context will further create a sense of how the diverse Latin speech-acts belonged within the community life of Cambridge, meaning both the life of the University community at large, and the more familial life of his college. "Familial," it should be noted, foregrounds the image by which both communities figured their life-relations; for every student was referred to throughout the exercises as the "son" of his college tutor as his "father."[6] By the same token one's peers were "brothers." We need

---

[4] See also Hale, *ML*, 26, 67.

[5] The term "pre-criticism" is adapted to Neo-Latin from work on Roman Latin by Gordon Williams in *The Nature of Roman Poetry* and other works: see John K. Hale, "The Pre-Criticism of Milton's Latin Verse," in *Of Poetry and Politics: New Essays on Milton and His World*, ed. P. G. Stanwood, MRTS 126 (Binghamton: MRTS, 1995), 131-49.

[6] There is also a vestige of *mater* or "mother" in the word *matricula* (diminutive of *matrix*, womb) or "register" which gives rise to the rituals of "matriculation," by which the freshman was first received as a member (limb) of the body of the University. The more etymologically aware these Cambridge Latinists were, the more would these metaphors come to life in use.

not insist that these metaphors were always taken seriously, but they *could* be so taken, to make a point or a special effect; and even as a dead metaphor the kinship-image shows the foundational, originary conception of the communal relations which defined their corporate existence. Assuredly, the metaphor will be found in Milton's speaking, there to be given many an expressive twist.

Foremost among the Cambridge Latin genres come the "exercises." Often enough summarized, these will be sampled in their own chapter: for the present it is more important to note that they comprise several distinct kinds and media of utterance. The set opening orations were scripted, though they might have to be performed from memory without notes.[7] Abundant examples survive. But what followed the opening oration mattered far more, especially the impromptu of cross-examination by the opponent, with further contributions by the opener's sponsor, the moderator, and ultimately anybody (which is how King James could have his say). For Milton, as for almost all disputants, only his opening orations survive.

Further Latin speech-acts had a sanctioned place in the exercises, for example the "varying" or "praevaricating" by a licensed parodist of the proceedings. His role was to relieve the intense, combative logic of the principal two disputants by mock-logic, by reductio ad absurdum, by any means. Some Praevaricator-scripts survive. Most of them are lamentably unfunny. But some, like Thomas Randolph's specimen, abound in real humour.[8] Although Milton did not perform this role on the University scene, it throws a flood of light on his college performances, as will be shown in Part Three.

---

[7] The most valuable work on the exercises for Milton's Cambridge remains the highly entertaining study by Father William T. Costello, S.J., *The Scholastic Curriculum at Early Seventeenth-Century Cambridge* (Cambridge, MA.: Harvard University Press, 1958). Costello is supplemented where necessary by works less specific to Cambridge, and by volumes of the *History of the University of Oxford*. Thus the point made above concerning performance from memory is an inference from the Tudor regulations for *Oxford*: see J. M. Fletcher, "The Faculty of Arts," Chap. 4.1 of *The History of the University of Oxford*, vol.3, *The Collegiate University*, ed. James Maconica (Oxford: Clarendon Press, 1986), 169.

[8] See Thomas Randolph, *Works*, ed. W. C. Hazlitt, 2 vols (London: Rivington, 1879), 2: 679-80.

"Act verses" were another regular component of the proceedings. Whereas the disputing existed in a shorter version for graduating students, and in a grandiose lengthy version for the July graduations, at which correspondingly praevarication also loomed larger, the act verses were required of all graduands. They had to compose (or commission) Latin verses summarizing the thesis which they would be defending. These summaries were printed, and distributed while the disputation was beginning. Because they were not performed aloud but printed on a broadsheet, many have survived. Although none of Milton's is among them, he refers in a letter to writing one. Two among his *Poems, 1645* have a relationship, currently unclear, to the act-verses.[9]

Students and seniors alike delivered "declamations," set speeches which resembled the opening speeches of a disputation, but lacked the aggressive impromptu of the disputational sequel. They shared many oratorical qualities with the set orations on great occasions, such as the effusions of the public orator when speaking on behalf of the University to royalty in its presence. A very notable example is George Herbert's accomplished performance as University Orator, greeting the King and Prince of Wales in 1623, when the latter found himself ironically the hero of the hour by so signally failing to win the hand of the Spanish Infanta.[10] Herbert most beautifully skates over the thin ice, pirouetting and serious by turns. As for Milton, though he never came near to such representative oration, his published declamations are among the glories of his early years. Not only do they deserve an even higher estimation than Tillyard and others[11] accorded them, but the way to perceive that is to engage with their Latin, on its own terms. Consequently the present work devotes not one but two chapters to case-study of Milton's achievement in this Cambridge mode.

---

[9] This is explained further in Chap. 2.

[10] I examine the issues and stakes of this event in "George Herbert's Oration before King James, Cambridge 1623," in *Acta Conventus Neo-Latini Cantabrigiensis*, ed. R. Schnur et al., MRTS #259 (Tempe: MRTS, 2003), 253-62.

[11] E. M. W. Tillyard, *Milton* (London: Penguin, 1968, but first published by Chatto & Windus, London, 1930); also Phyllis B. and E. M. W. Tillyard, *Milton. Private Correspondence and Academic Exercises* (Cambridge: Cambridge Univ. Press, 1932), referred to henceforward as "Tillyards."

Further University modes did not involve him, so far as we know. As a rough indication of how Latin saturated the public and curricular life of the Cambridge community it suffices to offer a checklist based on the researches of Jozef IJsewijn, Father Costello and James Binns.[12] Under "Drama," IJsewijn lists for Europe as a whole "Tragedy," "Comedy," then "Tragicomedy and Comicotragedy," then "Comoedia Sacra." Cambridge had its equivalents. Costello, discussing the exercises, mentions besides disputation and declamation (to which Milton did contribute) the following to which he did not: the "lecture," clerums, sermons, priorums and posteriorums.[13] Binns, for his part, enumerates the University's printed anthologies which expressed joy or condolence as appropriate, to royalty (*Latin Writings*, 40-43). Though Milton did not join in, his absence may be significant and will be discussed: he did join in the practice of copious handwritten funerary verse, in favour of the University's own worthies. Alongside the public and curricular life of Latin, Binns mentions Latin word-games, paraphrase, and translation, and records a long array of endeavours, varying by intellectual discipline or verse / prose medium, or occasion (Chaps. 4-5 and passim).

We should also distinguish the University's Latin happenings from those of the colleges, Christ's in particular. Much of the students' time was spent in the college chapel practising the disputing and declaiming which they were all required to perform in the University Schools. The main difference was that in college the audiences were fewer, more known and friendly than in the larger, less familiar version.[14] The Schools as auditorium would be correspondingly less familiar and larger than Christ's College chapel. These differences help to explain the variations

---

[12] Jozef IJsewijn with Dirk Sacré, Humanistica Lovaniensia Supplementa 14, *Companion to Neo-Latin Studies, Part 2: Literary, Linguistic, Philological and Editorial Questions* (Leuven: Leuven University Press, 1998), 149-64, the bibliography to Chap. 3; J. W. Binns, *Intellectual Culture in Elizabethan and Jacobean England: The Latin Writings of the Age*, ARCA 24 (Leeds: Francis Cairns, 1990).

[13] Costello, *Scholastic Curriculum*, 34-35. These are not as distinct nor recondite as listing makes them seem: his concluding comment is admirably balanced (35).

[14] A visit to Christ's Chapel and Hall then to the University Combination Room (part of the old Schools) helps to bring home the contrast of size and scope. Dimensions may help the reader's visualizations: Chapel 72 x 28 ft, Hall 54 x 26 ft, Schools 96 x 28 ft, approx.

Introduction

in tone and address when Milton disputed in college and in the Schools (Prolusion IV as opposed to Prolusion V).

Other genres belonged to college only. One was verse, in the sense that the best productions probably received a hearing, so existing in the ear as well as on paper.[15] Another presumptive occasion was the November 5 commemorations. These were compulsory, throughout the country and therefore the University. Annually the University marked the day of James's deliverance in 1605 with a sermon in the University church, Great St Mary's, in English in the morning, and then by a Latin speech in King's College Chapel in the afternoon. Milton would probably have attended the first but not the second. In the colleges it is likely that further rites were conducted: verse-writing might have led to a reading aloud there; and probably a less formal, more vernacular if not demotic partying ensued in the evening.

One genre not mentioned by Binns and the others, though Costello touches on it, is the salting. At a salting, held more secularly in the college dining hall, the year's freshmen were inducted to sophomore-status in front of their immediate seniors, with clownish tests and ordeals. The eponymous dosing with salt was a punishment for poor performance of a ritual test (through the pun on *sales,* "salts," Latin for Wit). It is therefore of special value to dwell on Milton's extant participation—not as initiand but as master of ceremonies—in this bilingual ritual. It occasioned his longest single undergraduate Latin text.

Diverse and numerous though the genres appear, they centre on the public deeds of an oral, performance-oriented community. All of Milton's have this dimension: they are not, as some of his English poems are, murmurings from an uncertain privacy, but are overt and social, sociable and kudos-seeking. They connect him with the life of his then community, whether college or University. Each one, in fact, may be understood in terms of its life-context, what biblical scholars have called its "Sitz im Leben." Conceding all needful difference between the oral and ancient genres of biblical tradition and the much more written early-modern ones of Cambridge, it still helps to ask of each performance by Milton

---

[15] Evidence that poems, or the best effusions, were rendered in colleges will be discussed in Chap. 8.

what is its "definite life-situation," its place "within [the] cultic *Sitz im Leben*, or setting of worship."[16] That is to say, several of the performances were "verbal [i.e. oral] compositions [which] stand in direct relation to life" at Cambridge, and "are themselves as it were events expressed in verbal form. . . . the funeral dirge is heard at the bier of this man or that woman, and so on."[17] Cambridge flowed with such dirges, handwritten and placed upon the hearsecloth; and Milton joined in, at least four times; University disputation speeches formed part of one's graduation; and so on. The Latin genres *did* something for the community which provided their audience. They not only involved performance: they were performative.

Another discourse has explanatory force, namely the anthropological commonplaces of transition and liminality. Often we should ask of a Latin genre which of the community's *rites de passage* it is serving. Thus the word "exercises" itself comes from the Latin word for the military training of Rome's *iuventus*: *exercitus* ("army") simply means "the exercised." Disputations, in particular, were structured to be agonistic. Declamations, too, were fundamentally adversarial. Act verses could be no different, summarizing as they do one side of a debate one-sidedly. The community's rites of passage are, however, more clearly visible in the optional than in the required genres. Certainly Milton stands closer to the rite and its anthropological quality in his attempts in these optional genres; indeed, they show him articulating it. For that reason, a pioneering anthropological explanation of the genres is provided. It is reserved for the later parts of the work, where the more optional genres are analysed.

In short, these performative and ritual or initiatory aspects of the Cambridge genres will be noted within the case studies whenever they make a significant difference. The performative ones will take pride of place in Part One, which deals with Milton taking a more usual, orthodox place within the University "at its exercises." Contrariwise, the rit-

---

[16] Bernhard W. Anderson, *The Living World of the Old Testament*, 3rd ed. (London: Longman, 1978), 20 n.6, 508.

[17] Otto Eissfeldt, *The Old Testament: An Introduction*, trans. Peter R. Ackroyd (Oxford: Blackwell, 1965), 9.

ual aspects will receive more attention in Part Two, where choice or opportunity afforded Milton more personal scope, and most attention of all in Parts Three and Four. These in fact consist of a study and an edition of Milton's college salting text, with translation. (The edition will be in some sense an *editio princeps*, in that it reassembles the bilingual portions of manuscript which Milton separated in the 1670s.) This is not to deny the presence of ritual in the University's exercising, nor of performativity in the more optional college genres; but it is a matter of felt emphasis, timely to be shown and best explaining the life of these now remote genres.

Classical Latin and Neo-Latin in the Cambridge Genres

The Cambridge genres, as presented so far, look thoroughly humanist. Not only do they resuscitate the Latin lexis of Rome, and for that matter preferably that of the most approved Latin authors, the "Golden" and "Silver" ones from Caesar to Seneca. Besides all of that, they draw upon Rome's history, mythology, and primeval cultus, as accessed through Rome's extant writings. To reiterate, philology serves *Philologie*. What is to be said, however, about the *non*-Roman aspects of the genres? Are Christian orthodoxy and terminology, and medieval scholasticism, not likewise important? Is their importance not a matter of words and things alike? Do not the Renaissance and Reformation make themselves felt, too, in both respects? Last but hardly least, do not these performers bring in their own collegiate Cambridge, alike in words and in substance? In short, does the foregoing generic account give an unduly privileged place to the classical world and its Latin? Does it occlude the distinctiveness of the world and language of *Neo*-Latin? While the full ramifications of these questions exceed the scope of the study as a whole, I should state my position, or rather my emphasis and competence.

As between *res* and *verba*, things and words, *res* are simpler. The Cambridge genres thrive on avoiding the above dichotomy. Cambridge is Rome, but also Athens, and a Christian place or the people of Israel, as occasion or local expressiveness requires. Equally it can be any combination of these. Milton and his congeners relish the opportunities of syncretism, and make free with it. With a corresponding freedom, the ensuing case-studies will dwell on any products of this kaleidoscope as need arises, without attempting to demonstrate all the possibilities, and without making an issue of the freedom. These genres do not problematize it; and though Milton's later English poems sometimes do, it is part of the freer world of the Cambridge Latin genres—something, indeed, to enjoy in them.

Verba, however, do raise problems. By training and reading alike I am better placed to explore classical Latinity than Neo-Latin. These studies therefore play to my strengths rather than expose known deficiencies. Four more points, however, modify this acknowledgement.

First, since the studies regularly look at examples of each genre composed by others than Milton, that entails attention to other Cambridge examples of Neo-Latin. Just as Milton emulates the ancients' Latin by his own, seeking to stand on the shoulders of those giants or make fresh honey from their flowers, so he is emulating those of his own time and place in these hallowed activities.

Secondly, scholarship is a shared and cumulative enterprise, which has advanced farther for some genres than others: prose genres in general and saltings in particular have not the same wealth of intertextual documentation in which the verse genres rejoice.

Thirdly, whatever the intertextual contribution made locally by Neo-Latin to each work, I perceive a more constant and pervasive as well as local dependence on ancient exemplars. These are always felt, indeed to be expected, whether or not scholarship has since added convincing proofs of Neo-Latin exemplars.

Fourthly, however, one genre does differ from another in these respects, as does one individual work from another, even regarding the same composer. *In Quintum Novembris* draws on Virgil, the Neo-Latin poet Buchanan, and Ovid in almost equal measure, thereby exemplifying the Neo-Latin freedom of combination. Declamations, on the other hand, strike me as relying mostly on the heroes of ancient *declamatio*. Disputations must deal in scholastic subjects, distinctions, and terminology, though in this case Milton manages to convey his repugnance. In the salting text it becomes part of the fun to employ some local or low-sounding words among the high registers. An example would be "Barnwellianos," never dreamt of by Cicero, but the name of the suburb where the brothels were, along with high expressions for low things: language too is on holiday, and becomes more nearly promiscuous. In such a rich field of enquiry, one which for some genres has barely begun to receive full philological attention, I see so much needing to be investigated that the studies here ought to follow their own logic rather than seek comprehensiveness or a balancing exactitude. It will be the best outcome possible if they prompt others to take up the search and bring back better, fuller discoveries.

PART ONE

Milton and the University Exercises

Ackermann's depiction of a disputation in the Oxford Divinity School, despite coming from another place and time, shows the unchanging performance-essentials. The thesis-proponent ("Respondent" in Cambridge-speak) stands in his special tall box on the left of the picture (Stage Right). His antagonist (the "Opponent"), who will try to demolish his argument by cross-examination, stands in his own special box (Stage Left). The Moderator, a senior academic, sits high and lifted up on his central throne. All wear full academic dress. Listeners, possibly Respondents and Opponents in waiting, stand or sit on the far side of a stylized partition fencing off the combat zone.

CHAPTER 1

DISPUTATIONS

Disputations are possibly the hardest of Milton's Cambridge Latin genres to treat justly. Not only do they seem obscure, quaint, and futile to ourselves: they received almost as bad a press from his century's best minds, including Milton. Consequently it requires conscious effort to recover their actual purposes, to become interested in their forms, and to gauge their tone and impact upon audiences. Only by doing these things, however, can we assess Milton's engagement with the celebrated genre, and find there what he found. What can we recover of his engagement from his two disputation-texts?

A distinction may help, between the Scholastic (neo-Aristotelian) subject-matter or thought-forms of the disputing, and its procedures. The artificiality of much medieval philosophy was notorious by Milton's time, or else English would not have possessed contemptuous expressions like "quiddities" (1539) or "quodlibetaries" (before 1631). Correspondingly, Milton's two prolusions address philosophical questions which did not attract him, or at least not as couched in their scholastic jargon. The procedures of the debating itself, on the other hand, although they may attract an equal obloquy from those who have undergone them and relinquished them for ever with relief, yet—like the sports, games, contests, examinations, and assessments of all *paideia* whatsoever—they had once engaged the participants, even when fear or loathing came into the engagement. Such activities are not end-productive. Their value comes from doing them. An appropriate comparison is with golf, or a team-sport you loved when aged sixteen. They build physical muscle and build character, not by intention yet not by accident either. A sort of homology inheres in paideusis, that just as from physical exercise comes physical muscle, so from mind-games like the exercises comes intellectual muscle.

It is necessary, or anyhow desirable, to unthink the obloquy of hindsight. Here is Mordechai Feingold's[1] temperate reversal of the hostile former consensus-view. That competitiveness, or healthy emulation, stimulated learning was a humanist axiom (222–23). Public exercises, especially disputation, brought students beneficial challenges, pressures, and thrills (224). Excellence in one encouraged emulation in the rest, though often enough producing misery and despair in some individuals (224–25). It was certainly an active way of learning, not passive like attending lectures. In particular, the predominance of logic as subject-matter for undergraduate exercises was utilitarian, and propaideutic (296). Logic was not a means to philosophic truth; it was mind-training (302). As Clarendon put it, "The art of logick ... disposes us to judge aright in any thing, and though we do not make our conversation in syllogisms, and discourse in the mood and figure, yet our conversation and our discourse is much the more reasonable and the better formed, by the experience we have had in that art, and in which we may have spent some time very merrily. And I must say again this most useful art was never well taught or learned but in our universities" (quoted in Feingold, "The Humanities," 301–2).

Clarendon's "very merrily" alerts us to the fact, seldom mentioned by its denouncers, that disputing could be fun. The fun aspect was actively encouraged, which helps to explain why the varying and subverting of theses was institutionalized in the century (303), and why large crowds attended the top combats (302).

Furthermore, the place of Aristotle in it all was changing. He was taken seriously even if his medieval followers were not. What is more, modern questions might replace Aristotelian ones—"*quaestiones* linguistic, moral, and contemporary" (303). Milton's own two instances are both Aristotelian, but show respect for the Stagirite himself in contradistinction to the Schoolmen.

Now although Feingold is describing the practice of Oxford not Cambridge, the two universities look alike to the outside gaze, even if it is heretical or disloyal to say so. Back then, the competition between the

---

[1] Again from "The Humanities," in *History of the University of Oxford 4: Seventeenth-Century Oxford*, ed. Tyacke, 211–357.

two[2] (in everything from patronage to printing) was acute; and competition implies sameness, strife within the same endeavouring.

We should not, however, think of this former Oxbridge as enjoying genuine intellectual freedom through its disputing. Whereas Aristotle and the Schoolmen had made many issues familiar and innocuous, might not the introduction of new ones risk disturbance to authority (authority intellectual, religious, political, the whole nexus of elements in the early-modern crisis)? No, this is not the case. Disputants did not debate truly hot issues, like whether the royal prerogative should be curbed or the Anglican settlement was a shabby compromise or the nature of God could not be known. The issues were chiefly innocuous through remoteness or generality, or the answer was often a foreknown orthodoxy. All that was needed was that something be argued pro and con, and that students adopt an alien view and advocate it effectively: no vote, and certainly no action, ever followed. The moderator could stop the debate whenever he wanted to, or to do so became prudent. That was the point: even if the pillowfighting would lead to careers in law or Parliament or the church, where blood might indeed flow as a consequence, the value was being found in the exercise of argument, but not in truth, nor in any commitment that would follow. It was all an As-If, all a play of imagination, however heated that might grow. What was at stake, for the better performers, was reputation and (possibly beyond that) preferment.[3]

To return to the young Milton, it is no surprise when he abuses Scholasticism. (Did he ever have a good word for monks or the Middle Ages?) It would be more of a surprise if, while engaged in disputation, he abused disputation, or its forms and sanctions, and especially the audience and judges. Even that, though it might straightforwardly convey disgust or rebellion, might instead be audacity or joking or detachment. Each tone of voice and stance, every fluctuating interaction between speaker and audience, should be judged in context. I shall be commenting on some moments of apparent detachment or reflexivity

---

[2] There were no other universities in England till much later. Trinity College, Dublin, and the Scottish universities were a source of competition not much felt by Oxbridge.

[3] Feingold, "The Humanities," 303 and n. 250.

in the course of analysing both the disputations which he kept and published. In doing so the distinction between scholastic thought and the procedures of Cambridge disputation will be tested.

As final preliminary to those analyses, here is first a summary of the procedures, followed by a comment upon the textual history of Prolusions IV and V (giving my view of its dubieties), and then similarly upon the state of the text and translations in modern editions.

Costello describes the college disputations as "friendly little affairs, where, if the student had stuck at a problem, the moderator first asked about among the students for a solution, then answered himself . . .".[4] A similar tone is felt in parts of Milton's Prolusion IV. But the grandest University version was neither friendly nor little: Costello compares it to a bullfight, and pressing his figure we might think of the Respondent as more in the position of the bull than of the matador. For the undergraduates making their statutory two appearances in the Schools as respondent and two as objector, the basic shape was the same. The greatest ordeal of the four was as Commencer-Respondent. At this, the moderator made a speech elucidating the question under dispute; the Father "makes a short speech on his pupil's behalf, then 'calleth up the Answerer [his pupil] who after his prayer readeth his position.'" During this brief statement his printed verses—act verses, the verse summary of the thesis—were distributed and read. Then the Father would interrogate his pupil on the thesis, this being done in such a fashion as to put him at ease. Then, however, the first opponent would rise, make a speech, and press his objections syllogistically. The respondent would reply to the syllogisms, in kind. The second opponent would be called and "engage in a long syllogistic scuffle as had the first opponent."[5] This was the heart of the event, and might go on for some time, and wax fierce. The moderator decided when to stop this, and whenever it stopped so did the disputation of that question. The assembly went on to the second, of the set pairs in which disputing was done (and the verses were printed).

---

[4] Costello, *Scholastic Curriculum*, 14, quoting the statutes of Trinity College (of "an.ii Eliz.," 171, n. 25).

[5] Costello, *Scholastic Curriculum* 19, based on the sole transcript of a complete Cambridge disputation yet known, that of one Boyes in the 1590s. By good fortune it happens to be on a substantial topic: whether the threat of punishment is a deterrent to crime. Costello's narrative is the best thing of all in his brilliant chapter of recreation.

It follows that in his two disputation-texts we are watching Milton merely warming up, making his opening set speech before the "syllogistic scuffling" starts. The effect of missing the sequel is to assimilate his disputing to his declaiming. At particular moments, nonetheless, we glimpse his conduct of the later impromptu, and his overall strategies and style of performance.

1674 prints the two disputation-texts as prolusions "IV" and "V." IV is a performance "In Collegio, &c." whereas "V" is "In Scholis Publicis." Thus IV is a practice-piece, delivered to friends (fellow-students) and tutor. "V" is delivered to mostly unknown persons, and a larger audience, though the tutor would be attending as Father to his Son.

Questions arising range from minor to very major. It is a minor puzzle to know what "&c." stands for in the title of Prolusion IV. It relates neither backward nor forward to another prolusion with fuller wording, so probably typifies the loose ends of *1674*. These loose ends include a very major issue, whether or to what degree Milton supervised the editing and printing, in his blindness and old age: thus we do not know whether the sequence of the seven prolusions is his or another's or a joint effort, nor whether it is chronological or qualitative or done for variety and drama. Because Milton in 1674 was blind and ailing and aging, and the papers were in disarray, but yet Milton was a determined character and concerned with reputation through publication, I assume a joint effort. Because no two scholars agree on a chronological reordering yet there are problems if the printed order is taken as chronological, whereas the printed ordering is sensible and varied and tasteful, I assume a joint editing which seeks to keep readers reading.[6] Of intermediate importance is the question whether the printed texts are what he performed. Some of them seem on the long

---

[6] Three declamations are followed by two disputations, after which comes a less formal piece which parodies both those forms, then his longest and finest declamation concludes. It is rather unlikely that the two disputations were composed just then, amidst the surrounding declamations. The printer's explicit statement that the papers were disordered ("haec forte juvenilia hic illic disiecta") and that he got the papers from the author through a common friend ("per Amicum utrique," "commune Amico") both point to a collaborative determining of the most effective ordering. The outcome is satisfying, much as (though of course lesser than) for *Poems 1645*. For a fuller summary of the arguments about sequence and dating see William R. Parker, *Milton. A Biography*, 2 vols., rev. Gordon Campbell (Oxford: Clarendon Press, 1996), 2: 775 n. 80 and 1226 (Campbell's updating).

side, when read aloud oratorically. We have no way of knowing, but (as I shall show) the scripts themselves imply orality, gesture, and interaction with audiences or individual auditors.[7] We can assume that where they come closest to oratorical delivery, *actio*, the scripts were performed accordingly. Certainly the opportunity must not be missed here to chart the implied histrionics, since he gained reputation by that; and the prolusions are the nearest we can now come to the very sound and motion of the man on his legs, orating.

The Latin text of 1674 is very bad. To quote the Tillyards (1932): "The edition of 1674 contains a long list of errata, which, however, is far from complete. The following list contains obvious corrections. In addition to these, the quotations from Greek authors invariably contain mistakes, which are however not enumerated here... No attempt has been made to indicate changes in the punctuation, since these are too numerous, the punctuation throughout being completely at random and frequently obscuring the sense."[8] This strong language is mostly merited. The Columbia text[9] corrects much, but even so makes substantive as well as accidental errors of its own (as will be shown below for passages discussed). A full textual overhaul is long overdue.

There are two main translations, Columbia's and Yale's.[10] Columbia is not especially accurate. Yale's is the Tillyards' again, reprinted with additional notes by Phyllis Tillyard in square brackets and more by Kathryn A. McEuen. Though Yale is very good because the Tillyards did a good job which Yale betters, it is vitiated for present purposes by its omission of the Latin original—even when a note discusses a point of Latin, which consequently reads like a bizarre shadowboxing. Columbia, accordingly, is used here for both text and translation: the serious reader of Yale has to have Columbia at hand anyway for the original Latin. Columbia's translation is used as well as its text, with its defects pointed out where applicable; but (whilst also translating some excerpts

---

[7] Like Shakespeare's texts, the words spoken entail gesture, body language, expression, and so forth.

[8] Tillyards, 143, "Textual Notes."

[9] *The Works of John Milton*, gen. ed. Frank Allen Patterson, The Columbia Edition, vol. 12: *The Familiar Letters* ed. Donald Lemen Clark, trans. David Masson, and *The Prolusions* ed. Donald Lemen Clark, trans. Bromley Smith henceforward cited as *ColWks*.

[10] *Complete Prose Works of John Milton*, ed. Don M. Wolfe et al. vol.1 *1624–1642*, henceforward cited as *YPW*.

myself where the published versions are inadequate) I prefer my own reader to consider my assertions about the Latin from Columbia's whole text and context, not solely from excerpts.

Prolusion IV: In Collegio, &c. Thesis.
In Rei cuiuslibet interitu non datur resolutio ad Materiam Primam

After these contextual preliminaries, necessarily lengthy because they relate to some further Cambridge Latin genres, let us plunge into Prolusion IV itself:

> Error an e Pandorae pixide, an ex penitissimo eruperit Styge, an denique ex terrae filiis in coelites coniuraverit, non est huius loci accuratius disquirere. Hoc autem vel non scrutanti facile innotescat, eum ex infimis incrementis, veluti olim Typhon, aut Neptuno genitus Ephialtes in tam portentosam crevisse magnitudinem, ut ipsi quidem veritati ab illo metuam....(*ColWks* 12: 172)

("In College, etc. In the destruction of any thing a resolution to primary matter does not occur." Whether Error broke forth from Pandora's box or from the lowest Stygian depth, or whether, in short, one of the sons of Earth conspired against the gods, is not to be investigated too closely at this time. Moreover it may easily be noted even by a careless observer that Error from the smallest beginnings, has grown to such enormous magnitude, as was once the case with Typhon or Ephialtes, son of Neptune, that I fear for Truth itself on account of him; for I behold Error contending not infrequently on equal terms with the goddess Truth herself...)[11]

At once, a disjunction is perceived between the Thesis or proposition and the exordial generalities. It is a set speech before becoming a specimen of logic. The Cambridge curriculum and the prevailing scheme of Latin genres may have distinguished between declamation and disputation, rhetoric and logic, but in practice both included both. It was later on, in the impromptu cut and thrust of interrogation, that logic held sway alone.

---

[11] *ColWks* trans., 173.

Meanwhile, here in the exordium Milton entertains his audience by flowers of rhetoric—by allusion and personification, by alliteration ("in coelites coniuraverit"), by strong verbs strongly placed ("disquirere," "innotescat"), and by prose rhythm whether internally or in clausula. He steps up this Latin eloquence as the flourishes continue, into "luscum et caecutientem (errorem)": Error is lambasted as "one-eyed and dim-sighted."

And thus he moves on into apparent hostility in "iam totis in Scholis dominatur immundus error" (174): "foul Error is lord and master in all the schools." Does this mean "among the Scholastics" or "in the Cambridge Schools"? That is unclear. It may be purposely unclear, though, since next he spots some listeners "submussitantes" (whispering), "quo nunc se proripit ille?" ("Whither is that fellow racing?", quoting Virgil).[12] A fair question: though "inveighing against error, he himself is wandering over the whole universe" ("ipse toto errat Coelo"). He is manipulating his audience by this time. So I take it that in *college* he can abuse "the Schools," the ordeal they all had to face later, with ambiguity and impunity. An easy rapport with a small, familiar audience can be seen, after all, in this quip. He does not tweak the Schoolmen's tails in Prolusion V, delivered "In the Public Schools."

Reading ahead now, we find that only after two pages of his ten have gone by does Milton get down to his set Questioning, with a prayer to Lua, goddess who expiates blood shed in battle. Is he serious, or is he not? Is he upholding the disputant's role or mocking it? My answer is that he is *performing*, and to see the performance straight we can refer to the Oxbridge context once more and to a Cambridge congener.

Rhetoric was part of making the logic pleasing, entertaining. More than that, rhetoric and logic together "offered techniques to all other arts . . . 'Logick without oratory is drye and unpleasing and oratory without logick is but empty babbling.'"[13]

In point of fact, Milton's two pages' prefacing out of ten looks normal, even austere, by comparison with (say) Alexander Bolde of Pembroke College. Bolde attacks the (fatuous) proposition that "Matter does not stir unless it is moved" ("Nullum corpus agit, nisi moveatur"). Fully

---

[12] *Aeneid* 5. 741.
[13] Feingold, "The Humanities," quoting Holdsworth (246).

half of the whole text consists of "introductory remarks, in which Bolde tries to put himself on good terms with the audience by suggesting that he is not the sort of pedant who enjoys nothing better than the labour of disputing. . . ."[14] No, not he! For in the second half, rather than staying with logic and confutation, he rattles off a string of puns on the key terms of the thesis, *agere* and *moveri*. Pedantic after all, he puns on the numerous idioms involving those verbs. Now this Bolde, who died in 1625, the year Milton arrived in Cambridge, was not only a Fellow of Pembroke but also University lecturer in Hebrew, and a regular performer of the Latin exercises at the University occasions. In short, the practised professional comes across as no less puerile than Milton the beginner.

Alternatively, of course, we could withhold the charge of puerility, as inappropriate to what the disputants had to do. Since they had to please by good Latin, and entertain by such wit as they could muster, it is no surprise when they combined the two as philological wordplay.

When we arrive at the logicking proper, we find that a good deal of it is chunks of a logic textbook, Suarez' commentary on Aristotle's *Metaphysics*. Compare this (Milton):

> . . . prior dependentia non est immediata, forma enim substantialis non informat accidentia, neque intellegi potest quod aliud munus exerceat circa ea in hoc genere causa . . . [15]

with this (Suarez):

> Prior dependentia non potest esse immediata, sed mediata; forma enim substantialis non informat quantitatem, vel alia accidentia, neque intelligi potest quo alio modo immediata circa illa exerceat munus causae formalis; ergo non possunt accidentia pendere a forma immediata in eo genere causae . . .

Be it remembered, too, that this paralleling is not an isolated example. Nearly twenty such "parallel passages" are listed by Thomas R. Hartmann.[16] They account for almost every one of Milton's arguments,

---

[14] K. M. Burton, "Cambridge Exercises in the Seventeenth Century," *The Eagle* [journal of St John's College] 54 (1951): 248–58, here 253.

[15] *ColWks* 12: 180; see Thomas R. Hartmann, "Milton's Prolusions" (Ph. D. diss., Columbia University, 1962), 137.

[16] Hartmann, "Milton's Prolusions," 135–145.

and the wording often comes as close to his as in the example cited. One is left wondering how much of the proof and thesis belongs to Milton. That is to say, the indebtedness is such that the meaning is clearer in the source. If this were an undergraduate assignment nowadays, it would attract a grade of about B minus, or else send the marker reaching for the guidelines concerning student plagiarism. What are we to think?

Hartmann thinks the prolusion "is essentially a satire on scholastic philosophy," and that "only the rhetorical portions can be attributed to Milton's own invention." What, then, is it doing in a 1674 *display* of Milton's powers as an exerciser? How could he ever have won a reputation for such a performance as this? The choice one has when reading the section, which after all is the heart of the proof of the Thesis, or such heart as it has, seems to lie between satire and intentional perfunctoriness. Not a feast of choice for us, but an awkward dilemma. Can it be resolved? Is there any further way of responding?

I have two suggestions. First, that a certain perfunctoriness is to be expected at this early stage of a whole disputation. The thesis is being opened up, no more. So at first we hear some flowers of eloquence, to please and predispose the hearers in the usual fashion (recall Bolde). Then, we hear a *summary*, of the main arguments for the thesis. The hard work lies ahead.

The speech's conclusion points in the same direction. We hear no final flourish whatever, no closure either; only that "I could produce many arguments on both sides." But such a listing would fatigue his listeners; so "at this point, therefore, it will be enough to sound a retreat." I read this in context as saying, I don't want to bore you, or give the opposition any easy handles. He is giving away as little as possible, in fact, by relying so heavily on Suarez and presenting the case the way he does, densely (in both senses of the word).

My second suggestion is to note, as all before me have done, how Milton makes a little theme of fatigue, boredom, his own and his hearers'. Since my first suggestion is that he wants to please his audience by considering its boredom-threshold as he closes, maybe the same tactic is operating at the more notorious first reference:

> Potui quidem, immo ac debui huic rei diutius immorari, ac profecto nescio an vobis, mihimet certe ipse maximopere taedio. (184. 18–20)

("I could indeed, nay, I even ought to linger longer on this point, but I am not sure whether I am boring to you; certainly I am very boring to myself.")

This sounds perfunctory, offhanded, and (whether or not also insolent or cheap) like an undergraduate playing for an easy laugh. The laugh would come from fellow-undergraduates doing this small-scale, in-college practicing. He is probably playing to the same gallery in his opening ambiguity about "the Schools." Equally certainly, his opponent's job will have been made harder to the extent that Milton has won the sympathy, laughter, and as it were connivance of his peers by such oratorical tricks. We can presume that they were not more absorbed in the thesis than Milton was, or lets them be. He is playing it cool. Whilst it may not be a way of winning a disputation, it may be a way of not losing—not losing what mattered, namely face.

Yet I remain not entirely happy with this reading. For one thing, it does not explain how the speech earned its place in *1674*. For another, it presents the speech as one where Milton appears *not* to play the Cambridge game for all it was worth, as I have claimed he does. An ingratiating histrionics is not a centrally relevant emulation. Still, my reading does explain the speech in terms of the context of its first delivery. It does keep the focus on performance. It acknowledges the badness of the philosophy, so staying in key with Milton's deprecation, dismissiveness, his knowing parroting of known nonsense; forms to be gone through with. Especially pertinent to my whole emphasis, it explains the badness and baldness of the Latin, so startling after the opening eloquence.

We are reading the bad, ungainly, and jargon-laden Latin of a talented stylist. Is he then, stylistically, playing a game with Suarez? He parrots such rebarbative post-classical words as "quantitativae"[17]

---

[17] Suarez abounds in such "-ivus" adjectives formed from an abstract noun: elsewhere Milton cleans up "relativorum" into "relatorum" for "relative terms, relatives" (Milton, *ColWks* 12: 180.19; Suarez cited from Hartmann, "Milton's Prolusions," 136). Similarly with Suarez' topheavy "essentiam actualem et entitativam" (cited from Hartmann, "Milton's Prolusions," 144), Milton slims it down somewhat into "verum et actualem essentiam" (188.12–13).

(182. 24)[17]; or collocations like "propriam entitatem actualem" (180. 8) and "de subjecto completo & integro (i.e.) de substantiali composito" (184. 25–186. 1). He not only parrots. He puts on show by contrast his own greater resources, of language and imagination. The rhetoric which had seemed to go underground once the proofs were reached turns out on closer inspection to weave in and out of the jargon. If we exempt all the borrowed reasoning, what remains? Hartmann calls it "the rhetorical portions" or "the oratorical links." I see it in more ludic terms, as a running commentary, as if a stylish and energetic vocabulary were adorning a humdrum football match, to give it what life it could: the life through wit and style of the commentator.

Thus we read that perception "raro hallucinatur" (184. 5). He would rather hear of "ghosts and hobgoblins" than those "philosophasters" (184.6–8).[18] They are seen to "snarl gormlessly"—"stulte et insubide ingannientes." The effect is of an imaginative energy and verbal resource which cannot be denied by the arid prevailing eristics, but must bubble out. By a different sort of transformation Suarez' colourless adverb "paulatim" becomes the mouthfilling, colourful "pedetentim" (184.16; Hartmann, "Milton's Prolusions," 140), "step by step" but literally "testing by foot," in which the root elements of the compound expose the original vivid metaphor, what with the adverb coming last in its sentence.

And when the last quarter of the game is reached (186. 10 and 22) Milton makes the running commentary more explicit. "The battle becomes violent and victory sways to and fro . . . Now the argument blazes up and boils over . . ." ("Adhuc incrudescit pugna, & nutat victoria . . . Gliscit jam atque effervescit contentio"). Later, near the end, we hear of the last "hope of victory"; there is a persistent image-cluster of contest and warfare, mockingly humorous since this is a harmless scholastic pugilism.

Images dominate, and they do matter. They are being assigned to Milton's opponents. He is anticipating their arguments: "occurrent adversarii," back at 178.11, is in the future tense. He is defending, then, by preemptive aggression, and increasingly as the climax approaches: the "they" who "press us keenly," "as if about to struggle to extermination"

---

[18] Contemptuous suffix from Greek, as in "poetaster." The Latin noun is found in Augustine.

(188. 23) are the opposition. We are reminded of the disputation-roles not only by this but more blatantly when Milton replies "Respondeo," first word in his sentences of anticipatory rebuttal at 186.20 or 188.5. He is the Respondent, and (in the oxymoron of some football commentators) he is getting in his retaliation beforehand.

What I am calling the commentary is a tacit claim to superiority made by two qualities of Latin tone. There is metaphorical verve, inherent in the strong muscular verbs and brought to prominence by the contrast with Suarez' fusty jargon surrounding. And there is a sprightly air of detachment, as if Milton were not so much conducting the battle as observing it from above (like the Father watching Satan's rebellions). The style is an active, entertaining one, more complex than first appears, more too than translations capture.

Something similar pervades that seemingly flippant remark about boredom, quoted earlier. "Immorari" means to "dawdle in a place or on a topic." Columbia's "linger longer" makes a jolly jingle, but is not so precise. The noun "taedio" is stronger than "boredom". It means "loathing, disgust, revulsion" (think of the *taedium vitae* in Aulus Gellius, suicidal). "Maximopere" is more vehement than Columbia's "very," especially with "taedium." The sentence is not a glib quip after all. I, and maybe you my audience, are feeling utter disgust at this talk of quantity following matter and quality following form. So let's get on, to forestall the opponents' arguments, if I can reduce those to "primary matter" or better still to annihilation. The self-reflexive punning begins in the *final* sentence, not in the one so often cited. It is better placed as a joke if it releases a tension, the tension created by a sudden ferocity in "maximopere sum taedio." That way, it will do more for the performance's reception.

Prolusion V. In Scholis Publicis. Non dantur formae partiales in animali praeter totalem.

Similar qualities enliven Prolusion V, even while that performance is conducted differently. We follow the continuities first.

Thus it is true that the speech "In Scholis" is shorter and more concise, and has the marks of delivery to a larger, less familiar audience in a more public anonymous place. It makes a loftier, more solemn beginning, and keeps its image-theme of the recovery of truth more prominent throughout, with the peroration in particular rounding it off with elegance.

Notwithstanding all of this, a replacement of jest and satire by formality and high didactic is only to be expected: it is the moving from rehearsal, possibly not even dress rehearsal, to the real thing. The peculiarities of Prolusion IV are not one-off aberrations, but are the marks of a usual and also personal style of performance. As to the personal I am thinking of the ebullient exordium, the metaphors of combat and the running commentary addressed to audience, the enlivening of routine summarizing by using muscular or vivid verbs. These are not done better now so much as in a higher register, because of the different audience. And as for the usual things of a performance, neither great advance nor decline is discernible. The usual things are being done in a usual way, though we can thereby see the usual more clearly.

Take the thesis itself, that "Partial forms do not occur in an animal in addition to the whole." Milton chose the topic to dispute as respondent, and also how he would treat it. How obscure is his choice this time? It relates, as he mentions (196. 14), to a passage from Aristotle's *De Anima*, "near the end of Book I" (411a27–411b29) Only he does not quote that, let alone analyse it. He declares that Aristotle favours his own view. He does not say why or how. Is this wilful or offhand, the usual thing or what? It looks simply the usual thing.

This is one of the times where Aristotle's otherwise lucid account of psychology does generate obscurity. For example, as W. D. Ross said, "The connexion of reason with the other faculties is one of the obscurest parts of his psychology."[19] Indeed, the ending of Book One of the *De Anima*[20] is mostly questions. Yet the persistent probing of what Aristo-

---

[19] W. D. Ross, *Aristotle* (London: Methuen, 1923), 135.

[20] Usually rendered "soul," as Columbia and Tillyard do. "Anima" translates Greek "psyche," which means "life" or "life-principle". The "psyche" of humans is most essentially that of consciousness, but Aristotle uses "psyche" to include the life of plants and animals also. Context makes it plain whether the more comprehensive or the distinctively human denotation is intended. "Psyche" or "life-principle" is the least misleading rendering.

tle left obscure remains a tribute to his penetration, not a waste of time or backhanded compliment. Truth is being honoured in the probing. In any case, Milton's immediate moving *past* Aristotle into Javellus shows that Aristotle left work to be done by his successors (who have not even yet exhausted his questions and their answers).

When the summaries of points and rebuttal of objections begin, the Latin becomes as technical and terse if not dense as in Prolusion IV. We have to remember, first, that a printed statement of the thesis was circulated at the disputation, and secondly that the audience were familiar with the thought-forms and jargon, but above all that the Respondent was declaring to the opposition the terms of combat, things to be taken up in syllogistic interrogation soon after. Seen in this light, what is opaque to ourselves now was presented by Milton in the usual way, with the usual brevity, and leaving room for the usual rhetorical embellishment.

In this conjunction of logic with rhetoric, philosophizing with embellishment, the demands of occasion preponderate. We must expect it in this most conventional and rule-bound of genres. It is vital to conviction, or even competence, that the speech should please by style, should entertain, should captivate and so persuade the listeners.

Accordingly, at the transition to Chrysostomus Javellus (196. 17), the otherwise intrusive swipe at Javellus' *style* (described as a dungheap with gold and gems in it: "stercorario," "Aurum & Margaritas") epitomizes the transition being made, from oratory alone to the thesis and its pros and cons, yet without forgoing irruptions of eloquence. What Javellus did not do, Milton will attempt. He will as it were flick the dung off Javellus' gemstones. The needs of occasion preponderate here too. It is vital to conviction, or even competence, that the speech should please by style.

Is there, indeed, a sort of "truth of style," a purity and energy in spoken Latin? Does this connect Milton's exordium with his logic after all? It is the case that what best differentiates Prolusion V from its predecessor is not its conduct of logic, but its more connected eloquence. I think of the enthusiastic opening survey of Roman conquest, or his closing Platonic myth of the Sun.

But the engaged verve of the rhetoric which links the logic shows up the disengaged drabness of the logic itself. In performing competently what was usual in the main, logical part of a disputation, Milton shows no special ability or interest, let alone flair. He does not aspire, is not stirred to direct emulation.

In fact, he says so: he will hide behind "Authores" to make his points (194.19), and can add nothing to such pre-eminent talents (20–21). That is quite true! Is he being modest or realistic or lazy? My primary sense is that he is being realistic, because he is content to summarize other arguments, and to postpone or avoid what he can. He never lights up with instinctive enthusiasm for an argument. Neither his heart nor his imagination is engaged. A slight reinforcement of this view may come from the contrast with some of the numerous disputation scripts or notes which can be read in manuscripts in Cambridge libraries. For example, in one the exact logical manoeuvres to be carried out are set out in a plan by symbols. Capital Greek *theta* means "major premise," a cross ("+") means a minor; "C" reminds the disputant of his "syllogism. hypothetici," "D" of his "syllogism. definitivus." Though we have no access to Milton's manuscripts let alone his working notes, we can perceive some contrast between his apparent insouciance and this carefully prepared itinerary.[21]

Milton seems so cavalier in some assertions, ready even to commit inconsistencies—which is to perpetrate the fundamental sin of a participant in logic and disputation—that we might suspect him of having some other agenda. He says at 194 that Truth is "tottering and overcome" ("labantem ... et profligatam"), yet in his peroration that it is invincible ("invictam semper"). We could read the apparent contradiction as ironic overstatement, or melodrama, to "create a sense of drama in the audience and urgency in the speaker's defence."[22] It certainly shows Milton's readiness to become excited with the rhetoric more than the logic: the life of the piece is in the stylistic glee. The same may be said of Prolusion IV, in whose exordium Truth is likewise endangered and must be defended (172). The difference here is that Milton offers a Platonic mythos, of the battling of truth with error and truth's fleeing to the heavens. In both speeches, nevertheless, Truth is a rhetorical de-

---

[21] Taken from Caius College MS 748–259: see also Costello, *Scholastic Curriculum*, 153.

[22] The perceptive comment comes from one of the readers for MRTS.

vice or flamboyant topos, not a theme let alone the question to be addressed. The life of both pieces resides less in the logic than in the stylistic glee.[23]

The answer to our initial question, therefore, what did he find in the Cambridge exercises, is in this first instance a negative. He found not enough, and possibly not much. He went through the required motions. He did not feel the pull of emulation.

To revert to the textual question for a moment, the placing of the two disputations as numbers IV and V among seven does suggest a certain modesty or even depreciation on somebody's part. What better way can be imagined to include some disputations (since they would certainly be expected amongst a gathering of the University prolusions of a famous practitioner) than thus prudently to tuck them away? My own analyses have tended to confirm the wisdom of their unemphatic positioning. Indeed, since the present discussion has tended to confirm the assessment by most Milton scholars who have considered the matter, it might be developed towards the position that Milton and his publisher in 1674 thought so too, both of them.

There is, however, one great exception to this sense of disappointment or non-event. Where heart and imagination do engage with the occasion is in the oratorical aspects. This bodes well for further genres, for act verses and declamations in Chapters 2–4, but leaves a conundrum for Chapter 5 on the impact of Cambridge upon his *Defences* of the 1650s. The *Defences* strike people now as excessively disputatious, yet on the face of it his training in the formal disputations did not go deep. Did he imbibe more than appears, or did he have to catch up, or did he separate the learning of logic from how Cambridge inculcated it?

---

[23] The topos of "Truth Lost" may have been a favourite to warm up a prolusion. Milton does something similar in Prolusion VII, where it has become the "republic of Fools" which is "tottering. " The reassembling of the severed limbs of truth is made the climactic mythos in *Areopagitica*. Thomas Randolph as Praevaricator in 1632 gives it a comical treatment, a hectic catechising of all the places and groups where Truth might have fled to, but none of them know or care.

CHAPTER 2

Milton's Philosophic Verses and the Cambridge Act Verses

Whereas his disputations evinced little spirit of emulation, and did not extend or affect their genre, his act verses show the exact opposite. He infuses this equally set mode of philosophical expression with considerable new life. He takes the conventional mode beyond its boundaries, to the point of renewing the mode itself. It is in *De Idea Platonica*, rather than in Prolusions IV and V, that the Cambridge disputations arouse him to intellectual energy. Chapter Two shows the dialectic of his progress, against a background of the Cambridge norm but dwelling longer on this quixotic, enigmatic poem.

Introduction: Act Verses Including Milton's

"Act verses"[1] are the Latin verses which accompany a disputation-thesis, summarizing the thesis in a printed form and distributed to its audience while the respondent is giving his opening speech. Thus we are to imagine Milton delivering Prolusion V to his University audience including examiners whilst copies of his verses on the thesis are being handed out to them. The verses themselves have not survived.[2] Whether or not the fact of print helps to explain why an exordium is digressive and lengthy, print was present alongside oratory and impromptu at the Cambridge commencements.

---

[1] An "act" in this sense means an official academic exercise, in the present context a disputation.

[2] They would be recognisable because they would advocate the thesis of Prolusion V, which would be printed at the head of the sheet.

Many of these printed act verses have survived.[3] They have a recurrent form, in respect of their titles, their length, and their logical shape. Each feature provides a useful index for Milton's versions of the genre.

The titles mostly make a statement or ask a question. They affirm a proposition (and hence have their verbs in the indicative mood), or pose a question "Whether" X is the case (and hence begin "Utrum . . ." or "An . . ." with verbs in the subjunctive mood). Much less commonly the title will be "about" X (and hence begin "De" followed by an ablative inflexion of the noun), or affirm by an expression in indirect speech (using Latin's accusative-and-infinitive locution), or use some other syntax.

By this yardstick, both of Milton's potential act verses—"Naturam non senium pati" and "De Idea Platonica"—have a less usual syntax. Although the indirect-statement form of "Naturam" does not differ in meaning from the much commoner direct form, a possible nuance is that its "statement-hood" receives notice; the "*That* Nature does not wear out." If so, the nuance calls attention to the poem as making a proposition which has been and will be contested by others—a small reminder of the poem's originating in disputation. As for "*De* Idea," the prepositional form of the title connotes less precision than do either of the statement-forms or the question-form: if pressed, "De" points to a more general area of thought, without saying which side is being taken. There is some precedent for this more elastic entitling, but as we shall see it is precise after all in Milton's use of it, because thus worded the title may arouse a flicker of dubiety: where does the poet stand? This "stand" is normally insisted on, by the nature of disputation. "*De*" *Idea* keeps us guessing.

In length, Milton's two poems conform much less to the norm. The length of a usual act verse is governed by the fact that normally a pair of them were printed on a single side of paper, in columns, of about thirty lines per column. But *Naturam* has sixty-nine lines, and *De Idea* thirty-nine lines, respectively. *Naturam* would not fit on one page of the standard size, nor would the two balance one another there. *Naturam*, though closer in its title and content to the usual act verses, is much too long to be printed in one column. It would fit across two, however: this

---

[3] Costello, *Scholastic Curriculum*, 17–19. Numerous examples are given in the *STC*, s.v. "Cambridge." See also Binns, *Latin Writings*, 77–79, "Versified Theses."

suggests that whatever it is it is not a set of candidacy-verses, for these did always appear as one column of a pair. Candidacies were always, statutorily, done in twos. These considerations are a further small indication that Milton's two poems are not the regular act verses, which nonetheless they resemble.

As for logical shape, act verses often close on an "Ergo," a "Therefore" or "Thus we see that"; with the ergo explicit, either within the verse itself or as a centred sub-heading to herald the concluding sentence, commonly a couplet. Milton is less explicit or mechanical: the nearest he comes is a "Sic denique," mid-line in *Naturam*, only then (in line 66) he takes his reasoning in a new direction. Once again, reference to the prevalent practice emphasizes that Milton extends it or departs from it.

If so, however, why do we need to consider the two poems in connection with the formulaic act verses at all? Compelling reasons are: (i) that Milton's poems share some, indeed many other characteristics of this little genre; (ii) that he will have written such verses when he defended a thesis of his own at a University disputation; and most decisively, (iii) that in a letter to his friend Alexander Gil, Jr,[4] he speaks of having composed some act verses for a Fellow of Christ's who had to perform in a Grand Commencement and felt he was getting too old for the concomitant versification. In other words, Milton ghost-wrote some act verses, for the University's greatest and grandest of disputation ceremonies. They would accordingly have been printed, and would have been his first printed poem.[5] Unfortunately, the verses have been lost, or not identified. Many scholars have wondered if one or other of his two poems on a philosophic theme of the Cambridge sort may be the ghost-verses. The possibility is exciting yet tantalizing, hard to prove or even to understand aright. I hope here to make new suggestions, which can advance our understanding if not provide a secure identification of his first commissioned poem. It does seem worth understanding the

---

[4] Letter 3 of *Familiarium Epistolarum*, dated "July 2, 1628" from Cambridge: see *ColWks* 12. 10. 10–22.

[5] A. H. Pollard, "The Bibliography of Milton," *The Library* n.s. 37. 10 (1909): 1, identified this lost poem as Milton's first to see print. I am reviving here his suggestion that this lost printed version was the "original form" of *Naturam*.

qualities in it which had gained him such recognition—especially considering his stormy start at Christ's and quarrel with Chappell, the fellow of this Fellow. In the end, though, it is more important to place and understand the two poems Milton published than to identify the missing ghost.

Relation of Milton's Poems to the Act -Verses Genre

Logically, both or one or the other or neither of *Naturam* and *De Idea* could be act verses, just as any might be the act verses which we know Milton to have ghost-written. Further, all of these eight positions could be examined here, with appropriate citation of the arguments of Masson and Parker and Bush and Miller and more.[6] I prefer simply to assume their work and recognise its inconclusiveness, and to give logic too a rest. After all, there are more than eight possibilities, of which one in particular appeals greatly. This is, that our two poems *began* life as act verses, which they resemble at more points than they differ; but that they have *developed* past that set form, to something more personal and expressive; perhaps expressing Milton's desire to move beyond the twofold limitations of scholastic thought and of act-verse formulae. The foremost concern is to see where he developed towards.

This position has incidental advantages. It may explain the absence of a dating for either in *Poems, 1645*. It may explain the absence of any other published act verse specimens, from an author who kept even school tasks in his work-box. It implies a reason—development, again, beyond the typical and formulaic—for the somewhat atypical syntax of both titles. It allows for the complicated form of the title of the poem which Milton published *after* the simpler poem of his pair: not only does "De Idea Platonica" have an unusual titular syntax, but with its ambivalently distancing appendage "Quemadmodum Aristoteles intellexit" ("As Aristotle understood it") it has travelled beyond the form and tone and scope of act verses.

The relationship I shall seek to demonstrate between the verses appearing in 1645 and their Cambridge matrix is of a development in self-confidence and scope. The generic comparisons enable us to trace

---

[6] A good summary is to be found in Douglas Bush, ed., *A Variorum Commentary on the Poems of John Milton*, (New York: Columbia University Press, 1970), 1: 209–12.

more exactly how Milton developed beyond the formulaic, by appropriating and reinterpreting it. We shall begin by examining some extant act verses. Because these are not lame but still no more than workmanlike, they suggest how Milton exceeds the workmanlike—something all the more worth observing in a genre which has been neglected or dismissed. Something big was stirring in Milton by the year 1628: he had achieved sufficient recognition by his other verses to be commissioned to compose act verses for the greatest and grandest of all the Cambridge rituals, the Great Commencement of July. These, to repeat, were his first printed poem.

Act Verses from around 1628

Now let us consider Milton's efforts in a context of this minor genre. Here are some hexameters[7] which support the thesis that "Non datur motus gravium simpliciter naturalis" ("The natural motion of weighty objects is not given without reservation," perhaps meaning that gravitation is inherent not in objects but in the constitution of the whole universe). These begin:

> Principio immensi cum primum exordia mundi
> Ceperunt, proprias retinebant singula vires,
> Pulchraque discordi constabat machina nexu.
> Haud placuit; sed contiguis quae sedibus essent,
> Officiis iunxisse iuvat; litemque diremit
> Hanc melior natura,[8] et amico singula vinclo
> Nexuit, alternisque agitat sub legibus orbem.[9]

---

[7] The two main metres in Latin verse, and in act verses, are hexameters and elegiac couplets. Hexameters (the metre of Virgil and Lucretius) all have the same line-length and metrical options, and so lend themselves to through-composition (enjambing), up to the scope of verse-paragraphs. Elegiac couplets, on the other hand, have the first line a hexameter again but the second line is a pentameter, divided—unlike the hexameter—into two equal parts, always hinged on a central caesura. The main resulting effect is that the shorter second line clinches the meaning of the longer first line. The effect is of very strong closure after each couplet: it is virtually a little stanza.

[8] Cf. Ovid, *Metamorphoses* 1.21, "Hanc deus et melior litem natura diremit." That the piece is patterned after this passage of Ovid is observed by Leslie McCoull.

[9] The verses are in the Cambridge University Library ms Sel. I. 24.2, and can be read in the *STC* microfilms Reel 1789: 4474. 123, tentatively dated to 1630. Author's name and date are not given. In general, the *STC* listing constitutes a valuable survey of act-verse subjects in the Tudor / Stuart period.

("At first, when the vast worlds first received their beginnings, individual things kept each their own powers, and the entire construction stood together in a linkage that was discordant. That did not please; but whatever things were in nearby places it was useful to have joined in duties, and so this strife was removed by benign Nature. She bound each together by a bond of friendship, and wields the world by alternating laws.")

This merits comparison with Milton's *Naturam* by using the same metre, by the scientific / cosmological subject, and by showing a related reliance on Ovid and Lucretius (for example in words like "exordia" or "machina," and the choice of hexameters for cosmological didactic). It shows workmanlike competence,[10] for instance with the enjambment, the varied sentence- and clause-length, and a concise argumentative quality. The verses do not, however, rise above the workmanlike: notice the otiose "primum" in line 1, the conventional word-order of line 3, the overworked invertebrate additive conjunctions "et" and "-que" in lines 5–7.

Consequently, the comparison shows connection with *Naturam* but then difference. Milton's sixty-nine lines argue "That Nature does not suffer old age," or (as we might put it in terms of the underlying principle of entropy) "Nature is not running down nor running out." The lines of an argument are all present, but all notably—audibly—differ from the formulaic. As we noted, *Naturam* at 69 lines in length could not be one of a pair on the usual printed page. Nor does it quietly or succinctly set forth an argument having independent existence, elsewhere, in prose. Milton starts with a forceful pair of exclamations (1–7). Then he poses a slightly longer set of loaded questions (8–16), after which comes a still lengthier drawing of absurd conclusions (19–32). Then as many lines as all so far are given to exempla supporting his own view of the subject (33–65). The conclusion springs a surprise, the animated vision of the end of time (65–69). The length and pace of units, the tone and stance, all vary as they go along. The poem could be performed aloud, whereas act verses existed for print.

---

[10] Latin verses can literally be written mechanically, working by rules of avoidance. In the nineteenth century, a versification machine—looking like a chest-of-drawers, but working like a primeval computer—was proposed. This noble invention is illustrated in Christopher Stray, *Classics Transformed: Schools, Universities, and Society in England 1830–1960* (Oxford: Clarendon Press, 1995).

Let us next take some verses on a theme surely congenial to the young Milton.[11] The theme is "That all men naturally desire to gain knowledge," which stands very close to Milton's theme in Prolusion VII ("Knowledge renders man happier than ignorance," [*ColWks* 12. 246]—a theme he explicitly says was congenial [12. 250 lines 14–20]). The act verses begin in sprightly fashion, opening up with the rhetorical question:

> Quis non Aonios latices, Phoebique fluenta
>   Quaerit, et Hyblaeo mella petenda jugo?
> Scilicet humanis haec est innata medullis,
>   Haeret et in nostro pectore sacra sitis
> Scrutari secreta Deum, viresque Parentis
>   Naturae, in tacito quas tenet ipsa sinu.

("Who does not quest for the Muses' liquids and the streams of Phoebus, and the honey to be sought for on the ridge of Hymettus? For of course this thirst is innate in humans' innermost parts and the holy thirst inheres in our heart, to explore the gods' secrets and the powers of our mother Nature which she keeps in her silent bosom.")

They follow through with vivacious, varied examples. After 24 lines (including more rhetorical questions) the examples go over into the negative ("Odimus" after "petit," "sitit" and "ausa est"). The last couplet begins with the expected, formulaic "Ergo," now neatly versifying the gist of the thesis:

> Ergo animis dedit ipsa sitim Natura sciendi,
>   Hoc lacte Infantes nutriit ipsa suos.

("THEREFORE Nature herself has given to our minds the thirst for knowledge: she has reared her infants with this milk.")

A pleasant vivacity in the examples, and the varied management of the arduous couplet form, make the verses better than competent.

---

[11] Cited from Costello, *Scholastic Curriculum*, 172, who comments, "The broadside bears no date, but it is inserted in ULC, sel. I, 24, immediately before a set of verses dated tentatively 1630." The text is normalized here, as there is no reason to make the verses look quaint by preserving original forms like "-q;" for "-que" or "&" for "et."

Milton's *Naturam* correspondingly enjoys its amplitude of exempla. We should, however, reflect on the choice of verse-medium, namely the absence in Milton of nimble elegiacs: how well do they suit real argument? Even Ovid took to hexameters for his philosophical poem, the *Metamorphoses*. Contrariwise, the present act verses use the less philosophical verse-medium for a more easy-going proposition. To overstate the difference, examples monopolize attention, being all there is, whereas they do not do so in Milton. By the same token his rhetoric wields more animation, and a more imaginative engagement with *his* thesis.

Yet a thesis, of the scholastic sort, it does remain. The last comparison is of both Milton's poems with act verses by Alexander Bolde, whose prose was examined in Chapter One, and whose notebooks in St John's College Library include disputation verses alongside his disputation-manuscripts. In this instance at least, we are measuring Milton by a near-equal, in the limited sense that Bolde was doing in person what Milton's elderly Fellow did by proxy: Milton's lost verses were to be judged as Bolde's were.

Bolde wrote two, for distribution together. The titles are conjoint, thus:

> Anno Domini 1615. Quaestiones a meipso defensae in secunda Solennitate Comitiorum quadragesimalium, his versibus explicatae.
> Prima. Saturni frigus frigidi cerebri figmentum.

("A.D. 1615. Positions I defended at the second solemnization of the Lent Assembly, set out in the following verses. First. That Saturn is cold is a frigid figment of the brain.")[12]

> Secunda. Actio et passio (eundem motum constituentes) non differunt gradu.

["Second. That acting and being acted upon (since they constitute the same motion) do not differ in degree.]

Bolde's "Prima" begins with a pair of questions:

> Siccior est bibula Lybiae Saturnus arena?

---

[12] The pun itself could be called "frigid" in yet another sense of *frigidus*, namely insipid.

Ismenia[13] buxo et gelidis pallentior umbris?

("Is Saturn drier than the thirsty sand of Libya? Is he paler than the Theban box-tree and the cold shades?") The question may as yet be open, or in view of the title be rhetorical, insinuating the answer "No, of course it couldn't be." Another follows, making clear if it was not already that the questions are leading ones: it is unworthy of a star to be cold, and do not stars shine by burning, therefore they neither experience cold nor emit cold –

> Nec patitur frigus, nisi frigora sentiat ignis
> Ignea supremo cum vis dominatur in orbe
> Isque situ errores longe supereminet omnes (9–11)

("Nor does he suffer cold unless fire feels the cold, seeing that the force of fire dominates the sphere of the heavens and he from his position far overtops all the wandering stars.") Besides, Saturn (the god, now) lived in Italy, and southwards from Cambridge it gets hotter not colder.

Ergo
> Cum neque participat frigus, nec id imprimit ulli,
> Saturni frigus fatui impostura cerebri est.

("THEREFORE since he neither partakes of cold nor impresses it upon anything, the supposed cold of Saturn is merely the imposture of some empty brain.")

The argumentation is an insouciant hodge-podge of assumption, common sense, and myth. Charitable interpretation might receive the mixture as witty, but philosophical or sequacious it is not. Nor is the Latinity unimpeachable.[14] Yet the weakest feature is the versifying, in that the hexameters seldom span the line-ends, and tend to come in pairs. Since Latin has elegiac couplets necessarily in pairs, it is denying Roman example to push the more plastic, discursive-argumentative hexameters back into pairs, being necessarily inferior to elegiacs when paired. (The ineptitude is like that of an English poet writing blank

---

[13] False quantity: the /e/ is a long vowel.
[14] I would have expected Bolde's causal clauses with the conjunction "cum" = "since" to take a subjunctive, not the indicative he favours.

Photograph of ms by Alexander Bolde, giving two sets of his Act verses in 1615, as discussed in text at pp. 48-51. The first set of Bolde's verses concludes at '... cerebri est.,' whereupon the centred words 'In 2am [=secundam] quaest; [= quaestionem] begin the second set of verses, which finish after eight lines of the RHP, at '... Plusve Minusve pati.' Both sets conclude by drawing the conclusion of their summarized arguments or examples preceding, with a prominent centred Ergo. This was the customary concluding formula, seen in the many extant verses whether printed or handwritten. Their absence from Milton's philosophic verses is thus a supporting reason for thinking those to be modeled on or extended from act verses rather than literally being such.

verse in unrhymed pairs, thwarting both ear and mind by falling between the two stools, heroic couplets and blank verse paragraphing.)

Bolde's second verses go better, perhaps because now he does compose in elegiac couplets. They argue, too: the first couplet gives two opposing views of the Quaestio; the second couplet says "I take a middle position." The fourth couplet says what an "Objector" might reply; then "Resp." (Respondent, the proposer of the thesis) rebuts in the fifth couplet. "Ob." has another go, in a sixth couplet; but "Resp." lays him flat, with three couplets of rebuttal. So we come once again to "Ergo":

> Quam quantum enixa est Virtus Activa movendo
>   Constat posse nihil Plusve Minusve Pati. (19–20)

("THEREFORE it is agreed that the amount of exertion by Active Power in its moving can be neither more nor less than what is experienced by Passivity.")[15]

The second set of verses do convey the back-and-forth of the Schools, whereby the thesis-summary anticipates objections, and keeps throughout to the lines and needs of the argument. There are no witticisms, no puns or myths, no poetical frills; and few poetical ineptitudes either.[16]

As for the comparison of both poems with Milton's two, however, neither of Bolde's is much like them. This can be seen best where some point of contact does occur, be it in subject or method or stance. For example, the "Saturn" hexameters begin with three questions, which turn out to be rhetorical, then berate error through a few lines: *Naturam* too berates error, then moves into questions which turn out to be rhetorical. At which point, however, sheer difference asserts itself. Exclamation precedes questioning, and both have much greater freedom and abundance. This is partly scale, and length, the absence of the act-verse cramping. This orator is writing for himself, not for one column of a thirty-line sheet. It is equally a positive presence, the sound and stance, of an impassioned orator:

---

[15] The rendering is clumsy partly because the Latin is. What does "Quam" mean or do here? The meaning is a sort of Newton's Law, that to every active movement there is and must be an equal amount of passive absorption of it.

[16] "Quam quantum" was awkward in sound as well as syntax.

> Heu quam perpetuis erroribus acta fatiscit
> Avia mens hominum . . .

("Ah! How perpetual are the errors which drive man's wandering mind to exhaustion! . . .")[17] This particular error will be exposed but by reference to a first principle of human mind. The Lucretian metre goes with a Lucretian attitude: Milton appropriates to his Christian belief the sound and fervour of Lucretius' denunciation of superstitions. In the body of the proof, a full-blooded Lucretian word-music is continuously heard.[18]

To put this another way, taking a point of contrast with Bolde's second verses now, no audience or occasion or disputation or opposing speaker is implied, because instead an indignant protest in the name of God's acts of creation and providence is the chosen goal. The tone of prophetic universality is a far cry from a set of act verses, yet the similarities and links have enabled it. The Platonic or theological animus against Error,[19] which has provided a starting-point or a grace-note for several of the act verses in this little survey, has become a theme and a passion, which leads to the final vision of the "Fire Next Time." I find nothing perfunctory or artificial about the composition. It has taken a stock idea from the university genre and found a muse of fire:

> Sic denique in aevum
> Ibit cunctarum series iustissima rerum,
> Donec flamma orbem populabitur ultima, late
> Circumplexa polos, et vasti culmine caeli;
> Ingentique rogo flagrabit machina mundi. (65–69)[20]

("In fact, then, the process of the universe will go on for ever, worked out with scrupulous justice, until the last flames destroy the globe,

---

[17] For Milton's Latin verses I use in the first instance the elegant prose renderings of John Carey's edition. The above example is to be found in John Carey, ed., *John Milton. Complete Shorter Poems*, 2nd ed. (London: Longman, 1997), 67.

[18] Cf. e.g., *De Rerum Natura* 3. 1058.

[19] Noticed in Chap. 1 above, regarding the two disputation-prolusions.

[20] Bush, *Variorum*, 223–24, for use of Lucretius, Ovid, and others here. In terms of diction and rhythm, once again, borrowing and pastiche have been appropriated, into a sound and a vision of Milton's own – ones which recur in his later greater works, including Prolusion VII.

enveloping the poles and the summits of vast heaven, and the frame of the world blazes on one huge funeral pyre.")[21]

If the development is so great, however, in what sense if any should we think of *Naturam* as the verses which Milton ghost-wrote, and refers to in his letter to Gil? Have I overstated my case?

In the first place, he kept most of his compositions. He used much less finished and compelling juvenilia than this for his *Poems, 1645*. Second, the form of the title is thesis-like.[22] The comparative rarity of its syntax may reflect a revision, too, putting a little distance now between the commssioned printed version and its more impassioned, oral development. Third, the topic suits the year following publication of George Hakewill's *Apology of the Power and Providence of God* (1627), which argues with a like Protestant fervour against entropy.[23] Fourth, the letter to Gil is often cited as evidence that the poem sent to Gil was a lost trifle because the tone of the letter is depreciatory; or else—going in the opposite direction—that the poem was *De Idea* because that poem is a "joking" one. Yet "leviculas illiusmodi nugas" does not mean "joking": it

---

[21] Carey, 68.

[22] This idea tallies with Estelle Haan's suggestion, in "Milton's *Naturam Non Pati Senium* and Hakewill," *Medievalia et Humanistica* 24 (1997): 147–67, that Milton's poem and the syntactical shape of his title alike relate to the controversy in print about entropy between Godfrey Goodman and George Hakewill: see below. Hakewill's work is *An Apologie of the Power and Providence of God in the Government of the World* etc. (1627, enlarged ed. 1630). He was answering Godfrey Goodman, *The Fall of Man* (1616, 1618, but with a new ed. 1629).

[23] The possible connection with Hakewill was advocated by Masson, downplayed by Bury, rejected by Parker, but left open as undecidable without further evidence by Bush (summary in Bush, *Variorum*, 213–14). See also *The Latin Poems of John Milton*, ed. Walter MacKellar (New York: Columbia University Press, 1930) 49–51. Estelle Haan has again proposed an influence in "Milton's *Naturam Non Pati Senium* and Hakewill." On the one hand, if Haan is right then Milton's acts of selection or departure from Hakewill (and from his sources and the opponent) may be seen as a clever interaction with them, although the force of this would be lessened by the time of publication, in 1645. On the other hand, the ideas themselves are widely found, and indeed (as Bush shows) reach back to the Bible and pagan antiquity alike. Nonetheless, the poem illustrates an important truth about Neo-Latin verse, that at certain points it derives its animation from the life of its time, to which in turn it gives heightened expression: other Latin poems by Milton at Cambridge refer to and illuminate quite different scenes from this life. See in general Hans Helander, "Neo-Latin Studies: Significance and Prospects," *Symbolae Osloenses* 76 (2001): 5–44; the point is taken up by a number of the commentators there on his paper.

is said from the standpoint of the Fellow, commissioning act verses because *they*, the genre, are now beneath him. Moreover, the depreciatory tone is largely mere modesty: if it is seriously intended, then it might apply also to Milton's next words, to Gil as a "keen judge" of verse, he being a "rerum Poeticarum judicem acerrimum" in general, (*ColWks* 12:10 15), and a very "frank" or "fair" judge of Milton's in particular ("et mearum candidissimum [judicem]"). I find it more natural, therefore, to conclude that Gil did what he was asked to do, and that his comments in reply provided the prompting to expand and improve the "nugae" into *Naturam* itself.

Naturam shows origins in the world of a Cambridge Commencement, but represents a development far beyond them. The poem exhibits a clear and strenuous emulation, one which extends the formulaic and required into the personal and voluntary. To put that point in another way, although the poem relates in its arguments to a contemporary theological controversy of 1627, what a reader responds to is the forceful, personal recombination of pagan topos and biblical orthodoxy.

How is it done, then? Can we recover the reading or imitatio which have lit up the poem, more clearly than its occasion? These questions raise the larger one, addressed in wider terms in the Introduction, of our poem's debt to classical or to Neo-Latin exemplars. I give my position on this vexed question as it affects *Naturam* before closing with an account of the poem's ending in that light.

Is the reading which the poem reveals to us only or mainly of Roman poets, or Neo-Latin ones too? What counts as proof that the poet has consciously, actively, been appropriating either sort of predecessor for wording, imagery, rhythm and so on? This is a distinct issue from whether the poem's *content* has imbibed arguments from the Goodman / Hakewill debate, and will recur in later chapters whenever a Cambridge poem by Milton is appraised.

I am more confident that Milton had read the Roman poets than I am that he had read the many Neo-Latin ones who evince parallel phrasing as recorded by editors and Neo-Latin scholars.[24] We know that

---

[24] See especially S. P. Revard, *Milton and the Tangles of Neaera's Hair* (Columbia, MO: University of Missouri Press, 1997), 4–6 and Chaps. 1 and 2; also Estelle Haan, *From* Academia *to* Amicitia: *Milton's Latin Writings and the Italian Academies, Transactions of the American Philosophical Society* 88.6 (Philadelphia: American Philosophical Society, 1998).

he read the Romans and drank deep of them, because he says so, because his own educational syllabus though radically reformist still bristles with Roman authors, and further because it was expected of versifiers, whether novices or at the highest levels. On the other hand, the more numerous are the Neo-Latin poems which are adduced as echoes, the harder it becomes to know which out of the many have probability as influences or sources; and so the appeal increases of the alternative possibility, *ancient* originals of topos, phrasing, cadence and all.[25] Thus although Neo-Latin remains one of the most intertextual of poetries, the intertextuality which counts most for me is the weaving—which is the root metaphor in "text" and "texture"—of the ancient exemplars into a modern *imitatio*. Just as with a Roman poem we look first and foremost at any extant Greek exemplars ("vos exemplaria Graeca . . ."), so with a Neo-Latin poem I prefer to go not very far into labyrinthine epigoni, and to stay close to its Roman starting-points. To do so remains both satisfying to the searcher and fruitful in secure findings.

Without wishing to invalidate other scholars' proposals, then, since they are based on wider Neo-Latin reading than my own, I do regret it when echoes or parallels (illuminating in themselves) turn during discussion into influences or even debts without due attention to probability. It is conceivable, after all, that modern scholars—who are older, who have fuller commentaries and dictionaries, and who in further respects work within a gathering avalanche of scholarship—have read more Neo-Latin than Milton (at age nineteen) had read.[26]

For the present enterprise, then, the primacy of the Roman exemplars is mainly upheld, along with a resolve to explore if not ransack them, for the sake equally of enlightenment and probability. We can return to *Naturam* for an example, its ending in a vision of fire.

---

[25] The picture is further complicated by the fact that without having read a poet he could read excerpts from that poet in composition-aids like Johannes Buchler or Ravisius Textor (Bush, *Variorum*, 10–11), where solutions could be sought to diction and prosody. The presence of a shared phrase or two may mean no more than that Milton had read these manuals, or studied from them at St Paul's School.

[26] A similar caution has been proved necessary in the case of Shakespeare source-studies. More and more parallels or analogues were being proposed. The more that were proposed, however, the less likely Shakespeare had read all of them, and that we were coming any nearer to knowing which one(s) he did read. Besides, he of all people could think for himself.

In a line like the closing one, "Ingentique rogo flagrabit machina mundi" ("the frame of the world shall blaze on its own funeral pyre"), Milton may well echo the thought of a multitude of writers and a dozen lines of other people's Latin; yet he gives a vision of the Lord's fiery final judgment which is his own. The most useful method of approach, accordingly, is to address the likeliest ancient originals.

"Cunctarum series iustissima rerum" brings into view Virgil's "series longissima rerum" (*Aeneid* 1. 641): we feel all the more, therefore, its difference, the difference between a very long process and a most just one. Milton's borrowing generates a new idea, one fitter to this context; indeed dare one say that since series are often "very long" Milton is less tautologous? In the next line "flamma . . . ultima" derives from Ovid, *Fasti*, 4. 856, "Ultima plorato subdita flamma rogo": "At last they set fire to the lamentable pyre" of Romulus' brother Remus.[27] Milton keeps the link of flames to a pyre, again a natural if not obvious link, but reserves the pyre to a later line. His "last flame" is magnificently revised, from being the straightforward habitual igniting at cremation to become God's torch at the end of the physical world. The shift theologizes Ovid, as Milton does elsewhere too and apparently likes doing.[28] This brilliantly calls up the biblical apocalypse of 2 Peter 3: 10–11, "But the day of the Lord will come as a thief in the night; in the which the heavens shall pass away with a great noise, and the elements shall melt with fervent heat, the earth also and the works that are therein shall be burned up." Only now the "final flame" will "ravage the round world" ("populabitur orbem"). Then, when the flame has "embraced the poles" and the "roof-ridges of vast heaven,"[29]

---

[27] Text from Ovid, *Fasti*, Book 4, ed. Elaine Fantham (Cambridge: Cambridge University Press, 1998), 82; translation from *Ovid's Fasti: Roman Holidays*, trans. Betty Rose Nagle (Bloomington: Indiana University Press, 1995), 128.

[28] The notorious "talia somnia" of Elegia III. 68, and the choice introduction of "nablia" at III. 65 (the Hebrew harps found in Ovid, turned into angels' paradisal ones): see Hale, *ML*, pp. 34–35.

[29] Grace-notes here include: "vasti" connotes "devastation" and so continues "populabitur" while of course denoting immensity; and the "culmina," being a collateral form to "columna," a column, give a glimpse of earth as a created city, now brought to nought by the God of the heavenly city who made both cities. Rome as the ultimate secular city is brought crashing into flames by the power of the God who made all cities. The *Fasti* is precisely a celebrating of Ovid's city and its life.

the frame of the universe will blaze on a gigantic pyre: "ingentique rogo flagrabit machina mundi." Whilst "machina mundi" is more of a stock phrase than "ultima flamma," its Lucretian origin (*De Rerum Natura* 5. 96) well befits the ending of this aetiological poem; being stock, of course, in fact obvious, makes the idea's appearance in Hakewill unremarkable. Rather, it is the flame which requires attention at the close: it spreads, from ravaging the round earth to a metaphorical, cataclysmic usage, in which Milton appropriates it to the igniting of the whole world's funeral pyre. A two-stage consuming is imagined: we move from a wildfire burning to death, to a ritual act of destruction of the corpse on the pyre.

This may be overinterpretation. Yet it does restore force to the continued metaphor, and removes repetition from within it. It gives more meaning to the Ovid allusion, and gives Ovid back his primacy. It takes the Roman reference seriously: Ovid is explaining the death of Remus, the founder's own brother. It links with Milton's characteristic best use of Ovid elsewhere: the *Fasti* in general for *In Quintum Novembris* (see Chapter Eight below), and the particular feasts honoured in *Fasti* 4, because the Book incorporates the birthday rites of the city of Rome and of the shepherds. The cremating of Remus and the fireleaping of the Palilia,[30] cunningly elided together by Ovid, caught Milton's eye as part of a wider fascination with the *Fasti*.

Herein resides the originality of the emulation. To recapture how it is done gives us conditions of understanding and our best guide to evaluation.

It is the same but even more so in the next poem discussed: this time, Milton creates the genre as well, since while still using commonplaces and shared tropes, and still showing many a connection to the disputations, *De Idea Platonica* is sui generis, one of a kind.

From 'Naturam' to 'De Idea Platonica'

The two poems come in this order, without any dating, in *Poems, 1645*. This can only mean that the self-editing Milton wanted them read in that order, and saw some progression. Since it is development which

---

[30] Ed. Fantham, 226–27, 240.

equally inheres in their relation to the act verses as a Cambridge genre, I will press the point concerning *1645*, to examine how *De Idea* can be seen as a development beyond *"Naturam,"* just fulsomely praised. First, it is more compact in delivering its rhetorical-cum-philosophic punch. Secondly, it moves outside the usual metres into that of Horace's *Epodes*—a virtuoso matching of medium to stance and subject. Thirdly, it is written much more dramatically, from the persona of an advocate who addresses several other personae, gods included (as no respecter of these personae): the tone is animated and abrasive. Fourthly, this is done so as to put in the dock the very last person one would expect Milton to put there, namely Plato.

It will surprise no one that Milton's latest venture in this rule-bound academic mode far exceeds the generic humdrum; but *how* he does it, as seen in the original generic context and its Latinity, should both surprise and please. For the present study, too, *De Idea* measures his farthest transcendence of any exercise-mode. The distinction between required exercise and voluntary is here dissolved into fiery complex bravura.

De Idea Platonica: Does Milton Really Ridicule Plato's Theory of Ideal Forms?

Opinion about Milton's Latin poem on the Platonic Archetype or ideal form changed with Coleridge, and has now come close to a consensus or orthodoxy. The view which prevailed before Coleridge had noted that the poem's voice attacks Plato's theory of Ideas and had assumed that Milton—in the poem—endorsed the attack. Coleridge rejected this view, saying: "This is not, as has been supposed, a ridicule of Plato; but of the gross Aristotelian misinterpretation of the Platonic Idea, or Homo Archetypus."[31] Masson[32] agreed; and so do most editors and commentators nowadays. Thus John Carey opines that "[The poem] is a

---

[31] Coleridge is cited, like others named in this section, from Bush, *Variorum*, 225, n. 1.

[32] David Masson, ed., *Poetical Works of John Milton*, 3 vols. (London: Macmillan, 1890), 1: 294–95, 341.

burlesque of Aristotle's criticisms of Plato's doctrine of ideal forms ... Milton speaks as a literal-minded Aristotelian."[33]

A few doubting voices are heard. Douglas Bush finds the poem a "half-burlesque."[34] One may wonder just how a half-burlesque works, and have doubts about Bush's doubts. Harris F. Fletcher finds ingenuity and wit as the poem's main qualities and (by implication) its raison d' etre, without however explaining why he thinks so. "To me the poem is strictly an academic exercise of great ingenuity, even wit, on a set topic, that was received with acclaim and even the kind of enthusiasm extended to a triumph among undergraduates."[35] Without knowing what Fletcher means by "strictly" here, he does face in the right direction, namely toward the spirit and axioms of the exercises.

Several other responses are possible. Besides the disfavoured predecessor to Coleridge's, and the positions sketched by Bush and Fletcher, we may posit a failed version of the two main ones. That is to say, the old view could represent Milton's design, but a design now taken as self-defeating or crass; or the present orthodoxy, though representing Milton's design, may expose it as too subtle to have its effect. Again, one could attempt a compromise or mixed position on lines different from Bush's or Fletcher's. It is time, at all events, to reopen the debate and to challenge the majority view.

To close this survey of opinion, here is C. S. Lewis, given the place of honour because he found qualities in the poem which others did not mention. He was moved to translate part of it, saying, "[The poem] was probably intended as a mere academic squib; but genius sometimes laughs at author's intentions. I hardly dare to hope that [my] version has preserved the goblin quality of the original: it will be enough if I send some readers to explore for themselves such a neglected and ex-

---

[33] Carey, 69.

[34] Bush, *Variorum*, 225–26.

[35] Harris Francis Fletcher, *Milton's Intellectual Development*, 2 vols. (Urbana: University of Illinois Press, 1956–1961), 2: 427. I shall be discussing the matter of the "set topic." I know of no evidence as to the poem's reception in Milton's own student milieu, but Fletcher is perhaps relying on the fact (which he discusses, following Masson) that the poem turns up in an anthology of students' wit-pieces a century later.

quisite grotesque."[36] Lewis is at any rate impressed with the poem, and his words "goblin" and "grotesque" have helped us all to enjoy it. However, he showed less respect when he chopped off the ending, saying "I cut the umbilical cord which, in the original, connects the fantasy with its scholastic occasion."[37]

We should *not* disconnect the fantasy from its scholastic occasion, or at least (since the exact occasion is a mystery) from its Cambridge Latin contexts. The Cambridge contexts can bring us to a fitter interpretation of the poem. Furthermore, the internal evidence—the topic and structure, prosody and tone of the poem itself—combine with that contextual evidence to redeem the poem from an orthodox valuation which I believe to be misguided and anachronistic. It will be contended that the orthodox view is an unexamined oversophistication, of an excellent and unusual piece of disputation. Though it is neither a prolusion nor act-verses, the poem is driven along by the spirit and excellence of both.

Here is the text with my own translation.[38]

De Idea Platonica quemadmodum Aristoteles Intellexit

Dicite, sacrorum praesides nemorum deae,
Tuque O noveni perbeata numinis
Memoria mater, quaeque in immenso procul
Antro recumbis otiosa Aeternitas,
Monumenta servans, et ratas leges Iovis, 5
Caelique fastos atque ephemerides Deum,
Quis ille primus cuius ex imagine
Natura sollers finxit humanum genus,
Aeternus, incorruptus, aequaevus polo,
Unusque et universus, exemplar Dei? 10
    Haud ille Palladis gemellus innubae

---

[36] Lewis is cited from Bush, *Variorum*, 226; he wrote in *English* 5 (1944–1945): 195.

[37] Lewis gives no reason for thus truncating a not very long poem. His version is lively, and I would have used it if it had been complete.

[38] The text is as prepared by myself for *BLN*. The translation is adapted from that in the same volume. It uses verse because Milton himself always used verse when translating verse. Some liberties are taken as a consequence, to convey in English the breezy eristic tone. The piece is a flashy Quod Erat Demonstrandum, one-sided and frenetic like the disputations.

Interna proles insidet menti Iovis;
Sed quamlibet natura sit communior,
Tamen seorsus extat ad morem unius,
Et, mira, certo stringitur spatio loci; 15
Seu sempiternus ille siderum comes
Caeli pererrat ordines decemplicis,
Citimumve terris incolit Lunae globum;
Sive inter animas corpus adituras sedens
Obliviosas torpet ad Lethes aquas; 20
Sive in remota forte terrarum plaga
Incedit ingens hominis archetypus gigas,
Et diis tremendus erigit celsum caput
Atlante maior portitore siderum.
 Non cui profundum caecitas lumen dedit 25
Dircaeus augur vidit hunc alto sinu;
Non hunc silenti nocte Pleiones nepos
Vatum sagaci praepes ostendit choro;
Non hunc sacerdos novit Assyrius, licet
Longos vetusti commemoret atavos Nini 30
Priscumque Belon inclutumque Osiridem.
Non ille trino gloriosus nomine
Ter magnus Hermes (ut sit arcani sciens)
Talem reliquit Isidis cultoribus.
At tu, perenne ruris Academi decus, 35
(Haec monstra si tu primus induxti scholis)
Iam iam poetas, urbis exules tuae,
Revocabis, ipse fabulator maximus;
Aut institutor ipse migrabis foras!

On the Platonic Ideal Form
as Aristotle Understood It

Say who, you guardians of the sacred groves,
And you, nine-times-blest mother of the Muses,
Memory; O say, Eternity, you who rest
Far off in your vast cave and keep heaven's muniments,
Jove's laws, celestial almanacs, daybooks of the gods: 5
Say who was that first Archetype, from whom
Skilled Nature fashioned all the human race?
Eternal, incorrupt, long-living as heaven,
Single and universal human template! 10
 Since he was not some twin of virgin Athena
Living unborn inside the mind of Jove,
Maybe although he shares in kind with all
He exists outside all, individual,

Wondrously limited to a finite spot?　　　　　　　　　　15
Maybe companioning the stars he roves
For ever through the sempiternal spheres,
Or dwells (earth's next-door neighbour) in the Moon?
Maybe amongst the souls awaiting bodies
By Lethe's stream he sits oblivious?　　　　　　　　　　20
Maybe in some far region of the Earth
He strides along, gargantuan Archetype,
Raising his head high to scare the gods witless,
Taller than Atlas who upholds the heavens?
　　Tiresias, with his blind seer's piercing insight,　　　25
Never perceived this Ur-Mensch; nor did Mercury,
Swift-flying god, reveal this mystery
In night-time seances to his band of sages.
No Assyrian priest has heard of him, despite
Listing the farthest ancestors of ancient Ninus,　　　　30
Primeval Baal, and the famed Osiris.
Even thrice-great Hermes, proud of his triple name,
Knower of secret things, left nothing known
To Isis' cult about this Archetype.
　　So Plato, lasting glory of Academe,　　　　　　　35
If you first introduced these bogeys to the Schools,
Call back the poets you exiled from your city!
Do it at once! For one of two things holds now:
Either confess yourself the ultimate fiction-writer;
Or else, you founder of the ideal State,
You'd better leave it!—Better emigrate!

External Evidence: Cambridge Contexts

Our poem sounds less like the act verses, of a versified thesis, than an "anti-thesis" so to speak, verse from the stance of an opponent not a respondent. Now opponents did not have to versify, opponency being the lesser of the two roles. Nonetheless, some light is dawning. Is it not in the *title* of our poem that we first register the contentious or tendentious sound of Cambridge disputation? We register it not through a named Cambridge genre, so much as in the subordinate clause about its Aristotelian standpoint; which standpoint by being named entails that there must be others. Critical debate, and ironic potential, are again kindled by the title. The announced topic is one about which there are rival views. We are being made ready, like the audiences at a disputation, to take sides. Milton is guiding us to absorb and enjoy the points of a one-sided diatribe.

Now the title may have been given it later, in 1645, when Milton edited his poems for his collected poems to date. It recognises the standpoint from which the persona speaks, without either endorsing or discrediting it. It is neither apologetic nor ironic, but helpful. It helps the reader by explaining that the poem is from a particular, named standpoint. One and all, act verses were done thus. This poem, a development beyond the staid and formulaic act-verse form, is an impassioned, rhetorical outpouring, by a well-dramatized persona. It is to be enjoyed and understood—like a prolusion—as advocacy. The very fact that the advocacy is of an anti-Platonic position confirms its relation to the exercises, because at times in the course of exercising the performer had to argue a position that was not his own, or even one which flouted his own. It was all part of the gladiatoring: the true performer would argue each case to the utmost, like a debater or mooter in our own world.

Equally, the poem is the furthest development by Milton of the scholastic modes; in musical terms, it is not an accompaniment nor an exam set piece, but a voluntary. This would help to explain why it gets printed after the simpler poem, *Naturam*, as if to say, "Now see what variations I can invent, upon a philosophic theme." Here, at the close of our treatment of Milton as disputant, we are moving toward the more voluntary pieces and optional genres of Part Two. A similar gravitation can be observed through the declamations, to be discussed in Chapters Three and Four.

Whatever the merits of this hypothesis may be, it must be recognised that the external evidence is suggestive, though not more. What it suggests is that the Cambridge contexts of Latin and scholastic logic conduced to an argumentative poem, less probably to a parodic one; but not to a conscious self-parody. To take those points one by one: (i) Our poem is certainly argumentative, in the one-sided manner of all disputation. (ii) Parody was prevalent, in fact allowed and institutionalized, as prevarication or salting, in Milton's milieu. Yet in praevarications the generally humorous, burlesque intention is never in doubt. Finally, (iii) I know of no self-parody. Whereas the present poem might be the first and sole instance of it, that sounds like special pleading, and anyway far too subtle for this public, oral, adversarial, aggressive world. People attacked. They attacked each other. What would be the point of attacking oneself, in public, in the eyes of this sort of public?

The Internal Evidence

It is time to address the internal evidence. It comprises these four matters: the choice of topic; the metre (leading to some remarks on historicity); the structure of the argument; and the tone.

The topic is a great one, potentially. This is the issue on which Aristotle parted company with Plato. In the *Nicomachean Ethics* Aristotle gave some seven major reasons for abandoning Plato's theory of Ideal forms—the theory that particulars are good, beautiful, and so forth, by sharing in some autonomous eternal absolute of goodness, beauty, and so forth. The first example he gives is Man. "In so far as both the archetype and the instances are Man, there will be no difference between them; and if so, no more will there be any difference between the archetypal Good and plain Good in so far as both are good."[39]

What raises the moment to a turning-point in the history of philosophy is the more personal preamble: ". . . such an enquiry goes against the grain because of our friendship for the authors of the theory of Archetypes. Still perhaps it would appear desirable, and indeed it would seem to be obligatory, especially for a philosopher, to sacrifice even one's closest personal ties in defence of truth. 'Both are dear to us, but our duty is to prefer the truth.'"[40]

Milton does not reproduce the fervent tone, nor most of the seven proofs. He does seize the first proof, however, instancing the same archetype—the human one. He argues the proof quite tenaciously.

What puzzles the Miltonist here is that Milton elsewhere attacks the Aristotelian emphasis of Cambridge, and often reveres Plato. It may be, of course, that he prefers Plato to Neoplatonism and Aristotle to Scholasticism: he relies greatly on the two philosophers, as distinct

---

[39] Aristotle, *Nicomachean Ethics*, 1096b1–3. The translation comes from *Nicomachean Ethics*, trans. H. Rackham, Loeb Classical Library (Cambridge, MA: Harvard University Press, 1934), 18–21.
[40] Trans. Rackham, 16–17, 1096a12–16 of the Greek.

from their supporters, throughout his working life.[41] We should try, at all events, to approach his present argument and its details without preconceptions. Is the speaker being forceful, or only crass, in pressing for an answer as to "where" we find this Archetype? The answer might be, "crass," in that the essence of humanity might be perceivable without having a whereabouts: "where" is intelligence, for instance, or malice? These are not to be found on a map either.

The speaker's utterance does sound "forceful," however, if listened to as rhetoric, a stream of rhetorical questions, all demanding the same answer: "Nowhere," "N'existe pas." Need we be surprised if the young Milton preferred a rhetorical, one-sided line of thought in 1628 at Cambridge? This was exactly what the University exercises comprised, encouraged, and rewarded. Even now, one can enjoy watching a Platonist belabouring Plato (having a holiday from reverence).

In short, although the vehemence is one-sided it matches the importance of the topic, that parting of the ways between Aristotle and Plato. Aristotle rejected his teacher's fundamental positons only gradually, belatedly, and with trouble. Fragments of these qualities enter into the vehemence of Milton, dramatizing that parting of the ways as a disputative Latin voluntary. The poem is venturesome in its topic, then; and so we find it also in its prosody, considered next.

He marks the occasion to the ear as well as to the mind, by the unique metre he chooses for his thoughts. That metre is iambic trimeters; that is, the rhythm of Plautus' senarii, but with stricter rules governing the patterning of sound-quantity into three metra.[42] The metre is to be distinguished also from the "pure" iambic trimeters of Catullus—"pure" in the sense that they use solely the pure, rising iambic (˘ –, six times over).[43] Nor is Milton using the iambic couplets, trimeters alternating with dimeters, known as "epodic" because often used by Horace

---

[41] Not to mention the third of this great triad, Socrates. In chap. 9 below he will "play in the Socratic manner." See also *Paradise Regained*, 4. 274–76 with 293–94.

[42] A metron is four syllables, typically ˘ – ˘ – or – – ˘ –. Three such metra make a "trimeter" line. It can be described as of six "feet," but the ancients heard this line in metra not feet.

[43] As in "Phaselus ille quem videtis hospitem": ˘ – ˘ – ˘ // – ˘ – ˘ – ˘ – (but the final syllable in this metre as in others is anceps, the long syllable replaceable by short because the final placing is felt as indifferent or unemphatic.)

in his Epodes. Nor yet have we the companionable or scornful "limping" ones (Greek "scazontes").[44] The choice begins to look challengingly particular.

We should ponder it further in terms of what Milton himself does elsewhere in iambic. He uses scazontes to console Salsillus, in his sickness ("Ad Salsillum"). He uses epodics, dignified couplets, to mark the death of the Bishop of Ely ("In obitum Praesulis Eliensis"). The present iambics, however, are neither lamed nor stanzaic. They are more continuous, more periodic and enjambed, than these other iambic types. If we ask to what ancient models are they indebted, I suggest it is to a combination, of Greek iambic practice in a broader way with the practice of Horace's outstanding poem in this "stichic" (non-stanzaic) way, the last of the Epodes, Epode 17.[45]

Greek iambics are the staple of drama; and Milton's poem shares its qualities of being aural, interrogative, or even invective. The name "iambics" also connects to *iambizein*, to abuse or attack, in the anonymous ritual iambic verses which had preceded the great exemplar of this mode, Archilochus. Milton's poem, whatever else it does, attacks.

In the Horace exemplar, Milton has felt a more formal, prosodic lure. This poem has most of its lines either purely iambic, or gaining a more massive effect by substituting a spondee in the usual places (first but not third syllable of each quadrisyllabic metron).[46] A few places, however, "resolve" the iambic into a tribrach ($\smile$ – into $\smile \smile \smile$,), or the spondee into a dactyl or anapaest (– – into – $\smile \smile$ or $\smile \smile$ –).[47] Milton does all of this. In doing so, he arouses the ire of one editor, Keightley: "All through this

---

[44] Scazontes as choliambs are "lame iambics", in which the last iambic is reversed into a trochee, giving the line a comic or bathetic or onomatopoeic bump or thud at its close.

[45] See the discussion of David Mankin, in Horace, *Epodes*, ed. David Mankin, Cambridge Greek and Latin Classics (Cambridge: Cambridge University Press, 1995), 14–22. I am grateful to John Barsby for this reference, which makes more sense of Milton's prosody in *De Idea* than Milton editions or commentaries do.

[46] By admitting a spondee in the first but not second half of a metron the ancients preserved the iambic pulse whilst enabling syncopations or other variations to be played around it. The same principle applies in dactylic hexameters and pentameters, indeed also in English iambics: variation in the first part of a unit (be it metron or line) is enabled by the resumed pulse in the second half.

[47] I found two dactyls in the epode, both initial; and seven tribrachs. See lines 12, 42, 63, 65, 74, and 78.

poem Milton makes too frequent use of the dactyl and anapaest."[48] Yet Milton is doing very much what Horace does. For example, Horace has several tribrachs; begins two lines with a dactyl; and in one line has no fewer than three resolutions, which exceeds even what Milton risks![49]

We ought instead to admire Milton's prosody here: it is receptive and absorbent of Horace's, well heard, with a practical understanding of it—an understanding which shows equally when he innovates.

Easy as it may feel to dismiss Keightley's unduly rigid prosodic canons, however, the truth is that a similar rigidity and preconception are spoiling the present-day reader's understanding and enjoyment of the poem. An improbable and unhistorical supersubtlety came in with Coleridge and has got stuck. When iambic is chosen for attack, we should compare iambic attack, not only in Greece and Rome but in early seventeenth-century England. To overstate for emphasis, iambic satire then usually attacked; attacked an outward target, in a blatantly obvious rather than indirect or ironic way.[50] The natural way to read Latin iambics which mock is as an attack on what is being mocked.

A more theoretical consideration may also find a place here. In Shakespeare studies, there is a well-attested tendency in the twentieth century to explain whatever is obscure or repellent in the Bard's actions by claiming it is ironical, tongue-in-cheek or self-exploding (as at the ending of the *Taming of the Shrew*) The tendency affects not only Shakespeare. Irony, by its nature, becomes pervasive, and recessive in the reader's mind: we find it everywhere, one irony within another, as we academics sit in our rooms and excogitate essays. Evidentially speaking, there needs to be something in a seventeenth-century satire, either about the context or within the text itself—clear external or internal evidence, and preferably both—to warrant the invoking of irony

---

[48] T. Keightley, ed., *The Poems of John Milton, with Notes*, 2 vols. (London: Chapman and Hall, 1859); quoted in MacKellar, ed., *Latin Poems*, 302.

[49] Horace keeps things regular and solemn till line 12, but then we read "alitibus atque canibus homicidam Hectorem" (dactyl, iamb, tribrach, tribrach, spondee, iamb: $-\smile\smile-\smile // \smile\smile\smile\smile--\smile \times$). Milton uses the initial dactyl in his first line; elsewhere he uses anapaests more than tribrachs for his resolutions—hearing a spondee not an iamb in the places where spondee is allowed?

[50] Indirect, self-exploding satire is of course frequent later in the century, with Dryden, then Swift and Pope.

so as to subvert the surface sense. Otherwise, we are giving ourselves carte blanche to disallow whatever discomforts a presentday taste. At all events, such thinking is most unsuited to *De Idea*.

Returning from this divagation to the immediate prosodic point, I would summarize it as follows. The poem attacks, using the metre of attack to give a metrical as well as other pleasures in the attack. These other pleasures include, notably, that of the structuring of the train of thought; the tone and its transitions; and the quarrel which Milton is picking.

The argument is structured as follows. An invocation of celestial wisdoms leads (with an imposing duplicity) to the question, "Who was that founding archetype or divine exemplar of humanity, from which we actual humans derive our humanity?" A fortiori, if the immortal wise ones can't say, we can't either. That is Step One, sentence One. Step Two is to give examples of where the archetype is not: not in the divine mind, but somewhere finite (line 15).[51] Step Three suggests a series of unlikely places, round the unknown edges of the cosmos. The argument entails that to situate the archetype so far from actual humans is not a convincing explanation of what those humans share, here on earth. Step Four takes a new turn, and a stronger grip. Why, pray, have not the great authority-figures of wisdom, not even one of them, left something revealed to disciples and worshippers about it? Why have neither Greek prophecy and religion, nor the *prisca theologia* and Hermetic tradition,[52] left us any word about the matter? Implication: there is nothing to say; they don't know; it's all false.

Then, tightening the screw one final turn, and confronting Plato himself, the speaker drives the point home: one of two things must happen now. Since you are shown to be as much of a fiction-writer as the

---

[51] Carey, 71: "Confined within definite spatial limits" (line 15). Should the Platonist have said, "Yes, within the divine mind; not in some finite location"? The argument conceals a dilemma: either the archetype is with God, or is God, so how does that help us, here, among particular material realities? or else the archetype is down here among them, in which case we are entitled to ask, where? How do we perceive it? and so on.

[52] Milton shows unusual erudition in lines 29-34 on the Hermetic traditions, the *prisca theologia*. He needs to show an informed acquaintance with what he nonetheless seeks to discredit (as he does in the Nativity Ode, composed about this time). Plato and his interpreters alike have erred: that is the thrust of the argument, quickening as it nears the dilemma it will pose to Plato himself.

poets whom you expelled from your ideal republic, either allow them back from exile, or go into exile yourself. The ending poses a dilemma, which hinges on several suppressed syllogisms. On this reading, a fast finish is more compelling, in terms of a poem which is making out a case, single-mindedly, than one which at an even exegetical pace makes the whole outcome explicit. This is where structure of argument crosses over into tone, which is considered next; but to anticipate somewhat, the rapid ending befits an argument which is narrow, forensic, and disputative; rhetorical as much as logical.

The reader should perhaps think of a mental duel. The poem seeks to lure the opponent into a dangerous position, then probe, then press, then open him up for a hit. It is a very palpable hit: the point of attack moves, from the Archetype itself, to the traditions of authority for it, to the great originator himself.

The tone suits this sportive, aggressive conception. Let us take the prosody again, because in Latin verse genres the choice of metre and the handling of it are what first establish the rhythm and sound of a poem; and hence, its tone. Milton seems well able to write an orthodox iambic trimeter most of the time, witness lines 2 and 4, or 7 and 12; so why might he resolve so many feet in other lines, and even resolve in ways not sanctioned by ancient authority? To cite Keightley once more, "Though the scazontes of the ancients sometimes commenced with a dactyl, we do not believe that this was the case in the regular iambic measure."[53]

There is a way to find decorum and pleasure, not incompetence or ignorance, in the unorthodox dactylic start. "Dicite," being an opening dactyl (– ˘ ˘), sounds like hexameter and on its dignity; then it tricks you. The prosodic pomposity carries on into the six-line invocation, only for the next two lines of the sentence, the main clause, to stick in the first barb; following which the last two lines of the sentence swell the iambic as pompous as it can go, dispensing with caesuras in the process. Far from censoring a heinous fault, we should watch with appreciation; that is, with enjoyment as well as recognition and understanding of an orator, making a case, and having *fun*.

---

[53] Keightley in MacKellar, ed., *Latin Poems*, 302.

The same impression, and a different enjoyment, result from a look at the syntax. Without analysing the larger units again, I note that the long sentences are expertly managed within the metre, achieving an expert and argumentative enjambment—more often and expertly than in earlier poems. Here, however, let us focus on something smaller and more measurable, namely the adjectives and their placement.

Adjectives are many and obligatory in neo-Latin verse, as signs of the practitioner's *copia* and competence, and knowledge of the ancients' practice. Milton elsewhere displays the expected patterns profusely, the Golden line and so forth, but often the effect is of padding, of insufficient meaning to merit such embellishment.[54] In the present poem, however, their orotundity and patterning do win admiration, because they swell the balloon till he bursts it. We feel, then notice, then appreciate, the grandiose compound at line-ending in "ordines decemplicis" (17); the straddling pattern of "citimum ... globum" and "obliviosas ... aquas" (lines 18 and 20), where the noun and its adjective as it were embrace the whole line. The pattern keeps changing, as Milton shakes his syntactical kaleidoscope. Though the next two lines again have adjective preceding noun, this time the adjective sits at the caesura while the noun sits at the line-end; thus, between them, controlling the line and insisting on the scornful point, the science-fiction remoteness of the all-important Archetype.

> Sive in remota forte terrarum *plaga*
> Incedit ingens hominis archetypus *gigas*.

Milton is having, and giving, pleasure. Maybe he enjoys his workout in iambics, which are not a usual metre of his. After all, that metre admits words you can never use in hexameters, because they are ineluctably iambic: mouth-filling words like *aeternitas* (4) or *caecitas* (25); or, very forcefully, *fabulator* at the climax. But although this technical pleasure shines through, it can hardly be the main point: the fact that Milton chose to use iambics suggests they fitted his meaning and its tone (rather than that he was finding a topic which allowed him to show off his iambics). The local felicities or flourishes help, not hinder, his onslaught.

---

[54] See John K. Hale, "Artistry and Originality in Milton's Latin Poems," *Milton Quarterly* 27 (1993): 138–49; and more broadly in, *ML*, ch. 2.

To repeat the earlier metaphor of music, because while images may be imprisoning they may (when changed) become heuristic: As when an organist, having practiced the tunes for the hymns (both Ancient and Modern) at the Sunday service, and seeking for something more adventurous and indeed personal by which to end the service with a joyous emphasis—loud enough, too, to drown out the post-liturgical chat—invents a flamboyant and innovative voluntary; so Milton, in my conception, sought out a theme and a diction and a metre which could express dissent, with much at Cambridge and even with his hero Plato.

Would Milton lavish these frisky embellishments on his persona in order that the persona should be thought *stupid*? This is not how Neo-Latin verse, at least in my experience of it, works. Can the supporters of Coleridge's view point to any congeners? If they can, this is where the debate should go next, to examine these. It is certainly time to ask that the orthodox view offer fresh and abundant evidence, of this sort as well as the other sorts which the heads of the present argument are identifying.

Conclusion

Throughout the discussion it has been asked, as if disbelievingly, Did Milton really ridicule Plato's theory of Ideal Forms in his poem *De Idea Platonica*? That is, surely he did not (Latin *Num*). My own answer, however is: Yes; he did; and Coleridge, even he, got things the wrong way round. My reasons include the following. (i) Milton may be obtuse; but his university studies trained people to be obtuse in exactly this way (and for a purpose). (ii) Irony is easier to perceive in the title than in the body of the poem. Like some other titles in the 1645 volume, the title seems to come from an editorial retrospect rather than from the time of the writing itself. (iii) Satire is not usually subtle when practiced by undergraduates in high spirits, nor by early seventeenth-century satirists; nor here by Milton, an undergraduate early seventeenth-century satirist in high spirits—and one whose idea of satire never later moved towards indirection or obliquity. (iv) Irony at one's own expense was rare till the novelists. It is quite a rare taste even now, outside high culture and Academia, because it so soon becomes a disabling tic.

Lastly, let me fill one large gap which has been left hitherto in my reasoning. I have not yet shown cause why Milton should attack Plato, Plato of all people. Even though we should not assume or guess that it was a set task, because I have not found a genre and occasion for which he could have been set such a task, nevertheless the subject feels thoroughly congenial. That is because it is a defence of poets, against their greatest and most influential calumniator. Milton the poet parts company with Plato on this issue because they are—for once—on opposite sides. Why should he not have fun repudiating the piece of Plato's wisdom which assailed him where his dreams of a poet's vocation lay? Sidney had done this in one rhetorical way, arguing suavely that poets portrayed a world better than this one, more ideal.[55] The young Milton, trained in verbal combat by the Cambridge scholastic system, gave his hero an eloquent breezy rebuke. He administered an ambush.

---

[55] "Poets only deliver a golden [world]"= They alone bring to birth a world of the highest value: *Miscellaneous Prose of Sir Philip Sidney*, ed. Katherine Duncan-Jones and Jan van Dorsten (Oxford: Clarendon Press, 1973), 78.

CHAPTER 3

Declamations

Though declamations preponderate among Milton's collected Cambridge performances, they are the least distinctive of Cambridge itself. Declamation is constituted more by ancient practice and paradigm. It has less of ritual and procedure than the disputations do, and—being a set speech, and not dialectical—has little interactivity. There is not a battery of local, Cambridge technical terms to be absorbed. Nonetheless, here is a mode which won Milton his first reputation, and in which he excelled; here is some of his finest Latin prose.

Here too is a striking paradox, that this prose has never to my knowledge been explored for its Latinity, though that is the prime thing about it. "In the declamation, style was the important thing."[1] I am therefore determined to explore that, giving it a longer treatment, in two chapters though the other genres receive one apiece. Declamation—more than the disputations and act verses—is fundamental to what Milton showed Cambridge that he could do, to his emulation and reputation there, to how he performed. Furthermore, it gives us apposite entry into Prolusion VI, because in that he parodies declamation.

Definition, Tradition, and Problems

Declamation, *declamatio*, is a more ancient and accessible Latin genre than the scholastic disputation. Milton liked declamations more, and composed and delivered more of them. For example, he introduced one where he had no need to, in Prolusion VI where the college festivities gave him a free choice as its master of ceremonies. We have seen already how he began his two disputations with substantial passages which are declamatory. To confirm the preference, and clinch its importance for

---

[1] Costello, *Scholastic Curriculum*, 32.

his 1674 collection, is the plain fact that the volume includes four declamations but only two disputations. Moreover, if as I have urged the arrangement of the prolusions is Milton's, he gives the declamations pride of position, first and last (I, II, III and finally VII).

What, then, is a *declamatio*? What is its history as a kind? How was it used at Cambridge? How did Milton himself employ it? How did he develop in it, or was he always so at home with it that he did *not* develop? A developmental view may seem foreshadowed by the conclusions of Chapter Two, yet those of Chapter One suggest it cannot be taken for granted. Costello, nonetheless, roundly declares that "if one compares the earlier flights of the [students'] notebooks with the fluent performances of bachelors of divinity, one is bound to conclude that constant practice in declamation achieved its end" (*Scholastic Curriculum*, 33). It would be strange indeed if chosen specimens by Milton, in a highly congenial mode, did not manifest striking development.

Cambridge *declamatio* included its Roman namesake,[2] but extended wider. The celebrated declamations of the first century of our era were the *suasoriae* and *controversiae*. In the *suasoriae*, anciently regarded as the easier and more enjoyable of the two, "the speaker gave advice to an historical character, or a group of persons, as to what his or their action should be in some crisis."[3] Should Hannibal cross the Alps? As such, it is a form of deliberative oration. The "historical" element received scant respect in practice, however, some speakers preferring the hilariously improbable.[4] The thrust of the thing was its appeal to the imagination, not to historical fact, as one would have guessed upon recognising the same elements in Ovid or Juvenal.[5] Milton's acknowledged liking for the Roman poets was a liking for the deliberative ora-

---

[2] Which as usual had Greek forebears: see Donald A. Russell, *Greek Declamation* (Cambridge: Cambridge University Press, 1983).

[3] M. L. Clarke, *Rhetoric at Rome: A Historical Survey*, 3rd ed. rev. with new introduction by D. H. Berry (London: Routledge, 1996), 89.

[4] Clarke, *Rhetoric*, 90; also 94. Examples can be read in *Roman Declamation*, extracts with commentary by Michael Winterbottom (Bristol: Bristol Classical Press, 1980). See also George A. Kennedy, *A New History of Classical Rhetoric* (Princeton: Princeton University Press, 1994), 166–72, 185–90, 209–15, 298 (index s.v. "declamation").

[5] See, e.g., Gilbert Highet, *Juvenal* (Oxford: Clarendon Press, 1954), 141, 263.

tions of their numerous personae.[6] The strength of the mode lay in the vivid or witty examples.

Much of this was found again in the *controversia*, "the imaginary case on some disputable point of law" (Clarke, *Rhetoric*, 90). These were often farfetched: "The law ordains that in the case of rape the woman may demand either the death of her seducer or marriage without dowry. A certain man raped two women in the same night; one demanded his death, the other marriage." Who shall win? Can both? Farfetched and tasteless as the case is, it flowed on into a thousand years of fiction, resembling the Angelo problem of Shakespeare's "problem play" *Measure for Measure*.

At Cambridge the subjects of *declamatio* differed, the general or abstract or topical being preferred to the historical or pseudo-legal or fantastical. Thus the themes of Milton's first three are "Whether Day or Night is the more excellent," "On the harmony of the spheres," and "An attack on the Scholastic philosophy"—respectively general, abstract, and topical.

Especial strengths of the *controversiae* lay in their rising towards *sententiae*, witty or smart or new rather than profound; in their exercise of and appeal to Pathos, strong emotion; and in the excellence of the performers, in their stand-alone performance, which drew large audiences, of rhetoric teachers and their pupils alike (Clarke, *Rhetoric*, 95–99). Thereby Roman declamation suggests a few more points of comparison; especially the performance, to teachers and pupils congregated to enjoy argument about what touched their own lives very little. It is this imaginary, freewheeling component which makes all three kinds of declamation an easy target for scorn, as superficial. Yet dismissal itself is superficial. The whole point of declamation, like disputation and indeed most Cambridge Latin genres, is their *dis*engagement from sober reality, from orthodoxy and conformism, from hot issues. Released from the pressures of a repressive everyday social life, one could con-

---

[6] Juvenal, particularly, writes in his satiric persona in the declamatory manner of the *suasoriae*, and though Milton's reliance on that poet has been little charted the evidence is not far to seek. Both at Cambridge and later on when he waxes satirical his manner is Juvenalian (caustic), not Horatian (laughing at folly) or Menippean (indirect).

centrate on the skills of argument and eloquence; and what is more, could try out new stances, experiment with ideas one did not affirm, give the imagination and the tongue a licence to travel. As D. H. Berry observes, "Declamation is in some ways comparable to a modern university education in the arts: the subject studied is not usually closely related to the future occupation of the student, but precisely for that reason it constitutes a general training of considerable value, while also being intrinsically interesting and enjoyable on account of its cultural significance" (in Clarke, *Rhetoric*, xv, emphasis added). At all events, the unrealities of the ancient declamation continued into its Cambridge namesake, with the attendant benefits and excitements.

These modes of declamation have an important kinship with the early works in which Milton takes up a point of view, to the exclusion of others and of judicious balance. *De Idea Platonica*, for example, is built upon the Aristotelian critique of Plato's idealism: "as Aristotle understood it" is manifestly not the only way of understanding it. *L'Allegro* and *Il Penseroso* are two opposite ways of regarding life itself, each resolutely persisted in from a partial perspective.[7] *Controversia* and *suasoria* required the speaker to look, respectively, at life-situations or topics with warm empathy and concomitant partiality.

Equally, however, we should understand Milton's declamations as *orationes*. (He sometimes calls them that. Terms like *oratio, prulusio, exercitatio, declamatio* overlap considerably in practice.) *Oratio* is a broader tradition. Milton alludes to it overtly in several prolusions. In beginning Prolusion III he cites the oracle, Cicero, to the effect that the role of the speaker ("Rhetor") is to "instruct, please, and finally persuade."[8] He is thinking of his own task as that of the orator. Here, accordingly, let us set out the usual threefold explanation of what oratory comprises: we need to bear it all in mind, even if much of it is vague, discretionary, or not quite what Milton does. A flexible or *pragmatic* analysis is foreshadowed for my treatment of the four prolusions.

---

[7] Their dating is unfortunately not clear (Carey, 134), but Tillyard's suggestion (Carey, 134) has merit from the present standpoint: he "contends that the twin poems grew out of the debate about night and day in Milton's first Prolusion and were written for an academic audience at Cambridge in M's last long vacation (1631)." In *some* sense, assuredly, they "grew out of" the declamation.

[8] *ColWks* 12: 159, "doceat, delectet, & denique permoveat."

The basic threefold orthodoxy from Cicero and Quintilian is succinctly summarized by Clarke (*Rhetoric*, 24–25). Oratory is forensic / judicial, deliberative, and epideictic (*iudiciale, deliberativum*, and *demonstrativum* respectively). The functions of the orator (*officia oratoris*) are: *inventio* (devising of matter), *dispositio* (arrangement), and *elocutio* (style or presentation); then *memoria*, and *actio* or *pronunciatio*. The last two, memory and delivery, are sometimes omitted from the ancient accounts, as being in the domain of nature more than of (teachable) art. The parts of a speech are: (i) *exordium*, (ii) *narratio*, (iii) *divisio* or *partitio*, (iv) *confirmatio*, (v) *confutatio*, (vi) *conclusio*. However, this sixfold division was only fivefold in Quintilian, while other ancients had four or seven parts. Perhaps the Romans were less sure and systematic than their subsequent interpreters: in practice it is hard to separate the five securely (or the four, six, seven, or eight!) typical parts in an oration, and certainly not in the case of Milton. I suspect that whatever number of parts are advocated, the scheme suited forensic orations better than the other sorts. Cambridge declamations are not forensic.

The doubt could be taken further. I have always found that the unity and force of Milton's declamations, when present, derive from the *un*structured flow of the eloquence. Is the structuring so perfect as to be unnoticeable? Is the structure what does the trick? Or is this a non-explanation, like saying an oration succeeds because it is composed in correctly-formed sentences? One is just as likely to notice the power of syntax when it departs from correctness, that is, employs the figure of anacolouthon or aposiopesis.

Cambridge itself had strong views about all this, but without clearing our own path after all. Modern writers on the syllabus rely on the instructions of Holdsworth or Duport.[9] For example, Costello cites Duport to the effect that "when you declaime you are not in genere demonstrativo dicendi [praising and castigating] but either in judiciali [legal or quasi-legal cases][10] or deliberativo [advising someone what to do]." This is distinctly unhelpful, in that Milton's declamations do praise. They do

---

[9] Costello, *Scholastic Curriculum*, 33, and (very fully) Fletcher, *Milton's Intellectual Development*.

[10] Costello mistranslates the word as "judicious."

not become judicial or deliberative in Duport's sense. How then would he have acquired any reputation, other than that of a rebel or a freak?

Since, then, neither the ancient *declamationes* nor the ancient practice and theory of oratory nor the Cambridge variations on the theme of declamation provide clear enough guidance to evaluation, and the names too are vague and elusive in practice, each tradition will be tapped, eclectically, as the need arises, in service of the broader aim of approaching the actual published orations on their own terms and their own merits.

Examples: Two Cambridge University Orators

Performance, aloud, is one such criterion. How does Milton regard and manipulate his audiences in each prolusion? Are they more or less of a felt presence than for the disputations? It will be a pleasure to approach these works afresh, in the terms which matter most, namely those of their Latinity. But it is a pleasure, before that, to present declamations or orations by others, for purposes of comparison. Those others are George Herbert, as University Orator in 1623, and his recent successor, James Diggle (Orator 1982–1993).

Because the examples chosen are not declamations but orations, laudatory ones, the comparison with Milton cannot be exact. The overriding consideration, nonetheless, is to set up instances of accomplished, distinctive Latin oratory from Cambridge, so as to measure Milton's performances (this time) with those of equals.

Herbert was delivering a speech of welcome to royalty, both King James and Prince Charles, in October 1623. It was the biggest occasion at which a University Orator has ever spoken, because the welcome was not merely for a royal visit but was the welcome to Charles upon his return from wooing the Infanta of Spain. It was a crisis; the nation was poised between peace and war because of the Spanish fiasco. Charles had failed, abysmally, yet received a hero's welcome for his failure! The Spanish alliance was feared by most of the nation, though dear to James's heart. Equally popular, maybe, was Charles's desire to go to war with Spain because of the huge snub. Herbert had thin ice to skate upon: he must welcome Charles for a glorious failure, a blessing in disguise, uphold the King's wish for peace not war, and even, if he could, put the Prince in a better humour, so that he could feel loved and not pursue a merely vindictive war. Herbert achieves it all, with panache and without compromise or crawling, as I have shown elsewhere.[11]

Audacity excused by joy fills much of the speech.[12] For example, he compares Charles to an elephant. Now the elephant is doubtless a noble, sagacious animal; but Herbert's conceit is sprightly and preposterous, as well as obvious and complimentary. When Charles went to Spain, why did he go alone, why oh why did he not take us all along with him: "siccine abiisti solus? cur non omnes tecum? cur non ut elephanti turres, ita tu patriam tecum portasti?" (451.7–8) The passage catches the fancy in several ways, from the engaging sound-pattern of the dentals through the quixotic image of Charles reversing the march of Hannibal, to the emblem or cartoon of the prince carrying the nation on his back, like a howdah. A serious point and a compliment are being made too: the heir-apparent does carry the nation's well-being on his back, and does it with ease.

In this image a rather special witty histrionics is on show. Herbert follows up this flashy conceit with another, less whimsical and more dramatic, one in which he secretes a stronger public emotion: "Sic tunc omnes strepebant: huiusmodi lamentis & quiritationibus plena erant fora, nundinae, conciliabula, angiportus, Maeandri" (451.9–11). The asyndeton certainly exaggerates, histrionically again, but the imaging is a beautiful arching, aural as well as conceptual. "Public places, marketplaces, places of assemblies, narrow lanes, winding ones." Here, just as the Latin words progress from shorter to longer and from simpler to grander, then diminish and fade away (from two to three to six syllables, then four then three, and in rhythm from trochaic to dactylic then aside into molossus), so the progression of ideas has equal lucidity: from places where people congregate, sell, and decide together, to their

---

[11] Hale, "George Herbert's Oration before King James, Cambridge 1623." The following paragraphs are abridged from that essay.

[12] *The Works of George Herbert*, ed. F. E. Hutchinson (Oxford: Clarendon Press, 1941), 445–55, hereafter cited as "Hutchinson." Reference is to page and line of Hutchinson.

journeying home. This they do in small bunches, then alone. Herbert is making vivid pictures, of the nation discussing its absent prince, and he ends plangently on their dispersal homewards, still obsessed, perplexed, deprived of their beloved prince. The exaggeration, and the conscious artistry, enhance the emotional implication by cloaking the serious thrust. The thought "How we missed you!" is after all not likely to displease Charles, and anyway this was exactly the anxiety with which his absence had afflicted his ailing father.

Now ensue two pages in favour of peace. It comprises reasoning, in which he gives war its due, but then eulogy of peacetime in a heightened register contrasted with wartime; then reasoning again, and so back into a grateful praise of a prince who has nobly sought peace at personal risk for his people. The prince is Charles, just as if he were not the chief belligerent of the hour, but rather were being tacitly incorporated amongst the peace-lovers, since peace was the real meaning of his wooing-journey. If this bemused the young man, so much the better, rhetorically.

Selections will best demonstrate the rhetorical power which Herbert exerts in this crucial passage, and especially in his transitions. Here is where he warms to his theme: "... certe fatendum est, anteferendam bello pacem, sine qua omnis vita procella, & mundus solitudo" (448.7–8) War as *procella*, a "commotion" or "hurricane" comes from Cicero and Virgil, the best of classical authors. Likewise, war as "solitudo" adapts from Tacitus the *mot* "ubi solitudinem faciunt, pacem appellant."[13] The emotional temperature rises higher: "Pace, filii sepeliunt patres; bello, patres filios: pace, aegre sanantur; bello, etiam sani intereunt . . ." (8–15). The ordered antitheses may be standard topoi, but honed thus to dense expression they become plangent. They strike strongly if the aging James thought back to 1619 when he buried his eldest son, Prince Henry, or ahead to the time soon coming when Charles would bury him. Herbert gives another three such antitheses, then caps the rising series of five with a couplet in Greek.[14] It is so finely said that those who want only pleasure can enjoy the stylish expres-

---

[13] *Agricola* 30, fin. Not the same point, but empowering Herbert's stronger, more disinterested one: "let us hang onto the real peace we do enjoy."

[14] ". . . pace, securitas in agris est; bello, neque intra muros: pace, auium cantus expergefacit; bello, tubae ac tympana: pax nouum orbem aperuit; bellum destruit veterem" (448. 10–13).

sion, but those who are prepared to be persuaded, through their ears and into their hearts, will be.

Now here is James Diggle, presenting Dame Janet Baker for the award of an honorary doctorate in 1984.[15] He speaks, in praise of music as much as of the lady herself, in a radiant prose which matches nothing so much as Milton's verses in praise of the Italian singer Leonora Baroni some 350 years before.[16]

> Scripsit haec ipsa uocem suam sibi a Deo non mancipio esse commodatam uerum hac condicione, ut eius fructum perciperent quam plurimi. nimirum, dum sublimes Iohannis Sebastiani modos, dum Angeli uerba somnianti Gerontio interpretatur, pro certo habemus, si quid in caelo musices futurum sit, huius nos uocem audituros esse caelestem. quod autem non rursus hanc pulpita uidebunt lugemus ipsi, lugent pulpita...

("I believe," she has written, "that my voice and power of communication through music were given to me by God, to be shared with others." When we hear her interpret the sacred music of Bach, or the words of the Angel to the dreaming Gerontius, we know that, if there is music in heaven, it will be her celestial voice. We weep that the stage will see her no more.[17])

If this should seem florid, we must remember what music can be for us, and what a voice Janet Baker's was, and reflect too that the Orator is thanking her for it to her face on behalf of us all—everyone who has ever been transported to nameless otherworlds by that voice channelling the music! The speech and the sentiment alike are beyond my power to praise; and only a brief analysis is worth adding.

The oration weaves in lines from Horace about Orpheus, and from Dryden about Saint Cecilia, and some words of the singer's own and an

---

[15] James Diggle, *Cambridge Orations 1982–1993* (Cambridge: Cambridge University Press, 1994), 10–11.

[16] Milton on his Italian journey 1638–1639 wrote three fine epigrams in praise of Leonora, each of which is a fine praise of music as mediated through her: see Carey, 257–60; Hale, *BLN*, 98–99.

[17] Diggle, 10–11. The translation is his own, quite free rendering. I have kept his spellings in case they help to recreate his actual pronunciation in the Senate House ceremony that day.

artful listing of her most famous operatic roles.[18] Rather than itemize these, however, though they mix art with life and all the languages in which she sang, a simpler appreciation of the Latin will do better. Its art is so good that it is *forgotten* in the contemplation of the subject, what music can be and can do. Never let it be thought that Latin cannot take wing, cannot praise absolutes worthily, cannot achieve a Pindaric radiance! Milton, in his declamations, moves toward a similar sublimity, in the last and finest of them, when he contends that knowledge makes us blessed ("beatiores").[19]

---

[18] See respectively Horace, *Odes*, 3. 11. 13–14; Dryden, *A Song for Saint Cecilia's Day*, 1687, 48–49; and for allusions to operatic roles, "subit denique quae uel maxime nos commouit Maria Scotorum Regina, exsul exspes splendida dolore," with its magical cadence ("perhaps most moving of all Mary Stuart, radiant in grief and despair").

[19] In case a false impression is being given that Cambridge oratory was always of such quality, and on such worthy topics, here is something more humdrum and Cambridge-parochial. The poet Cleveland, who was a younger contemporary of Milton's at Christ's College, went up several rungs of the Cambridge ladder before the Civil Wars supervened: he became Reader in Rhetoric as Herbert had done. Here, first, he begins an oration at an exercise "in Scholis publicis" as "Father" (*The Works of John Cleveland* [1687], 140): "Quam aequivocum sit Patris nomen, quota & quam discolor officii ratio, si non aliunde, ab hac varia frequentia (Severiores viri & lepidisssima proles) possem dignoscere?" ("How ambiguous the name of *Father* is, how great and diverse is the rationale of the office, I could discern—if from nothing else—from this present varied throng, O gravest elders and most talented youth!") He makes pawky puns as Bolde had done (Chapter One) or Herbert in his 1623 warm-up. Similarly balanced hypotaxis launches Cleveland's inaugural oration as Reader in Rhetoric ("cum Praelectoris Rhetorici munus auspicaretur," 144): "Quanta & quam divina sit vestra benefaciendi Indoles, quam pauperrima gratitudinis nostrae talio, nescio an diutinum meum silentium, an hodierna Oratio luculentius fuerit testimonium." ("How great and godlike is your disposition to benevolence, and how very poor is my own return of gratitude, I know not whether my own lengthy silence or my oration today will more blatantly testify!") This, once it has walked its way on stilts to its last word, will make the audience laugh, partly from relief. As a modesty-topos it is also somewhat precious, for example at "gratitudinis talio" (for which there are simpler words and ways to convey thanks). Throughout, it uses florid diction to dress up the simple as if it were weighty and complex. Now the cosy wit resembles some of Milton's personal asides in the declamations. The *display* of wit and vocabulary and allusion is the introverted side of Cambridge performance. It is on show in Milton's first declamations, but utterly subsumed into the theme in his best ones.

Prolusion One[20]: "In Collegio, &c. Utrum Dies an Nox praestantior sit?"

Milton's Prolusion I was delivered in college, which means—as with the disputations—that it was delivered among a smaller and more friendly audience than its University counterpart. The topic, "Whether Day or Night be the more excellent," is so empty[21] that the task is not so much to reveal the truth as to make a good show, to entertain and persuade by somehow pleasing. How will Milton do it, and how will the collected prolusions make a bright enough start—if it does?[22]

Indeed, at first sight the beginning seems gauche and offputting. Thomas Hartmann, for example, found that "He engages in a sarcastic defense of himself that could only alienate his audience."[23] Thus although an exordium should be "securing the goodwill of the listeners" so that their minds can then be moved to persuasion ("permoveri"), Milton claims he cannot do that because most of the audience look hostile and inexorable to him ("infesta in me capita," "non exorabiles"). The competitiveness of the Schools generates "hostile encounters" ("simultates,") which may include Columbia's "hatreds" (*ColWks* 12: 120. 2). But he doesn't care (120. 2–6). He does see some well-wishers, and prefers their approval to that of the prevalent ignorant (120. 7–15). Then he excoriates those ignorant, who logically include the majority of the listeners; and he does it at some length (120. 10 to 122. 2), likening them to empty bean-pods or frogs which can't even croak. It is a very curious *captatio benevolentiae* which flouts the first rule of oratory and proceeds to insult a large part of the audience. Is there no alternative to seeing the opening of the first prolusion as an arrogant, alienating misjudgment?

---

[20] The declamations are conveniently summarized by David Masson, *The Life of John Milton and History of His Time*. 6 vols. (Cambridge: Macmillan, 1859) I. 239–273, as a group; also, more scattered, in Parker, and in Fletcher, *Milton's Intellectual Development*.

[21] The topic is only a peg to hang the oration on, because it is like debating whether Up is better than Down: we need both, not least to define each other.

[22] Repeating the assumptions that the first is meant to make a bright start yet leave room to display growth in later effusions.

[23] Introduction to "The Prolusions," in *The Prose Works of Milton*, ed. J. Max Patrick (Garden City, NY: Doubleday Anchor, 1967), 5.

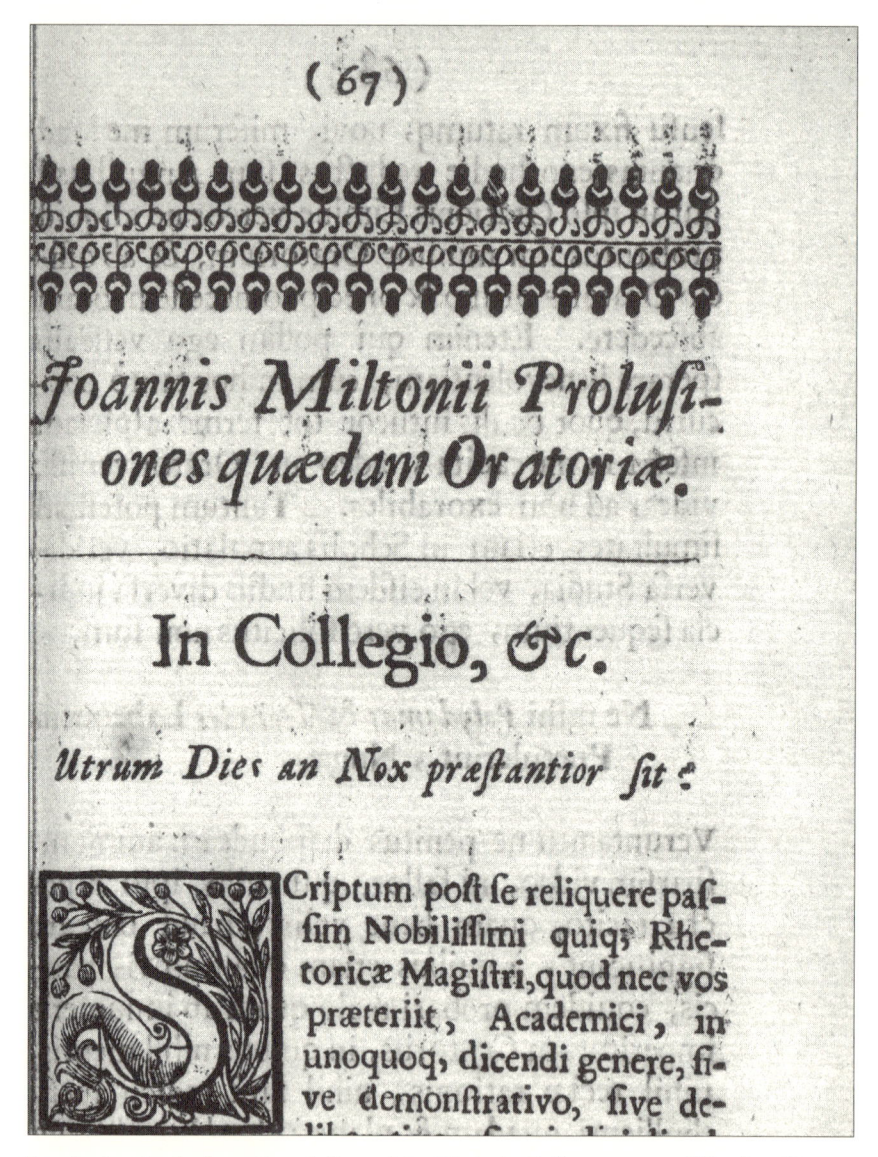

> (67)
>
> *Joannis Miltonii Prolusi-*
> *ones quædam Oratoriæ.*
>
> In Collegio, &c.
>
> *Utrum Dies an Nox præstantior sit?*
>
> Criptum post se reliquere passim Nobilissimi quiq; Rhetoricæ Magistri, quod nec vos præteriit, Academici, in unoquoq; dicendi genere, sive demonstrativo, sive de-

Proclusion 1, declamation delivered in Christ's College etc. on Whether Day or Night is more excellent.

> "It is a widespread maxim of the noblest masters of rhetoric, as you well know, my fellow-students, that . . ." He starts off slowly and with a truism, for the sake of establishing a dignified and speakerly register, which is further established by the formal address to "Academici," "members of the University of Cambridge."

There is. Everything depends on tone. Just as one can be appalled as an outsider overhearing the insults through which two friends put each other down, and then be disconcerted to find that they are actually enjoying themselves ("doing the dozens"), so here we find linguistic clues which make us revise the first impression, and recall the occasion and the audience, that collegial friendly closeness of which Costello spoke, and which will dominate Milton's performance in his salting (Chapter Nine).

Exaggeration is the first and plainest clue. He thinks of the task as a "certamen" (122. 7, "contest"), and more colourfully a "decertatio oratoria" (122. 16), a "decisive contest in oratory." A "decisive contest" or fight to the finish, it was *not*. If we press his final adjuration to his listeners (148. 2–3) that they should "adorn my cause with your votes," they will be voting who wins this "contest." Whether an actual clapping of hands concluded the declamation in the small college chapel we may doubt. What is certain is that this very minor engagement in *controversia* is being dressed up by Milton as if it was important. The over-emphatic metaphors suggest an in-house familiarity, not anxiety but ease.

A related but distinct feature of good Latin style supports this interpretation. If we ask how Milton keeps his listeners entertained with no help from his inane topic, we notice his extensive and resounding diction. While "diction" can appear an abstraction or etiolation, seizing upon individual words rather than the phrase or clause or thought of a Latin prose, Latin of the ancient or humanist sort cannot be appreciated without recognising, upon occasion, and at need, the one right word in the one right place. To take a small instance, James Diggle speaks about the voice of Elgar's Angel to "somnianti Gerontio," the "dreaming Gerontius." "Somnianti" alludes to the title of the text, John Henry Newman's "The Dream of Gerontius." Better yet, the continuous present of the participle pinpoints how the Angel comes to Gerontius at a critical point of his death-agony-dream. Crucially, the longer word takes its place in the whole clause, the rhythm by which it climbs through lengthening polysyllabics to a finality of rightness: "dum Angeli uerba somnianti Gerontio interpretatur." The climax of the prose is echoing the climaxing of the oratorio at this point. Slowing the pace to analyse it uncovers how the final five-syllable word is the most vital: "interpretatur," the Angel interprets, goes between, makes sense of it all for the dreamer. In a related way, Milton's longer words and their place within the rhythm of the limbs of the thought (both smaller and larger and largest) direct the attention of the reader, and still more of the listener, to the pleasures of the Latin style. Juvenile as it may seem to put so much weight on the well-chosen word, or tendentious to make it so important when the subject is so null, this *is* how Latin style challenges judgment; what it was aimed towards and how it was appreciated—anciently, in Milton's time, and not really so remote from (say) Flaubert.

With something of this emphasis in our ears, then, let us see where Milton puts his effort, where he calls attention to his diction and its rhythm. To take one more example, the "insulting" comparisons of the ignorant, perhaps including present company, to bean-pods and frogs:

> quanto nudiores Leberide conspexeris, & exhaustâ inani vocabulorum & sententiuncularum supellectile, μηδὲ γρῦ φθέγγεσθαι, perinde mutos ac ranuncula Seriphia. (120. 15–17)

("... you will find them even more empty than a bean pod, and when they have exhausted their meagre supply of words and little maxims, they utter 'not even a grunt', being just as speechless as the little Seriphian frogs.") The inarticulate are berated super-articulately, by a witty reverse onomatopoeia. The polysyllables swell up like waves, till the wonderful seven-syllable "sententiaculorum supellectile." It means an "equipment of piddling little maxims" (Columbia's English is tame and insufficient here): huge word for tiny thing, like Virgil's "exiguus mus" (Georgics 1. 181); alliteration with the following "supellectile"; then a learned Greek counterpart, the paradoxically croak-less frogs.[24] The ignorant are mute where they should not be. The mockery of dumbness—in both senses—charms by fluency, by the paradox of opposites and the verbal flow. The logorrhea may seem obscure or arrogant but its purpose is clear if we consider its place in the performance.

More readily to be admired is the later portion of the prolusion, because by then the theme is more overt and its embellishment entertains straightforwardly. That is to say, once the opening address to the audience is completed, Milton tackles his thesis through playful fictions. Thus

---

[24] Cf. Aristophanes, *Plutus* 17.

he plays fast and loose with the ancient cosmogonies to show that Day preceded Night (134. 14). He plays his own tricks with time: his speech begins in the morning (124. 16) and by its close Night is near (146. 22).

Mythopoeia is the staple. We sample its caperings, to consider as well their style:

> Abunde sane laudis hinc sibi adepti sunt, affatim gloriae, quod homines in sylvis atque montibus dispalatos belluarum ad instar, in unum compulerint locum, et Civitates constituerint, quodque omnes Disciplinas quotquot hodie traduntur, lepidis fabellarum involucris obvestitas pleni deo primi docuerint... (128. 11–16)

("As it is, they [poets] have won for themselves abundantly indeed of praise, enough of glory, because they have driven into one place men who were wandering in the woods and mountains after the fashion of wild beasts, and they have established states, and, inspired by the divinity, they have first taught all learning whatsoever that has been handed down to this day, clad in the beautiful vestments of fiction . . .") The idea is cheeky, tendentious, and excellent. It revises or updates the classic Greek reconstructions of how society began, such as that in Plato's *Protagoras* (320d–323a); but instead of humans settling into groups to exchange their labour, what made them live together was their need to hear poets, who concealed all needful knowledge in their compositions.

The language, however, has more mixed success. "Abunde sane" is a pointless jingle. "Laudis" and "gloriae" balance, but mean the same anyway. "Dispalatos" ("scattered," "straggling" in 12) is both good in itself and in collocation with "belluarum." The verbs following, however, seem too consciously alliterative on /C/ sounds. One can tire of polysyllables: words should stand out by meaning and rhythm, first, not by mere size, and why make them all large? Consequently, even the individually vigorous words of "lepidis fabellarum involucris obvestitas" could seem sluggish, for which word is the most important?[25] Could not the long words have been given, so to speak, room to breathe? "Pleni Deo" is the strongest idea, yet is overshadowed by the preceding polysyllabics and then muffled by "primi" following.

---

[25] Perhaps *involucris*, "coverings," pointing to allegorical readings of poetry; yet the powerful (non-classical) *obvestitas* tries to cap it. The effect on me is too rich and cellular.

Polysyllabics go on dominating, with ten more in the remaining twenty-two of the sentence. The obsession with large words is a sign of mere phrasemaking here. There are too many words in each limb, with the further result that the limbs do not quite balance with each other nor group into balanced larger wholes. Not that the number of words, or syllables, should balance numerically, indeed the contrary is a mark of good Latin prose style. But balance, somehow, they must: fewer words, and a higher proportioning of short ones to long ones, are needed to articulate both rhythm and sense. In short, while succulent, mouth-filling *words* abound here, they detract from rhythm, which is fundamental to basic speakability; which means in turn their comprehensibility to the audience; thus denying them pleasure.

Now whilst these strictures may not command universal assent, they do provide our discussion with a benchmark. They show the kind of thing which Milton improved later. The prolusion very usefully shows his capacity for play (something to recall in Chapter Nine on his salting prolusion). It shows by contrast what more he might do when his theme was more important and he was more engaged with it (as Chapter Four will be demonstrating). We do not notice hesitant qualifiers or clogging polysyllables when he is no longer filling in the time pleasantly but is possessed by his theme, and as Longinus puts it "sweeps away resistance" (*On Sublimity* 1. 4).

Prolusion II
"In Scholis Publicis. De Sphaerarum Concentu."

Already Prolusion II, "On the Music of the Spheres," has strength exactly where its forerunner was weakest. It is shorter, it has conviction, and conviction improves the Latin style, now impassioned and beautiful and genuinely argumentative. The change of occasion and venue may have contributed, for this oration is held in the Schools,[26] on some notable day of the University exercises. At any rate, the big names of philosophy now resound. Milton is lining up against Aristotle, with Pythagoras and Plato. He even fathers the daring conceit that the soul of Pythagoras may have transmigrated into himself now speaking (152); and though

---

[26] Similar advance was noted from Prolusion IV, in College, to V, in the Schools.

one takes this as conceit in two senses, it enhances (not disrupts) the listener's belief. Whereas any prolusion may release the imagination to adopt a different persona, to speak in a different voice, it begins to look as if Milton's imagination rises furthest when it goes with single-minded conviction. The theoretic ardour[27] of this prolusion leads not only to "Blest Pair of Sirens" on the same theme at Cambridge,[28] but to the more sombre majesty of the visionary passages of the *First Defence*.

The address to the audience is now simpler and more winning than in Prolusion I. He proceeds via a modest disclaimer for himself and a compliment to previous speakers, to praise for the occasion itself. Thus it is out of respect for everyone, not only himself, that (instead of embarking on some trite theme) he is "kindled to attempt a new one" ("ad novam aliquam materiem . . . accendit animum, & statim erigit") (148. 13–14). If any doubt remains, let the audience take his words "as if said in jest," ("quasi per lusum dicta," 150. 2). *This*—so apt, quick, and varied—is how to win attention and disarm objectors.

If any single passage sums up the advance in quality from Prolusion I, it is where he imagines his soul inhabited by that of Pythagoras:

> Quod si sic tulisset sive fatum, sive sors, ut tua in me, Pythagora Pater, transvolasset anima, haud utique deesset qui te facile assereret, quantumvis gravi iamdiu laborantem infamia. (152. 2–6)

("But if only fate or chance had allowed your soul, O Father Pythagoras, to transmigrate into my body, you would not have lacked a champion to defend you without difficulty, under however heavy a burden of obloquy you might be labouring!")[29]

Although putting "tua" and "me" together is merely the usual Latin way with pronouns, its neat quickness helps to connect the two persons, thus miming the meaning, the union of the two souls. Then, to apostrophize Pythagoras also mimes a personal relation, just as next to make their relation paternal is most disarming: the conceit seems much less conceited because of it. There may even be a witty glance at the Fathers

---

[27] George Eliot's phrase for Dorothea Brooke is apt for the young Milton also.
[28] Carey, 167–70.
[29] The rendering is Tillyard's (65) because Columbia's is laboured and inaccurate, rendering "sortem" as "necessity" and muting the decisive allusion to metempsychosis—Pythagoras' own doctrine applied to himself.

and Sons of the University exercises: if so, Milton is hinting that he has a better "Father" than the opposition do, since he has Pythagoras (the Gandhi of antiquity). The contracted form of the counterfactual verb, "transvolasset" for "transvolavisset," is Milton's usual preference, but how well it sounds, and with what agility it moves the mind onward into the nimble tribrach of "anima" (– ˘ – ˘ ˘ ˘). Rhythm is well served in the clausula, the labouring "laborantem infamia" (˘ – – – – ˘ ×). The well-managed closing onomatopoeia epitomizes the advance upon Prolusion I.

Milton goes on more argumentatively, and if anything more nimbly. Though not profound philosophy nor stringent logic, the move has the alacrity of both. The abstracting mind is catching fire, to move with ease into a conversation with Aristotle, whom he reckons to browbeat for being too literal with Pythagoras' metaphor:

> At vero quidni corpora coelestia, inter perennes illos circuitus, Musicos efficiant sonos?[30] Annon aequum tibi videtur Aristoteles?[31] nae ego vix credam intellegentias tuas sedentarium[32] illum rotandi Coeli laborem potuisse tot saeclis perpeti, nisi ineffabile illud Astrorum melos detinuisset abituras,[33] et modulationes delenimento suasisset moram.

("After all, we may well ask, why should not the heavenly bodies give forth musical tones in their everlasting[34] revolutions? Does it not seem reasonable to you, Aristotle? Why, I can hardly believe that those Intelligences of yours could have endured through so many centuries the

---

[30] Quadrisyllables, now, do not distract from the key idea (*Musicos . . . sonos*), but embrace and enhance it.

[31] He turns without warning to Aristotle, as if he were present (as he should indeed be in spirit, at a disputation). And he puts it to him, absurdly but pleasantly, "Fair's fair, eh, Stagirite?"

[32] The ear, though not the syntax, links the "Intelligences" (which govern each sphere in Aristotle's cosmology) with "sedentarium," as if to hint that the cosmology is static, compared with the dynamic beauty of the celestial music-making in Pythagoras'.

[33] The beautiful phrase turns the tables completely: if the Intelligences stay in their places, it is because they are held there, ravished by the music of their spheres. The clausula misses solecism by a whisker: – ˘ – ˘ ˘ – – is so close to the hexameter verse-line cadence, yet for that very reason the extra syllable adds alacrity and impetus. Then the last clause moves it all the other way, by polysyllabic spondees.

[34] Tillyard misrenders "perennes" here as "annual."

sedentary toil of making the heavens rotate, if the ineffable music of the stars had not prevented them from leaving their posts, and the melody, by its enchantment, persuaded them to stay.")

Milton has followed up two sentences comprising an assertion then a counterfactual wish, with two very short ones of question; then the lengthier exclamation just quoted, then one giving its reasons; then another pushing the supposition even farther. He is in top form. It has both variety and energy of syntax, and this time the long words realize their full potential, by coming in amongst shorter ones, to give the impression of weight. Is it the technique which has advanced from Prolusion I, or is all owed to the new engrossment by a congenial theme?

The new sentence has a tone of nimble satire, matching but extending the visionary hectoring of Aristotle:

> Quam si tu Coelo adimas sane mentes illas pulchellas, et ministros Deos in Pistrinum dedis, et ad molas trusatiles damnas. (152. 12)

("If you rob the heavens of this music, you devote [condemn] those wonderful minds and subordinate gods of yours to a life of drudgery, and condemn them to the treadmill.") In "pulchellas" the diminutive sounds affectionate, and simultanously rebukes Aristotle for being ungentlemanly. "How *could* you?" he is saying. Stronger in the follow-up, he asks how could you "betray the darlings to a treadmill"? The words "Pistrinum" (a "mill," hence "drudgery") and "molas trusatiles" ("hand-mill") are rare, and for that reason surprising, yet completely exact, therefore pleasurable. The idea is of ministering angels toiling in a dark Satanic mill. All the aspects work together, to make the listeners' pleasure.

Milton is by no means finished, or exhausted. He continues the conceit by imagery of Atlas released, dolphins, Arion, and larks in flight. The series of exempla ascends, so to speak; each is a vivid quick image. Audaciously, too, he cites as witness those who opposed him. He manages to be sly, combative, and sincere by the end. Throughout, he "speaks masterly."

From Prolusion II to Prolusion III, and Beyond

A still wider unity and progression can be discerned now. In Prolusion II Milton gave the leading role to Pythagoras, with Plato and—amazingly—Aristotle as witness. In Prolusion III, "Against the Scholastic Philosophy" (158), he calls as chief witness—whom but Aristotle again (171)? That is, he sets Aristotle over against Aristotelianism. He does the same, as we saw, in Prolusion IV (178); and again in V (196). We might at this point credit Milton with a temperamental purism, an advocacy of return to sources. The explanation, rather, is rhetorical: he is casting the major philosophers in a sort of prosopopoeia. They are becoming characters in his eristic drama, his morality play of removing the barnacles from the good ship "Philosophy." That is to say, the four declamations (I, II, III and VII) can be read as a coherent sequence: a critique of Cambridge scholasticism for being a throwback, which exploits the Cambridge forms to convey the critique. The first plays with the forms, the second praises what they overshadow, and the third will criticize them.

Seen in this light, Prolusion VI is like the official "Varier" or Praevaricator at the exercises, "varying" the thesis by turning it upside down and inside out. Parody joins the feast. A different varying is to be seen in the complex perspectives of the poem *De Idea Platonica*. In Prolusion VII, however, the contest is raised to a higher power than in any before it. Milton champions Knowledge against Ignorance, speaking with complete conviction in his finest rhetoric of all.

Prolusion III:
In Scholis Publicis.
Contra Philosophiam Scholasticam

The speech "Against the Scholastic Philosophy" begins by invoking Cicero's view that a speaker should instruct, please and persuade (or "move," "influence"—*permovere*). Very soon, though, he has promoted the second and third above the first. If this attack on the Schools' way of doing philosophy is to succeed, it will be by pleasing. He modestly concedes this may be beyond his capacities ("sit exilitatis meae," "my weak point"), but it is what he yearns for ("erit tamen desiderii summa," "the height of my desire"). His way of pleasing is by a mixture of caricature and encomium; namely, caricature of the Schoolmen as neither pleasing nor useful to humanity (160–168), followed by encomium of other studies, a wide range of them (168–170). The clincher is the final summons to Aristotle himself as witness (170–172).

Nothing here is itself philosophical, in the sense of an empirical case or one conducted by syllogistic control. It is a declamation, not a disputation, and it will persuade (if at all) by the rhetoric of critique and of praise. For Milton sees his task as "permovere." That word comes three times on the first page, and later. On 162 "promovere" does similar duty. He seeks to do what rhetoric can do; namely to have an effect, on the emotions through the imagination; to influence, even control.

His foremost means to this end are fivefold: diction (wide and dashing); imagination (caustic, then visionary); the use of figures; implicit stage directions; address to audience. All these have the further interest in the present study that they carry forward from their counterparts in earlier prolusions towards their fuller embodiments in Prolusion VII.

The five features can be seen cooperating in one of the many purple patches:

> Mihi credite, Iuvenes Ornatissimi, dum ego inanes hasce quaestiunculas nonnunquam invitus percurro, video mihi per confragosa tesqua, & salebras, perque vastas solitudines, & praeruptas montium angustias iter conficere; propterea nec verisimile est venustulas, & elegantes Musas pannonis hisce & squalidis praeesse studiis, aut deliros horum Sectatores in suum vendicare patrocinium... (162. 5–12)[35]

("Believe me, most illustrious young men, sometimes while I survey unwillingly these empty little questions, I seem to be undertaking a journey through rugged deserts and uneven roads and through vast solitudes and

---

[35] The punctuation pauses in places where a modern, logical pointing would not, e.g., after the first of a pair of words ("tesqua," "solitudines" or the adjective "venustulas"). I would hesitate, for the accidentals of such a poorly edited first edition, to claim that the effect is authorial. But it may be rhetorical, and thus point us to places where the orating voice would make a natural pause for effect; e.g., to make the listeners hear, and so savour, "venustulas... Musas." In general, unfortunately, it would be a herculean undertaking to disentangle the indicative pointings from the general muddle of the 1674 pointings.

precipitous passes of mountains, because it is not likely that the charming and elegant Muses preside over these shrivelled and obscure subjects, or that the silly followers of these lay claim to their patronage . . ." [163])[36]

He had first addressed his audience as "Academici," the more inclusive term, to pose as uncertain how best to use his allotted half-hour ("semihorula," 158. 22). But in the extract he calls upon his peers ("Iuvenes"), buttering them up as "ornatissimi" ("accomplished, excellent"). To call the scholastic exercises "empty little questions" ("inanes hasce quaestiunculas," line 6, large word for petty thing)) would please the young, not the old whose job it is to teach them: he has already called them the "joyous wranglings of *old* men" ("festivis *hisce* tetricorum *senum* altercationibus," 160. 4–5) in which "his<u>ce</u>" is emphatic and so hints at a better alternative, and "senum" points to the generation-gap. It is an impolite manoeuvre, but relevant to the theme and to winning his case.

The vigorous apt diction here goes with vivid onomatopoeia, obvious in its sibilant harshness. Imagination is developing a repulsive mental landscape, a continued imagery of the old learning as a wasteland (all three features cooperate in the mouthfilling "confragosa tesqua et salebras.") The rhetoric levers the listeners into revulsion by amusing them, their literal ears and their minds' eyes. The phrases of the intellectual "wasteland" make up into groupings which keep up a feeling of balance, credited (as in any dunciad) to the speaker alone, not what he castigates. He avoids the imitative fallacy.

The satire is not subtle, yet thereby befits performance to a large audience in the Schools: the speaker will contort his face as he grinds out each colourful expression of distaste, slowing the pace to rub in the rebarbatives, sibilance assisting contempt. In "Per confragosa tesqua et salebras, perque vastas solitudines" the sense is equally apt: "vastas" means not only "vast" (size) but "waste" or "wasted, devastated" (ruined for human occupancy by the schoolmen). The audience is invited to enjoy the caricature, moment by moment, confirming by sharing the shudders. The diction and image, the figures of speech and thought, these aural hints and guides to the audience, draw them into a constant complicity.

---

[36] "These" ("horum") are the "subjects" ("studiis"), while "their" patronage is that of the Muses.

Throughout this variation of address, he is doing what he has said he will do. He is relying wholly on an uncomplicated, forceful contrasting: Schoolmen (bad) vs new Baconian curriculum (good).[37] So next he moves to a more ideal syllabus, contrasting. *Permovere* returns with fuller and clearer force where he praises rhetoric itself. Note that rhetoric, which was also castigated by the reformers as privileging words over things, is not the villain here. Cambridge gives him the present scope to berate Cambridge.[38]

> Rhetorica sic animos capit hominum, adeoque suaviter in vincula pellectos post se trahit, ut nunc ad misericordiam *permovere*[39] valeat, nunc in odium rapere, nunc ad virtutem bellicam accendere, nunc ad contemptum mortis evehere. (162–64)

("Likewise rhetoric captures the minds of men and so pleasantly draws after her in chains those who are enticed, that at one time she is able to *move* to pity, another to transport into hatred, again to kindle to warlike valour, and then to exalt to contempt of death": 163–65).

Notable figuration here includes the strong verb "pellectos" ("seduced" as harlots—*paelices* or *pellices*—know how to); an unusual fourfold patterning of parallel verb–phrases, itself swelling from a pair of three-word phrases to a pair of four-word-phrases (held together economically by "in . . . ad . . . in . . . in . . ."); and a superb climax about removal of the fear of death. There are many other wonderfully eloquent passages of praise-rhetoric that could have been selected, but this one is on rhetoric itself and is concise. Moreover, its subject should surprise us, being the praise of *rhetoric*.

Would not Milton's icon, Plato, deplore all this, as rhetorical manipulation itself and advocacy of manipulation? He would; but Milton is not consistently or solely a Platonist (as *De Idea* differently attests). He

---

[37] Tillyard, xxiii.

[38] Cf. Feingold, "The Humanities," 247. The reformers sought to abolish both scholastic logic and rhetorical training. But humanists as well as reformers criticized the *abuses* of rhetoric. And moderns have taken the polemicists at their own valuation, because in the end they won, whereas our extract shows Milton using one of the exercises to criticize the other, in public. This is to the *credit* of the exercises and of rhetoric.

[39] My emphasis. Permovere = "thoroughly move" is seldom used literally in Roman Latin, where instead it is *the* word for exciting strong feeling, moving us deeply, as oratory does.

is eclectic, and in love with rhetoric. He has carried himself away also, for love of philosophy as *he* conceives of it.

The speech moves higher and higher, up a tacit chain or ladder of intellectual insights, all the way to the greatest enquiry of all, the mind's knowledge of itself ("quod adhuc altissimum est, seipsam cognoscere": 170. 19), and of "the holy minds and intelligences with which it will hereafter consort for ever." "The mind itself" passes on, even higher, into what it would be joined with: "seipsam cognoscere, simulque sanctas illas mentes, & intelligentias quibuscum post haec sempiternum initura est sodalitium."

There are two ways to receive this lark-ascending passage; either as a transporting rhetoric, Milton's counterpart to Diggle's praise of music; or as a fake philosophy, gushing ineffables without knowing what it means—the sort of thing which solider Aristotle would bring crashing to earth. Precisely as this doubt might intervene, Milton turns to Aristotle himself, for agreement. Rhetorically, this comes as a knock-out punch, because unexpected. It is not totally unexpected since a glimpse of the imminent peripeteia may be given by "intelligences," an Aristotelian concept and word; but the peroration now drives the point home. The Aristotelians have betrayed Aristotle; the Schoolmen have thrown out the baby with the bathwater.

Although the "proof" is only rhetoric, the rhetoric is a controlled master-stroke. It is not hard to see how Milton's Cambridge audiences accorded him high reputation for such performances. He closes by declaring his hearers are "moved by his name" ("permoveri," again, moved by Aristotle); inclined to favour his own case; oh, praise and thanks to Aristotle himself, then! ("laudem . . . illi debebitis et gratiam"). The elegant quiet further turn, and modest apology for his own "prolixity," show a newly winning orator.

CHAPTER

4

Milton's Last Declamation, Prolusion VII: (In Sacrario habita pro Arte. Oratio. Beatiores reddit Homines Ars quam Ignorantia.)

Milton's last[1] known declamation is quite simple. We hardly at all reflect how clever or learned this student Milton is. We are following what he has to say on a subject which has possessed him. The prose has a new quality, passion.

At this point, despite the risk of labouring the obvious, we might consider the matter of simplicity, both for better and worse, since simplicity is not a simple concept. We would not expect him to be artless when praising art.

Simplicity does suit the topic, "That Knowledge[2] renders man happier than ignorance," which has the same broad abstractness as Prolusion I (and many a debating motion today). Moreover, Milton can repeat his fine simple strategy of Prolusion III: an exordium addressing listeners about himself and them and the subject can be followed by praise of the idea which he is championing and by attack on its opposite, with final return to the listeners. *Copia* flows forth to fill out the simple opposition. He has a congenial topic, and is on the congenial side of the struggle.

---

[1] I think it the last for the general reason that it is printed last, and for the particular one that its title is fuller and more flamboyant than for the other declamations. It is also the longest declamation. While Masson (*Life of Milton*, I: 266) and Parker (*Biography*, 774) place it in 1631–32 but Gordon Campbell, *A Milton Chronology* (London: Macmillan, 1997), 41, places it in 1630, they all place it later than the other prolusions.

[2] Phyllis Tillyard explains why "Knowledge" is a clearer translation than the literal "Art," extant only in phrases like "the liberal arts," (*YPW* I: 288, n.).

Still, there are considerations which he does not address. If the topic is to be taken seriously, the strongest of the opposing arguments might merit probing. Why do people say that "Ignorance is bliss"? Why is a simple religious faith often stronger than a complicated one, and why did Jesus in the beatitudes ("beatiores"!) praise the poor in spirit, the meek, and the pure in heart? Why are the academically learned so often mocked, and why do we muffle our thoughts in preposterous jargon? Not even this modest degree of meditation enters Milton's oration. He reasons the easy way, by impassioned eloquence of exempla.

The answer to such misgivings is itself quite simple: "Non omnia possumus omnes," we cannot all do everything; Milton gratefully does what he is best at, praising the intellect. He seizes his chance to shine at this licensed sort of public performance. It was in his nature to shine and to perform, to emulate and excel. What the more high-profile exercise of disputation had not brought forth in him, he lets this congenial exercise achieve for him.

The strategy adopted here for charting how he does it is, first, to consider the title and occasion, these being unusually—suggestively—full. Secondly, the exordium is examined. Then I analyse major passages from the work, ones substantial enough to show how the thought keeps changing its angle of address to the subject, and how that governs the varying tone. It is the transitions of tone, quite as much as individual purple patches, which keep up the impact of simple, sincere passion. Lastly, we shall contemplate simplicity again, from the vantage-point gained, so that in Chapter Five we can survey what declamation and disputation together availed him of later when he wrote the *Defences*.

The Title and Occasion

The title has two distinctive features. First, whereas the previous titling of prolusions has been a general, brisk statement of venue, "In Collegio &c." [sic] or "In Scholis," the present oration was given specifically "In Sacrario," in the College *Chapel*. As college declamations were usually done there, some further meaning seems aimed at the reader. "In Sacrario pro Arte" juxtaposes the particular building with the theme, the oration in praise of Ars. The title connects place with theme, and hints at a connection, the possible sacredness of knowledge and concomitant devotion to learning of the learner. This is certainly a major motif in the body of the speech.

Secondly, the fullness of the title suggests a self-editing, whether at the time of the performance or in 1674. Prolusions VI and VII, which climax the volume and (I believe) were the latest delivered, are both given titles which contextualize them as to venue and audience. That suggests that whereas "In Collegio &c." (I and IV) is perfunctory, the greater care taken when entitling the final two in-college orations reflects a sense of their being big occasions; big, that is, for the performer himself.

All in all, this title alerts us to the link between speaker and subject, whereas in Prolusion VI the salting's title alerts us to the link between speaker and audience.

Speaker, Subject, Audience

The titling also reflects the primal triad of all public persuasion: the personal character of the speaker, or "ethos" as Aristotle termed it; how to put an audience into a fit state of mind, or "move" them to "pathos," strong emotion; and the proof or discussion or case or subject itself ("logos").[3] The triad is certainly primal because there cannot be a speech without some such threefold attention throughout, shifting the emphasis upon one or another and altering the combinations of two or three. This obviousness notwithstanding, Milton's oration is built upon the three, moving very simply amongst them; almost, indeed, taking them one by one. Than which, what could be simpler and more naive?

First, Milton explains himself to his audience, and gives a circumstantial narrative of how he comes to be speaking on this topic and on this side of the debate. He projects an ethos thereby, of one who would rather be enjoying *otium* in study than speaking at all. He insists that he hardly ever orates of his own free will or accord (246. 13). Whether or not this was winsome, it could be construed as disavowal of vainglory, or faintly echo the Roman mythos of Cincinnatus called from

---

[3] Aristotle, *Rhetoric* 1355b22 onwards, as summarised by Brian Vickers, *In Defence of Rhetoric* (Oxford: Clarendon Press, 1988), 19–20.

the plough to save Rome. At all events, his emulation is veiled. There is a modesty-topos, in fact several. The wish to be studying rather than speaking, however, is not grumbling nor irrelevant, because it characterizes the speaker as a lover of that which he is about to praise.

As for the audience, we gather they are in their gowns ("togati," simultaneously academic and Roman), and in a crowd (246. 7–8). This supports the title's implication of some larger than usual college assemblage.

Then, the logos or reasoning fills all the rest, up until the close: only an intermittent "Auditores" keeps the audience alert, or in print reminds us of their presence. Finally, however, the "Auditores" do come into direct gaze, at the explicit "Ad vos venio, Auditores." Here, but not before, he compliments them: "O Auditores intelligentissimi," "O my most understanding of listeners" (284. 5–6). Thereby they are being assimilated to the "understanding" side of the debate itself.

There is a simple, intelligent sincerity about the whole progression of attention from ethos to logos to pathos. It could be objected, naturally, that the sincerity is artful, not spontaneous. This issue will keep returning. Suffice it here that deliberate simplicity, by someone who knows how to be complex but chooses not to be, should be received on its chosen terms—like any work of literature, in fact, and certainly as a rhetorical performance must be if it is to be enjoyed. Simplicity may in fact come spontaneously when the subject is also one's passion, and the purpose is to communicate that. We should give Milton the benefit of the doubt, if any.

A different objection might be, that my division leaves the whole body of the lengthy oration as a single entity, whereas the mind needs to know the construction, the art of the praising of Art. Yet the relations of the proofs to the thesis are at no point unclear. Besides, though we are moved about amongst argument pro and argument con, and exemplum, and narration and critique and eulogy of particulars, so that one might tie the labels on to these aspects as they occur, the kinds of proof come round several times, making it needless to keep on identifying each. It seems better to lump than to split, so as to appreciate better Milton's unity of emotion and tonal mix, and his transitions. This principle has guided the choice and analysis of the passages which follow.

Transition to the Theme, Beatitude

As the four-page preamble is closing Milton restates his title, that "Beatiores reddit Homines Ars quam Ignorantia." He does it in terms of the cognate abstract noun, *beatitudo*. He must show what contributes to "illam in quam omnes ferimur, beatitudinem" ("that state of happiness toward which we are all borne along,"[4] 253. 17). Though the contributions are to be described, he has first claimed the high ground, the end towards which they are the means. What exactly does he mean?

"Beatitudo" is a more full-blooded word, in his usage, than it may seem from translation as "happiness" (Columbia) or "blessings" (Tillyard). "Beatus" in the Latin Bible and in Christian Latin is an ultimate state of well-being: "Blessed is the man who fears the Lord" (Psalm 112: 1). In the classical context of rhetoric and ethics, whilst it may include prosperity or a sunny disposition, it is rather the Aristotelian absolute, *eudaimonia*; human "well-being," the autotelic good of the mind's activity. It is not that all humans are high-aspiring of soul, since if they were no one would prefer to be ignorant and the debate would not be happening. But we are most ourselves when we are "beati." The thought embraces Aristotle, the Bible, and Plato.

The explanation is supplied because Milton does not give it. That may be because he is busy conducting a first transition. The transition is curiously done. Not only is there not time to define the all-important aim of life, but the Latin style is laboured until the transition is completed.[5] *Then* we feel the change of gear. Here is the English of Tillyard, given because Columbia's is clunky, beyond any labouring of the Latin. A lengthier extract than usual will be appropriate, to illustrate both the awkwardness

---

[4] I have changed Columbia's "hastening" because the Latin idiom is not active nor optimistic, but in the passive or middle voice: we pursue our happiness or well-being whether or not consciously. Tillyard has it more circumspectly as, "that happiness which is the aim of every one of us" (107).

[5] Not helped by the Latin text's being unparagraphed in *1674*, and still in modern editions. A modernized paragraphing is needed, and punctuation and spelling too, not to mention removal of the accents which make Neo-Latin look needlessly quaint to the eye accustomed to reading classical Latin. See Erwin Rabbie, "Editing Neo-Latin Texts," *Editio* 10 (1996): 25–48, and also Hale, *BLN*, 29–33.

and amplitude of Milton's bridgework at this decisive moment. Tillyard's version is not quoted whole but with commentary in square brackets interwoven, so as to interconnect the two for the reader.

> Verum, Auditores, sic ego existimo in re mediocriter laudabili maxime elucere vim Eloquentiae; quae summam laudem habent, vix ullo modo, ullis limitibus Orationis contineri posse, in his ipsa sibi officit copia, et rerum multitudine comprimit et coangustat expandentem se elocutionis pompam; hac ego argumenti foecunditate nimia laboro, ipsae me vires imbecillum, arma inermem reddunt; delectus itaque faciendus, aut certe enumeranda verius quam tractanda quae tot nostram causam validis praesidiis firmam ac munitam statuunt: nunc illud mihi unice elaborandum video, ut ostendam quid in utraque re, et quantum habeat momentum ad illam in quam omnes ferimur, beatitudinem; in qua contentione facili certe negotio versabitur Oratio nostra, nec admodum esse puto metuendum quid possit Scientiae Inscitia, Arti Ignorantia objicere; quamvis hoc ipsum quod objiciat, quod verba faciat, quod in hac Literatissimae Concionis vel hiscere audeat, id totum ab arte precario vel potius emendicato habet. Notum hoc esse reor, Auditores, et receptum omnibus, magnum mundi opificem, caetera omnia cum fluxa et caduca posuisset, homini praeter id quod mortale esset, divinam quandam auram, et quasi partem sui immiscuisse, immortalem, indelebilem, lethi et interitus immunem; quae postquam in terris aliquandiu tanquam coelestis hospes, caste sancteque peregrinata esset, ad nativum coelum sursum evibraret se, debitamque ad sedem et patriam reverteretur: proinde nihil merito recenseri posse in causis nostrae beatitudinis, nisi id et illam sempiternam, et hanc civilem vitam aliqua ratione respiciat.

The first sentence has 138 words, the second 76. Columbia and Tillyard both break them up into ten. However, the full force of a good Latin periodic sentence is felt only in the original sense-unit. Of these two instances, the first struggles, verging into a dribble of appositional afterthoughts. The second has firm control and a beautiful, mimetic shape. It comes as a relief, as if we had arrived somewhere. If this is the intention, though, it risked the imitative fallacy, indeed fell foul of it.

The contrast can be felt in the English despite the otherwise helpful division of the periodic sentences: "But, gentlemen, it is my opinion that the power of eloquence is most manifest when it deals with subjects which rouse no particular enthusiasm. [strange opening gambit!] Those which most stir our admiration can hardly be compassed within the bounds of a speech: the very abundance of material is a drawback, and the multiplicity of subjects narrows and confines the swelling stream of eloquence. [despite some flashing phrases like "comprimit et coangustat" the sense is thin and tedious so far, circling more than advancing] I am now suffering from this excess of material: that which should be my strength makes me weak, and that which should be my defence makes me defenceless [neat but mainly whimsical oxymorons, "vires imbecillum, arma inermem"]. So I must make my choice, or at least mention only in passing rather than discuss at length the numerous arguments on whose powerful support our cause relies for its defence and security. [Is this any more than trite methodological preliminaries? If any reader of this in a PhD thesis would shout "Cut!", how well does it suit an oral performance?] On this occasion it seems to me that my efforts must be directed entirely to showing how and to what extent Learning and Ignorance respectively promote that happiness which is the aim of every one of us. [The statement of the *telos* of life is almost buried, two thirds of the way through the Latin period.] With this question I shall easily deal in my speech, nor need I be over-anxious about what objections Folly may bring against Knowledge, or Ignorance against Art. Yet the very inability of Ignorance to raise any objection, to make a speech, or even to open her lips in this great and learned assembly, is begged or rather borrowed from art." (Tillyard, 106–7) [The closing paradox is sharper than all before it. Ignorance is *dependent* on Art, in the way that crime is parasitic on the law-abiding of the majority (as Plato-Socrates argued against Thrasymachus).[6]]

Now feel, even in the English, the smoother and more enraptured movement of the main argument when at last it is reached. The thought takes over. We are no longer being impeded by the twists and turns of oddly-assorted qualifications, like driving along a wriggle of backstreets, and continually slowed down by grammatical roundabouts: we are out on the highway, enjoying the proclamation. A noble myth is proclaimed nobly. An axiom explains us to ourselves. The sentence guides us at its close to the causes of our happiness, nothing less. *This* is the Latin we expect from Milton, for it anticipates the Platonic chorusing of the Guardian Spirit in his Masque. The thought and expression become *distinctive*. "It is, I think, a belief familiar and generally accepted that the great Creator of the world, [still hesitant, but *now* he unfolds it]

---

[6] In *The Republic*, Book I.

while constituting all else fleeting and perishable, ["fluxa et caduca,"[7]] infused into man, besides what was mortal, a certain divine spirit, a part of Himself, as it were, which is immortal, imperishable, and exempt from death and extinction [heavy reliance on pairing, but this time it is tricolon too: "immortalem, indelebilem, lethi et interitus immunem," the adjectival threesome opening up into the idea of our transcendence, like a flower blooming in front of us!] After wandering about upon the earth for some time, like some heavenly visitant ["coelestis hospes"], in holiness and righteousness, this spirit was to take its flight upward ["evibraret se," good corybantic reflexive verb] to the heaven whence it had come and to return once more to the abode and home which was its birthright. [We do not ask when or how this happened, or whether it is Platonic or Christian or Milton's own composite, because the noble vision nobly clothed in language preempts attention]. It follows ["proinde"] that nothing can be reckoned as a cause of our happiness which does not somehow take into account both that everlasting life and our ordinary life here on earth." What, indeed, could Ignorance, or the animal appetitive substrate of life, tell us about eternal life or the contemplation of it? The sentence has transformed the terms of the debate.

Milton possesses his theme, because it possesses him. Rhythms, phonetic and semantic patterning, figures of speech and of thought have by now come right. So it continues, when the rhetoric leaves the high altitudes of Platonic ideology to bestow splendours of particularity.

Studies of the Created Universe (p. 264)

The exempla burst upon us in another huge periodic sentence. It is followed by more of them, rhapsodizing over all the things there are to be known, a glorious catalogue of curriculums. I quote the first of these in full, before commenting.

It needs to be noted, as before, that the Columbia text misleadingly copies that of *1674*. Here, therefore, the apparent question-marks <?> are more of an exclamation. Nor do they close off a sentence. Rather, they let the thought run forward, as a single accumulating exclamation—remi-

---

[7] The fine hendiadys has an Augustinian ring to it.

niscent of similar thoughts and joyful particularity expressed by similar syntax in the Psalms or *Hamlet*.[8]

> Quinetiam si haec civilis beatitudo in honesta liberaque oblectatione animi consistit, ea profecto doctrinae et arti reposita est voluptas, quae caeteras omnes facile superet; quid omnem coeli syderumque morem tenuisse? omnes aëris motus et vicissitudines, sive augusto fulminum sonitu, aut crinitis ardoribus inertes animos perterrefaciebat, sive in nivem et grandinem obrigescat, sive denique in pluvia et rore mollis et placidus descendat; tum alternantes ventos perdidicisse, omnesque halitus aut vapores quos terra aut mare eructat; stirpium deinde vires occultas, metallorumque caluisse, singulorum etiam animantium naturam, et si fieri potest, sensus intellexisse; hinc accuratissimam corporis humani fabricam et medicinam; postremo divinam animi vim et vigorem, et si qua de illis qui Lares, et Genii, et Daemonia vocantur ad nos pervenit cognitio?

(Tillyard's version is again to be preferred: "Moreover, if this human happiness consists in the honourable and liberal joys of the mind, such a pleasure is to be found in Learning and Art as far surpasses every other. What a thing it is to grasp the nature of the whole firmament and of its stars, all the movements and changes of the atmosphere, whether it strikes terror into ignorant minds by the majestic roll of thunder or by fiery comets, or whether it freezes into snow or hail, or whether again it falls softly and gently in showers or dew; then perfectly to understand the shifting winds and all the exhalations and vapours which earth and sea give forth; next to know the hidden virtues of plants and metals and understand the nature and the feelings, it may be, of every living creature; next, the delicate structure of the human body and the art of keeping it in health; and, to crown all, the divine might and power of the soul, and any knowledge we may have gained concerning those beings which we call spirits and genii and daemons": 111–12).

Astronomy, meteorology, botany, mineralogy, animal then human physiology, medicine, psychology, then anthropology or the phenomenology of religion—the enquiries selected bear little relation to the seventeenth-century Cambridge B.A. curriculum! The empirical sciences are arrayed as a pageant to the mental gaze. What a march-past, for in-

---

[8] Milton may have remembered similar thoughts and syntax in the Psalms or *Hamlet*: Psalm 8:4 or 148:3–12, and Hamlet's "What a piece of work is a man."

stance, of the diverse forms of precipitation of moisture from the skies, all of them good and all good to understand. As in Psalm 148, to list the works of the Lord in nature is to praise him.

The main theme is never drowned in *copia* here, because the point is made in passing that such knowledges remove the fears which afflict the incurious ignorant. The ear, too, is awoken: strong, well-placed verbs ensure this (from the first, grandiloquently polysyllabic "perterrefaciebat" to the vivid "eructat" of the hidden forces, seen in their effects and understood by the searching mind). The theme, again, is withheld in the vivid description only to return enhanced by the glorying in intellection: "sensus intellexisse" (mind understanding perception, its own processes)—"divinam animi vim" indeed. Passage after passage of the immanence of God in the Eden of *Paradise Lost* is glimpsed.

In the listing of pagan spirituality ("Lares et Genii et Daemonia"), religion is approached, yet not reached. No theological certitudes are brought in to exalt, let alone end off the vision of intellection. The comprehensiveness of the vision, its embracing of all that can be studied, has been widened by its phenomenological thrust: spiritual forms merit study, whether or not they are the orthodox revealed ones. Milton as a student was captivated or interested by the pagan ones, and anthropologically poised to express that interest. It is an important moment in his life's perspective, because here something which died out from his speculative thinking later, or was subjected to the needs of polemic or system-building, receives enthusiastic expression for its own sake. A declamation can be offputting when it is freewheeling, but then *pari passu* enchant by liberal openness. The final word is the clinching noun: *cognitio*.

The marvellous eloquence next moves upwards, to a greater generality: the listeners' spirits can break free of this "dark prison-house" of the body, seeing beyond accidents and consequences to understanding their causes and nature.[9] The diction of this passage (266) has a quite exceptional range—moving in an easy leap from the splendidly sonorous condemnation of the body as "tenebroso hoc ergastulo" (266. 1. this dark drudging-house) to the philosophizing clarity of "casus atque

---

[9] There may be an echo and redirection here of Virgil *Georgics* 2. 490: "Felix qui potuit rerum cognoscere causas," "Happy the man who has succeeded in knowing the causes of things!"

eventus rerum" (266. 4) and beyond to the "power and authority" ("imperio & dominationi," 266. 7) which understanding gives.

The most impressive thing of all hereabouts is how Milton no longer inflicts his *copia* on the subject, not even here amongst exempla, but instead moves rapidly between registers. The nimble moving enacts the thematic point: the enlightenment which is being ascribed to the enquiring mind is reflected by the style.

Variations and Special Effects

If the reader agrees that there is something awkward in the transition from thesis to vision, those syntactical throat-clearings, it should be noted that a later "ascent" in moving from negative to strong final positive makes the ear labour to very different effect. Feel the clogged helplessness which Milton ascribes to Ignorance in his exclamatory vision:

> Quid autem ignorantia? sentio, Auditores, caligat, stupet, procul est, effugia circumspicit, vitam brevem queritur, artem longam . . . (272. 16)

("What, on the other hand, has Ignorance to say? I feel, my hearers, she is veiled in darkness, is benumbed, is afar off, looks around for means of escape, complains that life is short, art is long" [*ColWks* 12: 273. 19–22]) Asyndetons start the onslaught (every verb stabs). The clauses enlarge, as Milton is fond of doing; not in Virgil's favourite tricolon, but from one to two to five words. Ignorance has the nerve to *complain* of the glorious truth that "Ars longa, vita brevis." The stance confirms the ignorance of the speaker, who is a personified Ignorance.[10]

Soon afterwards comes the unflattering comparison of mental torpor with the working man's stamina:

> nihil arte praestabilius, adeoque laboriosius, nihil nobis segnius, nihil remissius; ab operariis & agricolis nocturna & antelucana industria vinci nos patimur; illi in re sordida ad vilem victum magis impigri sunt, quam nos in nobilissima ad vitam beatam . . . (272. 21–274. 5)

---

[10] As Leslie MacCoull suggests, Ignorance here is like an opposite of Boethius' Lady Philosophy.

("Nothing is more excellent than art, and nothing also requiring more labor: nothing more sluggish than we, nothing more negligent. We permit ourselves to be outstripped by laborers and farmers in nightly and early morning toil. They are more unwearied in humble matters for common nourishment, than we in most noble matters for an abounding life."[11] [*ColWks* 12: 273. 21–275. 4]). If scorn abounds in the asyndeton and expanding membra of the first passage, we find rueful reflection in the systematic comparisons of the second. The first has the energy of *copia*, the second toils along, like minds stuck in a rut. The picture of sluggish apathy is a reproof, because what is forfeit is happiness, *eudaimonia*, the life of blessedness.

The transition so far is all ascent, but the sentence actually closes in a would-be witty self-criticism. We are such feeble creatures that "immo pudet esse id, quod non haberi nos indignamur"—"it causes shame to be that which we consider ourselves unworthy not to be" (274. 7, 275. 7). I confess that I dislike litotes except when it is used very sparingly, whereas Milton used it quite freely, not least in prose.[12] Is not the impact muffled? It may be because "pudet" is such a strong negative idea, that we hear not a double but a threefold negative, in which the first negative outweighs the following two.

How soon Milton bursts out again. He does it, first, by a strong listing of disgust, at profligate reasoners who waste their potential "comessando, belluae marinae ad morem potando [a fine version of the cliché "drinking like fish"], inter scorta et aleam pernoctando..." (274. 12–14) Observe the lovely balancing here, of long and short words, rhyme and non-rhyme, verbs and nouns, comparisons and declaratives ("by eating and drinking after the manner of sea beasts, by spending the nights in debauchery and gambling . . .") Next he laboriously, gradually, builds up the opposite, or reformative possibility, to the point where moral fibre ("impetus . . . edomare") becomes unveiled as ascesis, the acquiring of knowledge perceived as a ritual of purification: "coelestem animi

---

[11] Masson's "abounding life" is interesting. It seems a little free for "vitam *beatam*" and so may glance at the gospels' "life abundant" (John 10. 10). This may be sprinkling holy water on a more secular beatitude.

[12] Its incidence was brilliantly charted and analysed by Annabel Patterson, in a paper to the Seventh International Milton Symposium, in 2002, "Milton's Negativity."

vigorem ab omni contagione et inquinamento purum et intactum servantes." In case the volley of the majestic words of intense zeal should surfeit, he expresses the outcome with an equally majestic simplicity: "ingens aequor eruditionis cursu placido navigasse videremur." If the singular steadiness and transparency of image and rhythm here owe something to Virgil and Cicero,[13] they are singularly appropriate mentors at this climax (274. 18–24).

They are brought in with force just where Milton begins to attack the Cambridge curriculum; and comprehensively, too. *Grammatici, rhetores,* logicians and metaphysicians; mathematicians, and especially lawyers, now get their comeuppance (276). All, it seems, are disciples of Ignorance, enemies of Ars. How so, we surely ask? The first two "abound in contemptible trifles" ("Quot sunt . . . nugae aspernabiles!") The logicians are like certain finches, they "feed on thistles and thorns" ("carduis & spinis vescuntur"). Most metaphysics is "rocks" or "swamps." Mathematicians pursue the "empty little glory of demonstrations" (Euclid?). The "itch of the hoods" ("cucullorum scabies") is completed with the "ranting pettifoggers" ("Leguleios nostros clamitantes"). Most of this is enjoyable rumbustious name-calling, itself a legitimate part of the orator's weaponry; but a few serious points are being aimed as well, like the grammarian's "childishness" or the law's unfathomable jargon. If Ignorance is deplorable, then must not a "gowned Ignorance" (*togatae*) be even worse? *Corruptio optimi pessima.*

The Transition to the Peroration

Where almost everything has such punch, such varied animation, how does Milton reach his peroration? More immediately, where does this circling variation go next?

Circling variation by no means precludes surprise. Next comes a vision, a sarcastic *muthos* to set against that opening positive one. Ignorance is on her last legs ("Expirat Ignorantia"). Her last thrust is to make modern learners despair: we can't equal the ancients, the world will soon come to its final pyre ("vicinus mundi rogus cremarit"), and

---

[13] Virgil (*Aeneid* 2. 780) for the image, Cicero for the cadence.

monuments of ability are a waste of time . . . (278). Oh woe! To this vision of doom Milton answers, not that it is untrue, but that the life which matters is the eternal one, in which lies *beatitudo*. To believe in the beatitude of Ignorance ("Ignorance is bliss") is to fall lower than birds, beasts, even trees and rocks; for all of them show providence and manifest Providence. Epicureans are below the brutes.

Though Epicurean *ataraxia* ought not to be dismissed so briskly in philosophy, this is rhetoric. Not leaving the audience time to reflect on that issue, Milton now turns to them late on, full on, to compliment them handsomely: "Auditores intelligentissimi," he calls them, "my most discerning listeners," singling out the attribute he wishes to work to his own advantage. Discernment means they will give him their vote.

Images crowd in upon them at the close. They the listeners are themselves proofs, nay weapons, against Ignorance ("non tam Argumenta, quam tela," 284), which "I shall turn against Ignorance." What a superbly, muscularly positioned end-word, "contorquebo." He has sounded a trumpet ("Classicum cecini"): rush ye into battle! Fight the enemy away from your "porticos and walkways" ("porticibus & ambulacris," from which Stoics and Peripatetics were respectively named)! This issue affects all of us. O my judges, forgive my prolixity as the natural excess of my zeal!

Images, imperatives, simpler diction and shorter sentences convince the hearers of the self-renewing urgency of the speaker (*ethos*), and the seriousness of the theme and situation (*logoi*), so engendering the required *pathos* in them. At the close, as at the beginning, Milton fuses the three aspects of *declamatio* as speech-transaction. Their conjoining well suits this transaction amongst human beings about being human.

All in all, the touch is light because of conscious exaggeration and caricature. The theme is simple, but yet intensely felt. The simplicities of structure and ideas serve the eloquence well.

In view of the consistency of the speech's enthusiasms—or equally its rejections—with those of Milton in his later life, it seems churlish indeed to doubt his sincerity. Certainly from the standpoint of the present study, Prolusion VII is demonstrating what he could do with the rules and tools of a Cambridge exercise, when—possibly for the first time—he could use them to speak from the heart.

Milton's Development in Declamation

Prolusion VII fully deserves its separate chapter in this study, being the longest and most eloquent of the prolusions. It shows Milton at his most ambitious and emulative, as is proved when this Latin foreshadows *A Masque* or other acknowledged Platonizing verse of the early period. Certainly a developmental viewpoint is warranted by its advances over the shorter, more perfunctory, less personal and passionate prolusions examined.

At the same time, the piece should not be overvalued, as can happen when only the best passages are read, and the grinding transitions or hiccuping qualifications are ignored. The youthful energy and enthusiasm are attractive; but a more measured and consistently muscular declamation is to be found in the defences of his maturity, to which we come in a moment.

In terms of the Cambridge Latin genres, too, it would be a mistake to admire the declamations because they read more evenly, and gratefully, than the disputations. The Latin verses of the period routinely surpass almost everything in the prose. This is reflected in the present study by the principle of division of the Cambridge output into Parts, termed "Exercises" and "Voluntaries." Interestingly enough, Milton himself makes the point: "I hardly ever undertake speaking of my own free will and accord" ("ego vix unquam mea voluntate, aut sponte ad dicendum accedam": 246. 13–14). Disputations and declamations alike, even Prolusion VII, are a damaging "interruption" to his study plans ('interpellationis damno," 248. 9). That contradictory mixture in his personality, of ambitious haste with unripe unreadiness, is at the bottom of these discontents. He has an overweening humility.[14]

Will we find the same in his Cambridge verses, or is the case altered for these voluntaries? Chapter Two has suggested so, and the suggestion will be tested in later chapters. Though the letter to Gil bespeaks some sense of constraint even here, his verses do stand free of the awkward bridgework and syntactical hesitancy. Possibly the demands of the

---

[14] Cf. Tillyard, xxxvii. See also xxxix: "[The prolusion] may be arrogant in parts, and it may be too rhetorical for modern tastes, but it is one of Milton's major works and one of the noblest expressions of the enthusiasm for Learning that held men's minds in the full tide of the Renaissance."

stringent verse-forms compel a greater conciseness of expression and directness of syntax. At all events, in verse the fiery advocacy flows unimpeded.

Prolusion VII in Performance

The oratory of praise has always been thought "higher" than that of critique or attack. Higher registers are possible, indeed, required for it. The orator can aspire to *hypsos*, sublimity, words of panegyric which sweep away resistance.

Examples have been shown from two Cambridge University Orators, one of them George Herbert at the height of his powers in 1623. All declamations are orations, but not all orations are declamations. Declamations are on set topics, of a set kind, and very often set by others or at any rate by a context of teaching. Within this smaller compass of his four Cambridge declamations, nonetheless, Milton is moving up the registers. As has emerged, he opens with an entertainment, before embarking on praise in his briefest declamation, and briefest prolusion. Critique governs his third declamation. Here in Prolusion VII, his longest and finest declamation, his highest and finest oratory is to be seen. Given the fact that as his life turned out Milton never preached a sermon, and his most vigorous mature prose was for print not performance, this present oration "Pro Arte" becomes by accident his latest and greatest *performance*. After its quiet start, it climbs and climbs. By its close, the long oration has become a Demosthenic avalanche.

CHAPTER 5

THE CAMBRIDGE EXERCISES AND THE *DEFENCE OF THE ENGLISH PEOPLE*

In *Behemoth*, written about 1668, Thomas Hobbes's two speakers (whom he imaginatively names "A" and "B") say this about the highwatermark of Milton's Latin prose achievement, his 1650s exchange with Salmasius:

> A. About this time came out two books; one written by Salmasius, a Presbyterian, against the murder of the King; another written by Milton, an Independent, in England, in answer to it.
>
> B. I have seen them both; they are very good Latin both, and hardly to be judged which is better; and both very ill reasoning, and hardly to be judged which is worse: like two declamations pro and con, for exercise only in a rhetoric school, by one and the same man—so like is a Presbyterian to an Independent.

The "two books" are the *Defensio Regia* (1649) by Salmasius, the peripatetic French humanist Claude de Saumaise, by then aged 61, and the 42-year-old Milton's *Pro Populo Anglicano Defensio* (1651), renamed his "First Defence" because he went on to write two more.

The witty reductive contempt of "B" here is refreshing. It is enjoyable in itself, as rhetoric or epigram, and as anticipating a modern consensus of distaste. Hobbes acutely and correctly seizes on the similarity—despite their opposition, indeed because of it—of the two contenders ("one and the same man"). It is a similarity of zeal as spokesman for an official viewpoint, such that black and white *sound* like each other. However, the sentence actually modifies this observation of tone of voice, in favour of a hit at the two contenders' churchmanship—finally attacking content not tone. This is the sting in the tail of the epigram: the fight was as futile as its conduct was. All in all, Hobbes's remark is itself contentious and partisan, for since the differences between Independent and Presbyterian had in fact been matters of the utmost importance during the Interregnum, we should not trust the aesthetic judgement of tone either without close inspection. Hobbes himself is rhetorical, obliquely advocatorial, grinding several axes at once.

He prompts valuable questions about our present subject. (i) Just how far is the *Prima Defensio* a "declamation" of the Cambridge "rhetoric school"? (ii) As declamation, did it so completely fail in its purpose, of persuasion? (iii) Does Milton rely solely on declamation among his Cambridge exercises and arts? (iv) What did he bring to the *Defence* from outside the Cambridge Latin activities? (v) Is the Latin as good as Hobbes's backhanded compliment declares? (vi) Exactly how "ill" is Milton's "reasoning," shaped as it was by a training in logic at Cambridge and then taught by him to pupils for many years? Pervading these questions is the larger one, (vii) how useful or harmful to Milton was his whole engagement with the Cambridge Latin exercises during the years 1625–1632?

The questions are taken in order, but first the context of Hobbes's epigram should be sketched. *Behemoth* is his caustic narrative of the years 1640–1660, with "behemoth" (a monstrous great animal, as in Job 40:15) his name for the Long Parliament. His dislike of that body was shared by Milton, and both wrote against it. The caustic tone is characteristic of Hobbes, so characteristic indeed that he had to explain that his cognate, earlier term "Leviathan" (Job 41:19) was *not* dismissive, but the name of the Commonwealth, that "mortal god" which keeps us safe in society. Even though Hobbes was in favour with Charles II, Charles prevented *Behemoth* being published in England. As intellectually bold as he was physically timorous, Hobbes was usually out on a limb. Milton and he felt respect but no admiration for each other.

For all of these reasons, we should approach with some caution Hobbes's easy dismissal of the debate which was the greatest event of Milton's public life; for even if the *Defence* were as intellectually null as Cicero's poems or Hitler's speeches, it would nonetheless need to be weighed up as a public event, a Latin speech-act couched in the forms of its time and genre. Still, Hobbes was an outstanding thinker, and wrote acutely about rhetoric as well as politics, not to mention that he lived through almost the whole of early-modern England's long crisis, from the Armada to the Succession Crisis of the 1680s. Assuredly, his opinion stands out among the responses to Milton's *Defence*.[1]

---

[1] See Parker, 588 for some others. The standard responses are either a partisan approval / revulsion, or the amusement of unaffected Europeans. Hobbes is unusual in challenging the methods of debate.

How far is the "Defensio" a declamation after the Cambridge manner?

It is at any rate not a disputation, simply because it is complete in itself, not the prelude to impromptu oral cross-examination. It is true that in demolishing the opponent's arguments and forestalling possible rejoinders, the work reminds us that similar tactics are wielded in both declamation and disputation. In the flow of rebuttals, and untiring attempts to convict the opponent of inconsistency (worst of all thought-crimes), we see how Milton as disputant may have done his interrogations. The work remains a written not spoken one, however, distanced by form and also length from disputation.

Declamation does come to mind. The opening preface is very much in the mode of *declamatio*. Indeed (as argued elsewhere)[2] the exordium is a fine example of it—majestic long periods, vivid imagery, apt quotation of ancient authority, and more. But Milton also goes beyond the requirements of declamation, to the life-and-death urgency which politics can engender. The conclusion of the work, for example, reveals the best qualities of the mode, but caps them with a fine patriotic urgency drawing upon Cicero. His philippic follows the *Philippics*, in many respects. It is not exercising, not play-fighting. It almost qualified Milton for the Restoration Parliament's death-list.[3]

In between the spirited preface and conclusion, however, comes the body of the argument against Salmasius, set out in chapters and addressing the opponents' reasoning and evidence point by point. Being bookish, detailed, and exhaustive, it seems to me to rely very little on *declamatio* or on flowers of rhetoric. Those which do enliven the reading of it are exceptions—special effects—which test and confirm the tendency. Examples include the colourful insulting pun which turns Salmasius into a henpecked globetrotting "gallus," both a cockerel and an interfering Frenchman.[4]

If the *Defensio* is a declamation, it is an intermittent one. So far as it is declamation, it resembles Cambridge's necessarily, since Cambridge *declamatio* was not distinct from ancient and universal *declamatio*. For that matter, Hobbes changed his mind about rhetoric, deciding (so

---

[2] See Hale, *ML*, 93–97.
[3] Parker, 570–76.
[4] Hale, *ML*, 93–97.

Quentin Skinner argues) that it was needed after all, logic not sufficing to persuade.[5] Where we should accept Hobbes's comparison to the "exercise" of "a rhetoric school" is in the combative and exhaustive mindset. As Costello concludes, the "mechanical forms" of the exercises were "a vital influence on the scholastic mind itself" and so are part of the general, intellectual background, helping us to grasp the workings of minds which were "trained to insist on an answer to an answer to an answer" (*Scholastic Curriculum*, 35).

As to the subject of Milton's work, it strikes me as distant indeed from those typical of Cambridge. The clash of abstractions such as Night and Day or Ars and Ignorantia is far removed from the question whether in any circumstances whatsoever a people could try and punish its monarch by death. In 1649–1660 that was a profound philosophical and jurisprudential contestation, which ramified into every sort of practicality as well, from where one would live, to how far to obey Might when it was separated from Right (Hobbes himself made submission to Cromwell's regime), to how one should read the Bible and Roman history . . . Milton's book was a part of all that, and to diminish it into a training-debate was to suppress the chief thing about it. Hobbes's dismissal seems itself to be a rhetorical device, minimizing both sides of a debate which did matter in its decade, and did command European attention.

As declamation, did it so completely fail in its purpose, of persuasion?

When Hobbes was writing, Presbyterians and Independents had alike been silenced. When Milton had written, however, the two were dominant forces, militarily as well as intellectually and spiritually. Hobbes can lump them together as much the same thing only because in terms of power they were both dispossessed by the late 1660s. In the 1650s, it was quite the contrary: both had great power, and both wanted all power.

The *Defence* is not aimed to express Independence as a philosophy, chiefly because the government which commissioned it was more

---

[5] Quentin Skinner, *Reason and Rhetoric in the Philosophy of Hobbes* (Cambridge: Cambridge University Press, 1996).

mixed. Nor is "Independence" the name of a single clear thing. In any case, the work was designed to persuade Europe rather than England. The better it expressed Independent views, the less likely that it would command attention on the continent. The issue of audience, and of occasion, is fundamental.

The *Defensio*, flanked and punctuated as it is by the elements of declamation, aims to win the *un*committed—or at least help them to stay neutral and do nothing. In pursuit of this aim, it first appeals to the emotions and seeks to give pleasure, the two inseparable aims of *declamatio* as a form of rhetoric. Having done that by an impassioned beginning, the work switches to argumentation; an argumentation so detailed and comprehensive and bookish, and so lengthy, that the reader's awareness of rhetoric has to be consciously reactivated at spaced-out points, for special effect. Conversely, the ending moves from detail and insult, up and away into the impassioned Ciceronian appeal to patriotism.

To see which passages derive from declamation it is perhaps sufficient to ask which could be performed aloud. The finely orotund exordium and ending show a high style of oratory, conviction-oratory such as Milton's declamations sometimes attain. The mass of the proofs, by contrast, sound oratorical only when denouncing or ridiculing: their low, thwacking style is heard during the declamations at points, but never as personal attack. Neither the lengthy proofs nor the personal abusing which dominate the *Defences* owe much to the declamations. Hobbes is wrong on this.

The *main* thrust of the Defence was to adduce fact, logic, principle, a sense of history, sacred authority, and of what is feasible within social living. This often entails rubbing the reader's nose in details of English custom and law or biblical exegesis, in a style and at a length far removed from declamation. Eloquence, of the beloved *declamatio* kind, was not the prime concern with this staple of the defence. European readers were not primarily being entertained by declamation, and their entertainment came also from other component sub-genres, like parody. Hobbes's emphasis on declamation misses the point. That Milton pleased some readers by sheer style is on record.[6]

---

[6] See Parker, 622 and 1044; also Hale, *ML* 98 and 102.

Does Milton rely solely on declamation among his Cambridge exercises and arts?

We have already seen that declamations were not his sole resource. If I am right in limiting the influence of *declamatio* on the body of Milton's defence, we should next look for influence from other Cambridge Latin genres. We should look for signs of the *disputatio* in particular, and Cambridge logic in general; for every student had spent much of his first year studying logic with his tutor, as integral to practising and performing *disputatio*.[7] Besides, logic and rhetoric cohabited in both the genres.

Hobbes's comment is not absurd, only partial. The *Defence* resembles a declamation in being a continuous, complete, adversarial advocacy, on only the one side of its question. But in its methods of reasoning, once it has passed the exordium and moved into detailed rebuttal, it resembles a disputation more than a declamation. Again, being a printed whole and not an oral cross-examination, the work has an impact like that of a printed declamation. Yet the body of it, read in close detail, gives us after all our best evidence of Milton's lost performances of the "syllogistic scuffling" which followed on the disputants' set speeches.

It is not a case of *either* declamation *or* disputation. Declamation and disputation *together* give us a valuable approach to the world of seventeenth-century debating. Costello's summary bears repeating: "It is impossible to understand such a phenomenon as, for example, the mid-seventeenth-century pamphlet war without understanding the mechanical workings of the mind which had been trained to insist on an answer to an answer to an answer" (*Scholastic Curriculum*, 35); for by the time Milton had answered Salmasius here, then in his *Second Defence* answered the rebuttal of his first one, and finally defended himself in the *Pro Se Defensio* against the answer which his *Second Defence* had elicited, he had done pretty much what Costello describes.[8]

---

[7] See, e.g., Feingold in Tyacke, pp. 276–306, and above, Chap. 1.

[8] To this day, too, universities have their share of such minds, though we are not unique; think of the correspondence columns of some newspapers, and the general relief which supervenes when the editor (like a Cambridge moderator) declares "This correspondence is now closed." The difference is that at Cambridge the closure was such that "All have won, and all shall have prizes."

Milton's methods will be sampled in a later section, where I shall be working mainly from examples of logic and the use of evidence. Here, though, it can be foreshadowed that the work's whole argumentativeness, its whole axiom that if the opponent's logic (*process* of reasoning) can be faulted the case too can be dismissed, is one which it shares with the disputations. Those disputations tended to be on topics which were too general or remote to matter, so that the logic was indeed all that mattered; victory or survival was measured solely by the *logical* conduct of a dispute. That measure, by the qualities of logic itself and perhaps too of those who excel at it, means that everything using logic becomes combative, adversarial, and just like the form of the disputations themselves.

This overinsistence on attack and rebuttal both is, and is not, the uppermost issue in 1649–1651. Outrage was bound to ensue when the King had been tried and condemned; and yet issues such as monarchy and sovereignty were not clear-cut, whether in theory or in practice. Again, Milton does not rely solely on logic; and yet for considerable stretches of the defence, and at many points within it, he does contest the reasoning of Salmasius' *Defensio Regia*. He must, if he wishes to demolish the royalist case in its every part. The generic expectation is of such a total demolition. Also, the Government in commissioning Milton may have required it. Zest and scorn vie as he rubbishes the opponent's hold on fact and evidence.

Cambridge forms and terms do not appear, scholastic ones seldom. But the Cambridge emphasis on valid and invalid argumentation does appear, as if the worst offence of all were to be inconsistent.

More incidentally, too, the *Defence* makes use of the rhetoric of praise and of scorn; and it uses versification for parody. Praise and scorn figure by turns within the detail: scorn for Salmasius' bad reasoning or bad character, praise for the English people for removing their shackles and the King's head. The parody re-words a passage of Persius (*Satires*. Prologue 8–14) so as to mock Salmasius' monetary tergiversations.[9] Thus virtually all of his Cambridge genres appear as *sub*-genres, or so to speak as episodes punctuating the "narrative," within the long work: parody, praise, denunciation, *imitatio*.

---

[9] See Hale, *BLN*, 168–69.

What did he bring to the "Defence" from outside the Cambridge Latin activities?

More than any of the exercises, Milton uses the scholarly analysis of texts. But this is not a Cambridge *university*-exercise, and indeed Milton's impressive scholarship owes more to his private programme of study in the 1630s and 1640s than to Cambridge. I have discussed part of this elsewhere:[10] for instance, Greek tragedians, for whom marginalia survive in Milton's hand, are enlisted into the battle. It is fair to assume that Milton worked in the same way for his other authors, including the Bible and its tradition, though no annotated texts survive. Reading of texts, including scrutiny of textual variations and castigation of blemishes, was a normal scholarly activity then, but not as part of the official or University curriculum. The position is similar with historical and biblical scholarship.

Milton brought classically-trained, as it were anthropological interests into his rebuttals. Whilst often being used only as a stick to beat the opponent with, they do show some continuity with his prolusions. They are not only handy specifics for ridicule. When invoking "nomoi," he shows awareness of the Greek word's doubleness: "laws" and "customs," custom in fact as source of laws. ("Nomos panton basileus," said Pindar: "Custom is lord of all."[11]) It is the source of the differences between society and society. This helps Milton's argument, since he is naturally better able to explain England's customs than the foreigner Salmasius can. More than that, he explains our *nomoi* against a background of the known world's variety, difference manifested across time and place.

Is the Latin as good as Hobbes's backhanded compliment declares?

In the body of the work the Latin is mainly functional, hence plain, because it is subdued to the immediate purposes of argument and proof. Because Milton dutifully answers every single point of Salmasius, chapter by chapter, the zest and invention seem at times to droop.

---

[10] Hale, *ML*, Chap. 4.
[11] Pindar, *Fragments* 69. 1.

Zest and invention do enliven the opening of the proofs, early in Chapter I (*ColWks* 7: 42): "Nevertheless, be careful not to attribute to yourself (what nobody grants you) the ability to state the facts of a case as a right orator ought; for you can play the part neither of an orator nor a historian, nor even of a hired partisan advocate. Like some itinerant hawker, instead, touting from fair to fair, you in your preface kept raising great expectations of next day's performance . . ."[12] This reminds one and all of the Roman models, glancing at the rules for right oratory and historiography which humanists should follow. Then the register coarsens: Salmasius is not "orator" nor "historicus" nor even "causidicus" (hired pleader), but a "circulator," a pedlar crying himself up by craft learnt at markets. Though it is only abuse, it has verve and makes vivid cartoon images. We notice the parenthesis, however ("what nobody grants you") : it adds no suggestion or persuasion, but by overinsistence evokes playground name-calling. This is partly the syntactical hesitancy remarked on in Chapter 4, but more the win-at-all-costs Cambridge eristic.

As for drooping, take the closing stages of the detail. Milton has to speed up, but awkwardly and perhaps unpersuasively. What could the continental reader have made of replies like these: "And as for our being 'subjects,' all such subjection, as our own laws declare, is limited to what is 'honorable and beneficial.' Leg. Hen. I. Cap. 55" (7: 532. 8–9); or "For the matter of the Irish butchery, you 'refer the reader to the king's well-known work the *Eikon Basilike*,' and *I* refer you to *Eikonoklastes*" (532. 20–22) The writing is tired, and the opening flair is absent: how many readers would have access to copies of the lawbook and the two pamphlets, or (having reached p. 532) would bother to look them up? The points are being made for the record, for completeness—exhaustive but exhausting.

Declamation, where it does take centre stage, is indeed done well, just as Hobbes declares. The exordium and the peroration are especially fine, and would speak aloud brilliantly (Milton as Cicero).[13] But speaker

---

[12] This time it is a pleasure to quote the Columbia translation: Samuel Lee Wolff captures the Latin's caustic verve well.

[13] They are analysed in Hale, *ML*, chap. 5, and translated as well in idem, *BLN*, 156–73.

"B" is opting for the *bon mot* rather than objectivity. Although rebuttal of an opponent was a part of declamation, if boringly done it would merely detract from the excellence of the Latin, the goal of pleasing so as to persuade. Undue length would also hamper the end-purpose. We might indeed propose the paradox that the *First Defence*, not to mention the sequels, is not like *enough* to a declamation. In the cumulative, or pullulating, detail, at any rate, Milton does not rise above the limitations of the school where he practised and performed his rhetoric. The implication, rather than the overt content, of Hobbes's backhanded praise holds substance, in the sense that much of the excellent Latin, and much of the whole piece, do not transcend its occasion. However, *that* was urgent, indeed overmastering.

How "Ill" is Milton's "reasoning"?

Here is the heart of the matter. Modern writers have tended to agree with Hobbes. Yet Hobbes's testimony cannot possibly be held typical of his time. It is the judgment of the whole intended and actual readership which counts, since for them the issue was hot and undecided, and all were trained up in this kind of Latin. Did they laugh at the jokes, for instance, though Hobbes did not? Above all, did the uncommitted laugh (for on a contentious political matter we can always expect one set of partisans to laugh and the other set not to)?

There is some contemporary evidence about this.[14] But a selection of analyses will give a fairer test. Even if to analyse Milton's rebuttals is to risk tortuosity myself—the tedious impact of analysing analysis of an analysis—some concreteness is needed here. I quote from Chapter II, using this time the fine recent translation of Claire Gruzelier.[15]

First, illustrating the relevance of Cambridge's syllogistic scuffling, we can consider the great story of David rebuked by Nathan (2 Samuel 12). Nathan gets the king to agree that the rich man in the fable who stole the poor man's sole possession deserves to die; then

---

[14] Parker, 622.

[15] *John Milton. Political Writings*, ed. Martin Dzelzainis, trans. Claire Gruzelier, Cambridge Texts in the History of Political Thought (Cambridge: Cambridge University Press, 1991). Dzelzainis / Gruzelier 97 corresponds to *ColWks* 7: 120.

accuses him, David, as murderer of Uriah and stealer of his wife Bathsheba, with the minor premise and the conclusion. "Thou art the man; *Now therefore* the sword shall never depart from thy house" (verses 7 and 10, emphasis mine). So the Bible relied on a sort of syllogism, and Milton draws that into his rebuttals: "Ipse se condemnaverat," "He had condemned himself."

It is not stated as a syllogism, however, and is used only as an incidental within a convoluted rebuttal of Salmasius. Again, a pertinent contextual point might be that David is king under God, on conditions, his kingship revocable like Saul's. But that is not Milton's point, either: rebuttal is all, in this case the desire to discredit a biblical argument from God as sole judge of King David to "no man judges a king but God." Milton has to argue that David's "against you only have I sinned" (Psalm 51:4) means "against you chiefly" (120. 4). The reasoning is tortuous; not syllogistic in form; and verges on special pleading. Cambridge forms do not come into it, but the urge or need to win by any means whatever certainly does. Hobbes was right to be unimpressed.

A series of examples now following does show Cambridge logic in action. One form is to expose an opponent's inconsistency to ridicule. Another is to uncover in the opposition's case an unpalatable dilemma, whose twin horns are both damaging to the case. (The metaphor is scholastic, *argumentum cornutum*, meaning your case is being impaled on one horn or the other of some fierce horned beast. Either way, your argument is dead.)

Milton accuses Salmasius of striking self-contradictions, "insignes repugnantias tuas" (*ColWks* 7: 122. 3). The Israelites both did and did not prefer being ruled by tyrants to being ruled by the Judges. But this contradiction is not striking at all: circumstances altered cases for Israel, and the two horns are not the only positions available.[16]

The next "repugnantia" is more intriguing (*ColWorks* 7: 122–23; Gruzelier, 97–98). Just as God gave Israel a king as punishment (for *their* sins), so the Pope has been given to the church as its ruler (for their sins)—so Salmasius had argued, in his earlier work on the Papacy.

---

[16] The *YPW* commentator recalls (363, n. 81) the point, familar in Tudor homilies, that when a tyrant does rule he must not be resisted by the people but left to the wrath of God.

Whether or not Milton is hitting below the belt by going outside the present controversy, his corollary is amusing: "So if your comparison holds good, either God gave a king to the Israelites as a punishment, and as an evil thing, or gave a pope to the church for its good and as a good thing." Salmasius is wrong either way, it seems; or rather, "either you are mad or you are on my side."

However, why should God be presumed only ever to have a single reason for appointing a king? And what does the Papacy matter to the main issue, which cannot be that all kings whatever are evil seeing that Milton actually needs to persuade continentals who live under assorted monarchies? Hobbes's pragmatism must have been felt though not articulated by most people of the time, but Milton stays on the level of Old Testament precedents, and the convolutions of its exegesis. What force of *reasoning* is to be found in any "similitudo" (comparison, parallel)? We may be persuaded, perhaps, but—despite the argumentative vocabulary—parallels do not *bind*, as logic exists to do.

A further attack is about evidence, or rather authority: Salmasius has failed to demonstrate ("non ostendisti") his point from Scripture or any trustworthy authority. The proof would have to come out of books, it seems, not facts. Both controversialists want to do it out of books, and Milton is perhaps just following suit. In that case, Hobbes's rebuke applies to both gladiators.

The argument reaches a central issue: who is worthy to rule, and who decides who is worthy? On the first point "it is not fitting nor worthy for a man to be king unless he far excels the rest" (126. 13; Gruzelier, 99). However, "When many men are equal, as the majority are in every state" power is equal and should be granted in turn. And certainly "equals should be not be slaves to their equal . . ." These are mainly hopeful, positive axioms. Things go better in attacking the opposite position: Christ's being a descendant of kings does not justify kingship now, any more than those kings who were tyrants get any merit from Christ's being their descendant. Anyway, Messiah is unique, so no parallels whatever should be drawn. These negative inferences appeal to me more (and suggest as a corollary that in *Paradise Lost* the kingship of the Father has no implications for kings on earth—the uniqueness drives in an absolute wedge). A giant "Distinguo!" is Milton's method here, and though he does not call it that, nor use the verb "distinguo," he does exploit that favourite manoeuvre of those who want to win an argument—or at any rate not lose it—by seeing a crucial difference; splitting where the opponent has lumped.

Nonetheless Milton reverts to futility next. There is much talk of "sequitur" in the sequel (128. 3, 7, 8), but the reasonings are indiscriminate scuffling. "Meanwhile royal government, which has been entrusted to unworthy and undeserving people, as most commonly happens, is rightly considered to have brought more bad than good upon the human race. Nor does it follow directly (Nec continuo sequitur) that all kings are tyrants. But let us suppose that it did: I grant you this in case you think me too obstinate. Now you use what I have granted. 'These two implications follow,' you say ('Haec duo sequuntur'): 'God himself would have had to be called king of tyrants, and indeed would be the greatest tyrant himself.' If one of these implications does not follow, (Horum alterum si non sequitur), there certainly does follow (sequitur profecto) that circumstance which almost always does follow from your book (toto tuo libro fere sempre sequitur)—that you perpetually contradict not only the scriptures, but yourself, since in the sentence immediately above you had said that 'one God is king of all things, which he himself created.' But he also created both tyrants and demons; and so in your opinion he is their king too" (Gruzelier, 99). The *word* "sequitur" is being used in too many senses for the argument to proceed clearly. The arguments are miscellaneous, short-circuited and weak. Some of the thrusts are mere verbal quibbles.

But should one be so austere, or censorious? Is it appropriate? Is Milton not trying to amuse the reader, by a quick or elliptical patter; by running rings round a big-name opponent? David is twirling his sling and teasing his Goliath, by making up quick chains of reasoning which shall embroil Salmasius in unpalatable dilemmas or commit him to ludicrous positions. The playful aggressive wit resembles what happened in disputations of the Cambridge type. Locally at least, there is something youthful, not grinding, about the display. Wit which makes the reader dizzy may help, not hinder, the cause.

As to the central point, nevertheless, he is not rightly scorned as some moderns scorn him, for believing sovereignty should be with "the people" even though this is only some portion of the people, the "worthiest" of them. Suffrage seems universal only till we ask about its starting age, and whether senility or insanity or imprisonment disqualify. Milton has been blamed for his ostensibly vague view of "the people" as "those worthy to vote" but it is the conventional wisdom of his time.[17]

To the Miltonist, as to Hobbes, the one-sidedness may not appeal, but it is endemic in political polemic. Milton is making it as varied as he knows how; light and knockabout here, downright and vituperative elsewhere, serious and orthodox when trying to frame a "social contract" theory, nimble in *reductio ad absurdum* about the contentious[18] moment when ancient Israel had moved to monarchy. It transpires that although at Cambridge Milton disliked exercising his powers of logic upon questions of scholastic philosophy which he deemed outdated, in the debate upon the King's trial he gladly exercised them on a burning issue of the time. "Gladly" is the operative word: willingly, and with zest, his interest being thoroughly aroused.

I myself find him *refreshing* when argumentative, at least in small doses. For instance, even though Salmasius is being assailed too indiscriminately for our taste—must he *always* be wrong?—I would compliment Milton for making the telling comparison, of the death of Mary Queen of Scots with that of her grandson Charles.[19] It is not that Charles' trial could ever be legal, but the stubborn fact remains that one *monarch* ("Good Queen Bess") had already consented to the trial and execution of another. The royalists' shock and horror are thereby seen as over-righteous because conveniently selective.

---

[17] Dzelzainis, *Political Writings*, ed., xxiv.

[18] "Contentious" in the Bible itself: Samuel, the prophet who brings it about, and is the last of the Judges, protests about it (1 Sam 7:15 and 8). Milton joyfully turns the biblical embarrassment into a ridicule of any conclusion Salmasius might draw from it: see Gruzelier, 101, "So either the right of kings was not what the prophet expounded ... or that right, by the testimony of God and the prophet, was evil; or lastly, which it is sacrilege to say, both God and the prophet wished to deceive the people."

[19] Mary is mentioned three times; see esp. chap. 1 (*ColWks* 7: 46. 16–19).

How useful to Milton in the Defence was his whole engagement with Cambridge Latin?

To put that question another way, would he have attained the same knowledge and the same skills in polemic without Cambridge? As to the knowledge, he surely would have attained it. He matured as a historian, exegete, and textual scholar *after* leaving Cambridge. As to the skills in polemic, they were all part of the intellectual and educational thought-forms of his time, not peculiar to Cambridge. The Cambridge variations grew from the same ancient stock. Moreover, logic is logic, and evidence is evidence, whether or not Cambridge had put its trademark on them. They are not cultural constructs, and Milton does not call our attention to any Cambridge trademarks.

But when the defence is childish or threadbare or ruthless or excitable, or gamesome and captious or petty, perverse in pursuit of victory, we are hearing echoes from the Cambridge duelling-chambers, with eristic rhetoric dominating real logic to the point of abuse of it. On the other hand, when the defence is most eloquent, be it in panegyric or vituperation, we can hear the voice of Milton's best Cambridge *declamatio*. The Cambridge Latin genres contribute local felicities as well as mixed effects. They helped considerably to equip his arsenal when the need came for a Latin war of words. He shows, after all, Cambridge's combative glee.

PART TWO

VOLUNTARIES

Though Milton devoted much energy during his student years to performing the University's required student exercises, the disputations and declamations, and though "performing" them meant that he delivered them aloud whilst standing before literal, physical audiences of college or University, he gained a reputation at Cambridge for further sorts of performance, which hold at least equal interest to us because they were voluntary. The anonymous biographer speaks not only of his "performance of public exercises" but of his "choice verses, written on the occasions usually solemnized by the universities."[1]

There appears to be a distinction here between exercises "performed" and verses "written." That is, the exercises were done orally in public, whereas the verses existed first and foremost on paper. Accordingly, in moving on to consider these voluntaries, we shall have to consider whether any of the verses, having come into existence on paper, were performed out loud as well, to a college auditory. In so far as they were written, they were more voluntary, yet they may have received oral exposure too, on merit. Furthermore, we shall go beyond the occasional verses composed for "solemnities" to works composed for less formal or more intimate audiences; for these are no less revealing of how Milton used Latin to perform to Cambridge.

The word "solemnized" likewise deserves some attention. The word connects with Latin *sollemnitas*,[2] a solemnity, festival, or celebration of a day. For the seventeenth century the Oxford Dictionary gives "observance of ceremony" (sense 1) and "occasion of ceremony . . . festival" (sense 2) and "a ceremonial procession" (sense 3). Oxford's sense 4, however, "being solemn, gravity," is not recorded till the eighteenth century.[3] Solemnities are always serious and ceremonial, but not necessarily

---

[1] Parker, p. 114; the Anonymous Biographer's remark is discussed earlier, see Introduction.

[2] Or *solemnitas, sollennitas,* or *solennitas.* It is curious that the word for what is customary and formal should have an unusually volatile spelling.

[3] The word may be glimpsed shifting its sense in the phrase "usually solemnized," in that "usually" is otiose unless the word is becoming fluid and needs this unconscious glossing.

solemn. That depends what rite is in question. The biographer is probably thinking of the November 5 celebrations as well as of funerals, and maybe even of the college parodying of the exercises at a salting. The important constant of the Latin voluntaries is that they belong within ceremonies, which they help to perform. Milton still performs in a role, but now he has sought it or been offered it. Part Two examines poems addressed to community but in which he seems to have sought a role, while Part Three considers the salting performance which seems to have combined an appeal from his college combined with a willingness to accept the distinctive role offered.

In Part Two we shall take some account of how *Latin* rites of passage inform their Cambridge successors, because of the Latin medium and the humanist attitude to Latin alike.

Funerary poems lament a dead worthy of the community (elder of the "tribe"). They draw on the funeral practices of Greece and Rome to "escort" the dead person across boundaries: the body crosses over from air to tomb or pyre, the soul from this world to the underworld. Christian orthodoxy may well be employed alongside, but for Latin verse the Latin accoutrements of funeral often bulk larger. Not to grant this is to miss one special pleasure in Milton's funerary poems, in which he finds a strong and beautiful pagan sorrow by which to build for the Cambridge worthies a ship of death.[4]

The greatest of all these rites of transition is the subject of his longest Latin poem, *In Quintum Novembris*, where the nation England (like Elizabeth in the Ditchley portrait, and like Israel out of Egypt) moves from darkness into glorious light. Through the Lord's saving act, England survives, and celebrates, and will do so for ever.

Such anthropological affinities will be pointed out where appropriate within the case-studies of the ensuing chapters. They become stronger and more pronounced as the genres follow one another. Part Three concerns the most nakedly ritualized of the genres, because a salting is a blatant rite of initiation. It is the most highly ritualized of all the Latin

---

[4] As in *Paradise Lost* and elsewhere he expresses feelingly the ancient and lost quality of the pre-Roman religions, the "Etrurian shades" which so impressed D. H. Lawrence later. (However anachronistic that may seem, there are points where Milton and Lawrence touch hands.)

genres. As a mode of initiation into the tribe it shows us Milton as tribal hierophant and mystagogue.

In Part Two, however, the emphasis on ritual is less because print form is more firmly established than any putative college performance. Evidence that Milton went beyond print in his funerary poems is completely absent, and unlikely. For his November 5 poems it is more possible, and the case will be argued. In any case, the subject matter of these poems is a rite of passage, and Milton presents himself in discernibly ritual roles.

CHAPTER 6

Praising Dead Worthies, 1626

Poems for University funerals were not required but optional. The exact measure of voluntariness would vary, so that (as with those act verses) Milton might have received a nudge or invitation; but we know nothing of this sort regarding his four funerary poems of 1626.[5] Such evidence as survives points in a different direction. We know that in his first year at Cambridge he was in strife with his tutor: *Elegia Prima* speaks obliquely of this, and centrally of the pleasures of being *away* from Cambridge.[6] He changed tutors, and things went much better. It was probably in his second year, 1626, that he founded a reputation, because we notice a cluster of signs that he made a particular effort in that year to found one.

---

[5] On important occasions he speaks of feeling unready, or overpersuaded, to write: the Letter to Gil is modest about the act verses, in *Lycidas* the speaker feels unripe, and sonnet VII is all on the theme of unripeness. Is this a mere modesty-topos, a way to get started, or a sign of the psyche trembling on a major personal occasion — so that when not expressed the occasion is not a major personal one? If the second and its corollary could be affirmed, we could take their absence from the funeral poems as a sign of only a small personal engagement, and hence more likely to be an impersonally couched claim to public attention. Contrariwise, we do thus register personal involvement in the modesty-topos which begins Prolusion VI, his salting-script.

[6] The evidence for Milton's first year being extraordinarily troubled is a passage in Aubrey's life, communicated he says by Milton's brother Christopher. Milton had a row with his first tutor, Chappell. He received "some unkindness from him (whipt him)" and was afterwards transferred to another tutor though this "seemed contrary to the the Rules of the College." Though this is called a "canard" by Carey, 20, it is hard to see why it ever arose unless true. Aubrey is not taking off from *Elegia Prima*, but from Milton's own brother: external and internal evidence tally. *Elegia Prima* is emotionally and tonally in key with just such a traumatic début, mentioning as it does the "threats of the teacher" and "things intolerable to my spirit," and saying that after a good period away from "reedy Cambridge" and its unpleasing philistinism he is going back to its marshes and its "raucae Scholae" (the disputations?). See esp. the poem's opening and ending.

The evidence is plainest in his four poems for the deaths of Cambridge worthies. Had they been college worthies, a college audience would be primary, if not sole. But since they were all University ones, unconnected with Christ's, there is reason to think he designed them for a wider audience, as well or even instead. (A bid for *college* reputation may be present in the same year's production of several poems about the Gunpowder Plot, to be discussed in Chapter 8.) That the funerary poems' appearance has to do with reputation can readily be seen from a context of manuscript publication of funeral poems, in the Cambridge and Europe of the time.

The Context of Latin Condolements

Verses, handwritten, could be put in prominent places at an important public rite, for all concerned to see. For example, when Queen Elizabeth visited the two universities, poems were affixed to the church doors.[7] As for funerals in particular, when a notable member of the university died, poems would be fixed to the tomb.[8] In Europe it was the same: a late instance is recorded from Louvain (1765), where the university press printed together the official eulogy of the dead and "a series of Latin epigrams which had adorned a monumental catafalque."[9] Upon a catafalque, a structure raised like a stage above the hearse, verses would attract an even more public gaze. Routinely in fact, important deaths were theatricalized, and poems in manuscript were part of it.

As for Cambridge funerals, the typical practice was for verses of condolence to be pinned to the official hearse-cloth, where the hearse lay in state. Such verses were often termed "lacrimae," tears, and were collected together as a part of the funeral observances.[10] Although or-

---

[7] Binns, *Latin Writings*, 35–38, using John Nicholls, ed., *The Progresses and Public Processions of Queen Elizabeth*, 3 vols. (London: 1788, 1805, 1828), 1: 7–9: "'The whole lane, between the King's College and the Queen's College, was strawed with rushes, and flags, hanging in divers places, with coverlets, and boughes; and many verses fixed upon the wall.'" Also, "The west door of King's College was 'covered with verses.'"

[8] Binns, *Latin Writings*, 38: "valvis ipsis affixi versus" when Martin Bucer (Butzer) died at Cambridge in 1551.

[9] Ijsewijn and Sacré, *Companion to Neo-Latin Studies*, 2: 176.

[10] Carey, 244, on *Lycidas*, line 14 ("some melodious tear").

chestration or collaboration might come into it, it was usual for an *individual* to pin his tribute to the pall. Milton speaks of the entire university making the dark hearse wet with their tears, which suggests a scattering of individual *lacrimae* upon the pall.[11] For royalty there would also be the corporate, directed effort of an anthology; and *Iusta Edovardo King* shows a more personal, peer-group effort of the same sort. For all that, the individual could act alone. So Milton did, I infer, in late 1626 when a succession of Cambridge notables died.

Most of such verses were Latin, because of the felt suitability of Latin and its permanence to funeral rites. Latin was the language of choice for memorializing, as seen in the Latin of the tombstones (and also statues) of the ruling classes till much later. It implied a community of Latin-speaking, within a community which sought civility by being Roman in its ways and forms of living. Verses were likewise esteemed as a harder, more pithy and weighty, utterance than prose: they held *dignitas*, weight and worth and authority (what Polynesia calls "mana"). By a felt fitness or buried pun, worthies were held to be worth this. Milton offered Latin verses for the four University dignitaries, just as he offered English ones for non-University funeral-occasions.[12]

In what sense, however, can we speak of them as "performances"? The records speak of handwritten papers, attached to the hearse, never of verses read or declaimed out loud. Certainly the speech-situation is unlike that for the prose exercises, so that "performance" is a more figurative expression now. Nonetheless, it was public. All sorts could, and did, come along to read them. Thus it was self-display, a means to attract notice and reputation, even preferment. "Such occasions offered an opportunity to poets and would-be poets to display their practical talents by the writing of appropriate poems."[13]

Having set Milton in this context, then, we shall look at the four poems to ask what talents he put on display. In what ways are the four poems appropriate to their occasions? What qualities make them better than merely not inappropriate? To what extent if any do they transcend their occasion? Should they be read as a group of poems, as a composite bid for reputation?

---

[11] Elegia II, line 22: Carey, 26.
[12] His own niece; the Marchioness of Winchester; Hobson; Edward King.
[13] Binns, *Latin Writings*, 34.

The Group

It may appear perverse to consider the four poems as a group. Composed and affixed to the hearse-cloth one by one, can they be considered a group at all? After all, nobody knew that those four people would die then, nor that their funerals would be handily spaced out through the autumn term of 1626! Moreover, in *Poems 1645* Milton did not print the four as a group, preferring a metrical arrangement—the two laments which were composed in elegiac couplets going into the *Elegiae*, as II and III of their series.

"Paradoxical," however, is a better word to use than "perverse." Milton was clearly working on poems on the same subject and for the same public outcome throughout that term, availing himself of the same opportunity and fulfilling a similar general intention. They do comprise a group in this sense. He never wrote like this again.

As for *1645*, having divided the Latin poems by metre into *Elegiae* and others ("Sylvae"), and also having chosen a mainly chronological sequence within each bunch, he had no choice but to number his poems on the University beadle and on the Bishop of Winchester his *Elegiae* "II" and "III", and to put the other two into the *Sylvae* at a comparable place. Just the same, the two pairings appear in a similar position, because of the chronology. Thereby, in the early stages of each section of the *Poemata* a funerary note is first felt, then confirmed. The two 1645 acts of selection and positioning turn out after all to suggest a second-year interest in funeral verse.

To look at 1645 more widely, too, just as it is natural to connect his later obituary poems on Edward King and Charles Diodati,[14] which are in different languages and spread across two years yet close off the English and the Latin poems respectively, it is equally natural to connect—to reconnect—the four earlier Latin ones. It can hardly be chance that he wrote only four such poems, and all in the same term.

---

[14] *Lycidas* and the *Epitaphium Damonis* are both pastoral laments, and respectively conclude the English and Latin sections of *Poems, 1645*. (Though *A Masque* does follow *Lycidas*, it is marked off by having a separate title-page.)

If we do consider the four as attempts at a single sort of occasion and its decorum, we find they cultivate variety within the broad similarities of occasion. The variety is at many points impressively inventive. We shall focus here on the metres chosen, the length of poems, their pairings within the foursome, and the stance of the poet-persona as beholder. A separate section will discuss the metres again, only this time not as recurrent general schemes but in terms of the particular rhythms, aural and often onomatopoeic.

Variety

As to metrical scheme, two poems are in elegiac couplets, one in alcaics (the ode stanza made famous by Horace), and one in iambics (alternating trimeters and dimeters). Since elegiacs were always the most frequently used metre in funeral verse and the University anthologies, this choice of Milton's is fulfilling expectation. The choice lets him avail himself of the Roman elegists as exemplars, especially Ovid. Its use from the Greek origins onwards was always for diverse subjects, ranging from drinking songs to laments, and from erotic to dedications, and epigrams to epitaphs. This meant that Milton could—indeed, by the norms of composition, he should—use words or phrases, even half-lines and epigrams, from any sort of Roman elegiacs. He does this. For example, he shows his understanding of the relevant capability of the elegiac couplet as the close of one poem: "Fundet et ipsa modos *querebunda* Elegeïa tristes," "May *plaintive* Elegy [personified] herself pour sorrowful harmonies forth."[15]

Alcaics are a more complex metre, mainly because the individual component lines come from different metres to make up a demanding, mixed four-line stanza: two lines of hendecasyllables, then a change to one line of iambic dimeter plus anceps, and a change again to a freer-running, dactylic line. This metre appears much less amongst the anthologies, because of its subtler rhythm and greater demands on syntax;

---

[15] *Elegia* II. 23; trans. Carey, 26, but emphases mine.

it is, however, favoured by the experts and professionals.[16] Its use by the 17-year-old Milton is therefore bold, and he handles this rarer, arduous metre excellently.

Because the iambic couplet is rarer still,[17] its selection is even more of a statement, a sign of versatility and accomplishment. It consists of a trimeter and dimeter, alternating like hexameter and pentameter in the elegiac couplet. (The "metron" of which a trimeter has three is not a "foot" but a pair of them; ˘ – ˘ –, not ˘ –.)

Examples follow, with their quantitative (not accentual) scansion added. "Quantitative" here means that the sound-pattern depends on vowel-length, or "ictus," more like note-length in music than accent or pitch in speech.

Elegiac couplets:

> Te, qui conspicuus baculo fulgente solebas
> – – – ˘ ˘ – / ˘ ˘ – – – ˘ ˘ – ×
>   Palladium toties ore ciere gregem
>   – ˘ ˘ – ˘ ˘ – / – ˘ ˘ – ˘ ˘ ×[18]

Alcaics:

> Parere fati discite legibus
> – – ˘ – – / – ˘ ˘ – ˘ ×
> Manusque Parcae iam date supplices,
> ˘ – ˘ – – / – ˘ ˘ – ˘ × (virtual repeat of line 1)
>   qui pendulum telluris orbem
>   – – ˘ – – – – ˘ – × (change to iambic)
>   Iäpeti colitis nepotes
>   – ˘ ˘ – ˘ ˘ – ˘ – × (change again, to quicker-moving dactylic, changing once more to trochaic clausula).[19]

---

[16] In his study of the British tradition of Latin verse, David Money gives pride of place to Anthony Alsop (1669?–1726), as the "English Horace." This is both his own age's and the modern scholar's appreciation of a poet drawn by "the fascination of what's difficult," namely ode and its metres. See D. K. Money, *The English Horace. Anthony Alsop and the Tradition of British Latin Verse* (Oxford: Oxford University Press for the British Academy, 1998).

[17] Rare, e.g., among the University anthologies, discussed in Chap. 7.

[18] *Elegia* II. 1–2; Carey, 25.

[19] *In Obitum Procancellarii Medici*, 1–4, Carey, 31

Iambic couplets:

> Adhuc madentes rore squalebant genae,
> ˘ _ ˘ _ _ / _ ˘ _ _ _ ˘ _
> Et sicca nondum lumina;
> _ _ ˘ _ _ / _ ˘ x[20]

The audible, though simple, sort of variety found among the choice of metres carries over into the poems' sizes. First, the four divide up, into two of 68 lines, and two of a varying lesser length. Compare this with the metres: two in elegiacs, two in two other metres. Secondly, the two longer poems are not in the same metre. Both the long ones are to bishops, but the bishops get different metres. Pretty clearly, Milton is ringing the changes, and though he satisfies expectation he provides also for variety, and a mild surprise.

In all this, too, the four poems manifest contrast within continuity, whether we feel it as binary patterning or musical variation. The impact is of a poet who is artful, in all senses. Although such art may seem extrinsic or artificial now, in its own world "artificial" was a word of commendation ("skilfully made": OED II.i, † –1738). Artifice was commended in the architecture of an intricate stanza-form or the cunning massing of poems in groups.

A feeling may persist, however, that it is not as hard to vary one's metres or to achieve these many binarisms of form as it is to speak memorably about deaths, plural—the deaths, too, of public figures of no known personal significance to Milton.[21] It is true, but still insufficient, that the binarism recurs abundantly in the subject and theme and treatment of each dead worthy. The two university officials receive a purely Roman, secular treatment: the two bishops receive a Christian one. Each member of a pair is treated differently in this respect from the other member. Nonetheless, all of this could be true of funeral poems which were merely perfunctory or slick, the sort of public poem which knows the ropes but remains mechanical; the bane of decorum, and the

---

[20] *In Obitum Praesulis Eliensis* 1– 2, Carey, 27.
[21] Parker, 32, speculates that Gostlin had taken a benign interest in Milton's first-year troubles. As he gives no reason, I presume it is a back-inference from the tone of the poem.

test of real merit and of strong critique alike. Does Milton achieve any newness or even inspiration, in this clichéd arena?

Newness and inspiration can both be found in a further aspect, namely his self-positioning within the poems; the roles and stances he imagines for himself, in relation to the dead person as a character in the little fictions. The fictions, by the way, divide up yet again, and subdivide, in twos. The Milton persona is narrating or speaking for the two Romanized deceased, but listening to a speech in the Christianized ones. Within the Roman ones, he speaks to one deceased, and to other people about the other. Within the Christian ones, one bishop speaks to him, and he overhears a mysterious voice speaking to the other. Furthermore, these differences serve each poem's narrative, thematic, and dramatic or even visionary purposes. They may even be intimating that the Roman dead do not speak to us, whereas the Christian dead do. This is intriguing, for a poet who was so sternly Protestant, and writing for a church which had abandoned canonization. Though it may be mere poetic licence, figure of speech or flight of fancy, we should note that the decorum of occasion and the Roman modelling have let loose an unusual vein of thought in Milton. Do they allow him to entertain unorthodox imaginings within the requirements of ostensible orthodoxy?

Now these ideas need substantiation, if they are to prove that Milton was displaying to Cambridge mourners and connoisseurs more energy, and rhetorical conviction, than the genre usually did.

For the Esquire Bedellus[22] Milton sets up a picture of this university "marshal" (*praeco*) being "marshalled" off stage by death in a punning peripeteia (like that of the Hobson poems, a case of the biter bit). Then the grim conceit yields to kindly remembrance of the man at the height of his powers. The stance is of an unseen watcher and listener, modulating finally into a more overt and speaking role for the poet-persona: he

---

[22] Richard Ridding. This official is prominent at ceremonial functions of the University, and a guardian of them. He carried the mace before the Vice-Chancellor in procession. This is referred to in the opening line, where "baculo fulgente" is the shining silver mace. It is probably not relevant that the Duke of Buckingham, when elected Chancellor in the same year 1626, gave a resplendent new mace to the University: Ridding had been Esquire Beadle since 1596, and Milton is making a point rather about his being a long-standing public symbol ("solebas . . ciere greges," the continuous use of the imperfect tense).

laments the loss of the good while drones live on (compare *Lycidas* for this personal and judgmental opinion), then issues a bedellical order of his own, to the University. This reverses the first reversal: it gives orders to death, then stands in for the dead Bedellus in telling the University how to mourn.

Milton's "marshalling" is comprehensive, and quite vivid and eloquent. Let all ranks wear mourning (21). Let some put their weeping verses on the black hearse (as he himself is doing figuratively, then literally, 22). Let the elegies sound out together in sweet sorrow: is oral performance envisaged here (23)? Let lamentation of every sort (verse, prose, any and every ululation?) resound among the lecture-rooms: thus involving the entire University, undergraduates and all. Whether or not the expression of this climactic urging is merely slick, the confident *invention* should impress.

I have written admiringly elsewhere on the ode to Dr Gostlin, admiring it all the more from translating it into verse.[23] Suffice it here that the poet's implied stance is changing and intensifying. Slow meditation and self-admonition on death commence the poem: it seems more of an *ubi sunt?* than a *memento mori* (1–28).

Then the address turns directly to Gostlin ("tuque," 29), remembered as the "ruler" of the University. They, perhaps including himself, are romanized as "gentis togatae," the "toga-wearing people" of Cambridge. This has greater particularity than is at first apparent: "gentis" declares the University a community or nation, visualized as all who wear the distinguishing clothing, like a Roman citizen's. It is then metamorphosed into a Greek "Palladio gregi," Athenian-like devotees of Athena (33). An equally vivid ancient dying is lamented, Gostlin riding on Charon's ferry (34). The goddess of the underworld is jealous of this medical man's powers to save life (37–40).[24] Sombreness is ruling the tone by now, except that Milton springs a surprise. He makes a new turn, one of those sudden transitions which so characterize ode and give it its distinctive sublimity.

---

[23] Hale, *BLN*, 48–53.

[24] This does seem an exaggeration or ingratiation, as one does not imagine an octogenarian Regius Professor of Medicine in seventeenth-century Cambridge doing much general practice.

He turns to pray for the Vice-Chancellor, as if he were no longer watching the soul's descent to underworld judgement, but standing beside the body's grave. May your limbs rest gently, may roses grow on the tomb (*busto*). May the gods of death judge you equally gently, so that you attain the Elysian Fields. I find an amazing plenitude of restrained compassion here, all the stronger for being restrained—doing that as ancient tombstones do it, by the absences and understatements of the drapes and veiling.[25] This excellent poem is very Roman and yet distinctive! Being worthy of its hard high genre, ode, it states a strong claim for the odist.

The bishops receive a lengthier, less surprising treatment. First, though, as their chronology and sequence have been disputed, I should make my own view clear. Andrewes of Winchester died first, on September 25; Felton of Ely died on October 5. Since the poem for Felton refers to the poet's recent ("nuper") weeping for Andrewes (lines 1–4) and paying due honours to his tomb (lines 5–6), the natural assumption would be that Milton "wept" his "lacrimae" in Elegia III, then did the same for Felton later. However, two factors complicate the matter. Allusions to a newly deceased general and his brother in the Elegy (lines 9–12) seem to postdate the poem to late November, when news of Ernst von Mansfeld's death reached England (Carey, 51). Andrewes' funeral was not till early November. But the complications are beside the point. Andrewes' funeral was still too early for the identification with von Mansfeld to stick. In any case, Milton plainly says that he wept for one then the other, and his weepings must be taken to follow one after the other, just as the two bishops' deaths did. These two laments are poems about grieving, not about funeral rites—another difference between the first and second pair of poems.[26] They are consolations, in which the dead console the living.

If the sequence is as argued, that makes Felton's poem, not Andrewes', the culmination of the series. Would one not expect the greater

---

[25] The dead person is veiled: the fall of the drapes continues the grief into objects.

[26] For example, Binns, *Latin Writings*, 60, distinguishes *epicedium* (praise and commiseration, spoken over the corpse before burial) from *naenia* or dirge (sung at the pyre in ancient times, inscribed on the bier at a Christian burial). Because I cannot match up Milton's four stances exactly to Binns's or other classifications of sub-genre, I take it rather that Milton is making his own recombinations, in the usual humanist manner of innovating by new mixtures (as a bee makes honey).

and elder bishop, Andrewes, to have the place of most honour, with elegiacs brought back to round off the series which it had begun? Just because this is what we might expect, but I am urging that Milton wants an element of surprise, let us seriously consider the alternative view. Since Felton was Cambridge's own bishop,[27] his death would have the bigger practical impact on the churches and university within his diocese. The judgment that Andrewes' poem is a more impressive one is an aesthetic one, next to be considered. We should rely on Milton's explicit statement of the sequence; not only because he might have fictionalized his own order of composition to gain a rhetorical effect, which indeed it does gain, but because the opening *may* be persuading us to read ahead and see how one grief is capped by another, and in his estimation one poem too by its twin. This novel idea seems worth a run for its money here.

Certainly the iambics are a technical surprise. The change from elegiacs to iambics resembles in reverse the more secular lamentations' change from elegiacs (24 lines) to alcaics (48). The fact that 48 is twice 24 suggests advance in importance and weight from Bedellus to Procancellarius; 68 for both bishops, however, suggests a deliberate equalizing. (The decision in 1645 to separate elegiac poems from mixed-metre "Sylvae" meant Milton did not have to declare a preference there.)

The story-lines suggest equality, too, being largely parallel but with differences made noticeable by the parallelism. In *Elegia III*, the weeping complaining poet has a dream-vision of Andrewes' reception into heaven, a heaven replete with images from the Apocalypse, and he hears a voice welcoming the bishop. The poet weeps again, but now because the dream has ended: comfort because of the vision is implied, and—in words based on Ovid—he wishes for more such dreams. In the *Ely* poem, the weeping but now angry and indeed cursing poet hears the voice of the dead bishop, explaining the justice of God within death's apparent rampages and describing his own soul's glad ascent from its "foul prison" (46), up beyond the stars and sun and Milky Way to the heavenly palace of crystal. The poem ends in a brief burst of images from Apocalypse, and the bishop's joy to be there. He gets the last word, the poem not reverting to the listening poet.

While one could prefer the dream-vision ending of Winchester's poem, the palm may be too easily awarded to it. There is no reason to

---

[27] Its Bishop resides up the road at Ely.

think Milton was awed by Andrewes' celebrity as bishop, scholar, and preacher. In general, Milton's dream-visions are many and enjoyable, but so are his celestial travels. Imagery of voice is more biblical (and in the end Miltonic) than that of vision. The ending of *Ely* is admirable, all sadness being transcended by the report of sublimity; the conclusion not brought back to earth by the reappearance of the poet in his own voice, but left with the dead saint's speaking.

One need not insist, because Milton gives us both bishops and their evangelium from the heavens *equally*. We have the parallel of *L'Allegro* and *Il Penseroso*, for Milton's doing the same thing two ways so as to bring out difference-with-equality. Yet just as readers may want to see if Milton is, by whatever judicious fraction, *more* of a penseroso than an allegro, so here it may defamiliarize both poems for my own readers if I risk stating an ultimate preference.

Many features point in the direction of the Felton poem. Is there not a less interesting architecture in the poem which closes upon the usual funerary elegiacs, brought back at the close as a sense of coming home, than in the new metre taking us (as the treatment of subject and theme does) in a new direction and leaving us there? Is not this more exciting, and cognate with Milton's preference elsewhere for the Petrarchan over the Shakespearian form of the sonnet?[28] But the best proof of such advocacy lies in the managing of the more adventurous metre, and to this I turn in a fuller, separate analysis.

Interactions of Rhythm with Diction

The metre is that of some of Horace's epodes, and of not much else that is noteworthy. Now Horace's subjects and tone are very different from Milton's—cocky and abrasive at times, and worldly.[29] Using the metre

---

[28] A predecessor who seems to have the same slight preference is MacKellar (*Latin Poems*, 49), who finds "more warmth of feeling" in this one of the four poems. Masson, quoted by MacKellar (291), thought the space-travel moulded on Dante and the *Somnium Scipionis* but better done!

[29] The Epodes have a dozen poems in the metre, and the subjects are sex, drink, friends, and politics. Most are light, all are secular. The political ones are solemn or reflective or sombre when contemplating the Civil Wars. There is no poem remotely like Milton's in use or subject.

for this heavenly vision is as much of a leap as alluding to Ovid's erotic to cap the other one.

In shape and scope the iambics resemble a speeded-up version of the elegiac couplet. Each trimeter has twelve syllables, each dimeter has eight; and the two schemes alternate throughout. The impact is of two-line stanzas, balanced not by length (as English heroic couplets are), but by a subtle symmetry or weighting, namely a semantic tightening or summarizing or sententia in every second line. The natural run of the syntax is to close after each couplet. This is overcome at times, for effects of variation or onomatopoeia; even so, there is usually a pause where there is not a close. In all these respects, the iambic couplets are doing what the elegiac couplets do. What are the differences, then, despite which, or for the sake of which, Milton set himself this new challenge?

An obvious one is the number of syllables. Elegiacs must have at least 14 then at least 12, which can go up to 17 then 14 if all the variable metra are given dactyls instead of spondees.[30] The iambics are at least 12 then at least 8. This is a much tighter sort of couplet. It does contain some "resolutions," the resolving or loosening of some long syllables into two shorts. We find this in 12 of the 68 lines. It bestows 13 and 9 syllables respectively on ten of the resolved lines. Further, two of the trimeter lines resolve twice, giving 14 syllables. Yet this still comes short of the maximum number of syllables which the ancient version of the couplet would allow through resolutions, and is much less than the allowed upper limit of syllables in the elegiac couplet. The figures demonstrate that Milton is not allowing himself frequent resolutions (useful though they might be in maintaining an arduous new metre). He plays by the rules, the ancient practices.

In particular I noted that the resolutions he does allow himself do not begin till the metre has established itself in the ear by complete regularity for nine lines: in other words, he introduces the slight variety when the ear knows the norm and might wish for a change. Similarly, there are fewer resolutions in the final third of the poem, as if to reaffirm then uphold a purer iambic quality in the closure. It may be an onomatopoeia—prosodic purism for the vision of purity. The lines

---

[30] See Horace, *Epodes*, ed. David Minkin (Cambridge: Cambridge University Press, 1995), 14–22.

about heaven and the bishop's declarative conclusion are firmly iambic; unwavering, and credal.

> Amoenitates illius loci, mihi
> Sat est in aeternum frui.

The technical nature of these findings may not be appealing, but they are at any rate specific and verifiable. Arising as they do from the approach normally used for Roman verse, they are highly relevant for the enquiry into how Milton would have tried to convince his readers, who had ears well tuned to the practices and laws of Latin poetry (and who were no doubt avid to pounce on blunders). If they were dons, instructing students in verse composition and composing themselves for anthologies and the like, this was their *profession*. These are the audience Milton seeks to impress, by technical correctness and fluency, and ease with his metre and its diction so as to beget the appropriate conviction.

A second aspect of metre is fortunately less skeletal, namely the impact of the unusual metric choice upon diction. In elegiacs, dactylic elements are needed quite often. Contrariwise, some words will not fit the stanza at all. "Imperator," for example, scanning $-\breve{}-\breve{}$, cannot find a legitimate placing there. But when the stanza is iambic, dactylic words in turn are unwelcome: they are either impossible or distort the iambic pulse by excessive resolution. Contrariwise, words inadmissible in elegiacs get an unusual chance. It is not being suggested that Milton would be short of words, nor use a word merely because it was at last metrical, but I do see the diction of the poem as a mixture of a new freedom and a beneficial compulsion, offered by the unusual choice of metre. He uses words (and phrases) which occur nowhere else because they would not have fitted the metre or register of any other poem. This is not a misfortune but an opportunity gladly taken.

Examples are of course everything here. Words abound which could not be used except in iambic: "devovens," "diriora," "erraticorum," "formidolosi," "pratervolavi" (55), "velocitatem," "crystallinam," "smaragdis," "amoenitates" (67), all these and more. At other times, we note inflexions rather than words per se which are unavailable to elegiacs, such as "ebulliebat" (16, $--\breve{}--$), "carnea" ($-\breve{}-$, 37), "volatilesque"(47, filling a half-line thanks to the suffix -que), "formidolosi"(53). These too abound, but the ones selected all yield special effects, too numerous to explain because the poem riots in them.

Instead, let us dig deeper into a few, because diction is not a mere matter of individual word-choice (as if composing a line of verse was like solving a crossword-puzzle clue), but of the collocation of words, in phrases and clauses played off against the metrical shape of the line and its couplet.

There is a noticeably high proportion of five-syllable words among both lists. This is partly because words of that size must so to speak declare their hand metrically, must have an iambic rhythm within the word to fit the metre (and so could not have appeared in elegiac). This is too crude an explanation, however: Milton did not have to use a five-syllable word at all, because with his fluency he could get his rhythm from a larger number of smaller (more flexible) words. He *chose* the long ones. Why?

It is because their placement at the opening of a trimeter fills the whole sound-space up to the normal point of caesura. (Another frequent placement is monosyllable, usually a conjunction, plus four-syllable word up to the caesura.) Or is this, again, too mundane and superficial as explanation? Milton created nine trimeters and six dimeters by such polysyllabic words, so many that he must have heard something desirable in the rhythm and weighting for his stanzas. They seem to cluster, too—after line 10, in the middle, and at the close. Is he not giving weight and mass and emphasis to his meaning, as well as to its sound (and dutifully fulfilling a metrical requirement)? This *solemnity* is essential to the poem's whole idea (and possibly helps him avoid the skipping or bawdy associations of this metre). The solemnity is manifest when the polysyllables are heeded closely in conjunction with what follows them: "Wintoniensis praesulis" (6), a whole line occupied by the title alone; "ebulliebat fervida" (16), a mimetic alliterative boiling of anger (b/b/f/v sounds); "Volatilesque faustus inter milites" (47), lovely nimble circumlocution for the conceit of angels. This one is almost frisky: angels not just winged but joyriding? "Praetervolavi" (55) does the glee of flying differently. As the flight goes on and on, past the sun, it goes steadily, through regular iambics, word-placing and phonetic patterning: "Praetervolavi fulgidi solis globum" (– – ˘ – – / – ˘ – – – ˘ x). There is an accompanying, thematic joy in the creating and wielding of new words or inflexions: what about the line "animasque mole carnea reconditas", "souls buried under the fleshly mass" (37)? This simultaneously finds a new, intensifying metaphor for the body as prisonhouse, balances two four-syllable words at the line-ends, and by a witty turnaround buries the flesh inside the soul's phrase.

Now though some of these particular points may be deemed fanciful, together they make good the general point, that fresh onomatopoeias are being reaped throughout. Self-inflicted metrical necessity becomes the mother of inventions.

Here is one more example, a whole couplet this time:

> Ventum est Olympi, et regiam crystallinam, et
>   Stratum smaragdis atrium (63–64)

This trimeter overflows into its dimeter, miming the idea of the soul's arrival in heaven itself, and the life abundant therein. The riches of the heavenly vision spill out into the huge adjective. "Crystallinam" is now *not* at the line's beginning, but deep within it, impelling the thought onwards. So does the enjambed "et / Stratum." The "outpouring" sound and sense and image of "stratum" ("strewn, scattered") moves delightedly on again, into what is strewn, the emeralds underfoot![31] His excitement, this quickening, need to be felt by the reader, because that is the last such detail we are getting from the bishop: "sed hic tacebo" (65). Diction, imagery, metre and sense work together to create this eager climax.

Seen from this technical perspective, then, Milton marked the lying in state of Cambridge's own bishop by a virtuoso display, and a rousing finish to the series of four. "Performance" is the right word, too, for verses which sought to impress his erudite Latin-loving community, because among the readers / mourners would be a very high proportion of versifiers. In all of the four there is much to catch and hold their attention. In the fourth and last there is much to gain their admiration and applause. It makes one think of an organ voluntary, like Bach's Toccata and Fugue in D Minor or the Great St Anne.

---

[31] The emeralds derive from Revelation 21:19, where the fourth foundation of the wall is garnished with emerald. Milton's three details — gates, palace, forecourt — come from Chap. 21 but are rearranged, the more clearly to make our gaze travel with that of the new arrival. That he reduces then breaks off the rather prolonged riches of John's vision shows a fine economy, here at the poem's climax.

The Four Poems as Performances

Two main conclusions emerge. First, the Latin funeral pieces are performances which consciously bid for University, as distinct from Christ's College notice. Secondly, Milton engineers a varying interchange between the rites of funeral perfomance which included "Lacrimae," poems of lament, and his own Lacrimae here which at points, with conscious diversity, incorporate the funeral rites. As the fish is in the sea and the sea in the fish, or as Shakespeare's comedies include festive rites and the rites include comedies, so the poems are Cambridge rites and the rites enter into the poems.

The first conclusion depends on both external and internal evidence. The internal signs of a virtuoso self-display have been argued in sufficient detail already. The external evidence may therefore bear repetition instead. We have it on record that Milton's Cambridge reputation was not only for the set prose exercises but also for "choice Verses," written on "the occasions usually solemniz'd by the Universities." Of such we have only one clear piece of external evidence, his reference in a letter to some act-verses. The verses sound more like University than college ones. The only other Latin verses extant for University occasions are these four poems. Milton kept the best of his poems, if not all of them, lifelong, and published most in 1645. The funeral poems were composed in a series, close together, in late 1626. Since the verses were composed so closely together in time and were conceived as a group having conscious diversity and interactiveness, the next link in the chain of inference is to infer that he intended the series as a bid for recognition.

The second conclusion has begun emerging from the analyses of structure and texture, but needs a fuller statement now. Incorporations of ritual detail are more frequent in the two more Roman, secular poems.

The occupation of "Praeco" is the central conceit of the first poem, with special mention of his mace. There is alignment of Cambridge with Athens and Rome. The poem closes by calling on the University to honour the funeral with proper rites, naming garments and verses of the funeral rites, and elegiac lamentations (like Milton's) among its lecture rooms. By mentioning Elegeia, elegiacs personified, Milton is inserting his own poem amongst the other ritual observances. The rites are in the poem as the poem is among the rites.

The interchange is less explicit in the poem on the Vice-Chancellor's obsequies, the main conceit now being his medical profession. The "people of Cambridge" wear "togas" and are a "Palladian" flock, continuing the previous melding of Athens and Rome into a Cambridge self-idealization. There is a new attention to the tomb, with the grass around it and flowers growing from it ("ex tuo . . . busto"); life around death, balancing the "Et in Arcadia ego." Death is the dominant theme; yet the poet addresses the dead personage directly, twice. Cambridge and ancient observances combine, in a more ambitious poem and a less usual metre.

In the verses for Andrewes, the scope is again wider, not totally Christian or biblical but syncretistic. Local rituals are absent in this effusion. The Roman goddess Libitina is complained of ("querebar," 15), in the lengthy lament section. In the poem for Ely, on the other hand, the poet does picture himself paying verse tribute at Andrewes' tomb ("maesta charo iusta persolvi rogo," "I paid my sad respects," 5) Ely himself is called "rex sacrorum," an exact and witty Romanism because that was a Roman priestly title. His cathedra is named, nearby at the "Eel-isle" ("insula . . . Anguillae," in Old English "Elig"). Cambridge references are fewer and slighter for the two bishops, who had not resided in that town for years and were not being buried there: their corpses lay there in state only symbolically, a cenotaph but under the same hearse-cloth.

In his solidity of specification Milton makes the most of what he is given. The varying circumstances of the deaths yield appropriate variations of stance and imagery. The interchange between rite and poem is clearest in the poems for the two purely Cambridge worthies. A sense persists of his poems as rituals of tribute, incorporating those of others and assigning themselves a place. His occasional verses have a continuous sense of occasion. The cumulative performance is a conscious rising to the series of University occasions. In a general way, it is a display of powers by the rising poet, *vate futuro*, in the University's singing-contests. In a more particular way, it looks back to Homer and Virgil, to the epic episode of funeral games, where to show skill or strength was both to honour the dead and to achieve personal prowess.

For the ancient world there was a sense that the *arete*, excellence or prowess, of the dead hero was to be served by the different *arete* of bards or athletes. Cambridge's obsequies, including orations and poems, conducted its worthies' send-offs in a kindred way, for the worthies are dead kindred, former "fathers" or controllers at the exercising of many "sons." The young Milton entered the lists of this poesy: other lists, as the next Chapter will reflect, he did not.

CHAPTER 7

The University Anthologies

This chapter concerns a genre, strictly a type of printed volume, to which Milton did *not* contribute. While prolonged discussion of an absence could become unduly speculative, this particular negative prompts pertinent questions. Did Milton have any choice about contributing to the University anthologies, or was he not asked? What is the relation of the official University anthologies to others where he does contribute, and to his self-collections? Is it the language-medium—Latin versus English—which governs what he does? Does his practice change at all over time? Though not all of these questions can receive secure answers, the questions themselves deserve to be explored in the context of his changing personality and attitudes, including his attitude to Latin and to Cambridge itself.

Positive benefit, too, may come from comparing Milton's funerary poems to ones from the anthologies. This is because to relate his work to the typical is to show whether and when, and where and how, he transcends the typical. One particular specimen will be made subject of a comparative case-study, namely the ode which Milton's close friend Charles Diodati contributed to the Oxford anthology tribute to Camden: the ode is in the same arduous metre in which Milton later wrote for Dr. Gostlin. Some other specimens are examined, composed in the more usual medium of elegiac couplets, from the anthology which came from the press during Milton's first year at Cambridge. Such comparisons provide relevant conditions of understanding and criteria of evaluation.

The Cambridge University Anthologies 1625–1632

Through the sixteenth century and into the Stuart era the custom established itself at both English universities, and the Irish and Scottish ones, of collecting up or commissioning tributary verses for royal occasions.[1] Royal deaths, coronations, marriages, or births were marked by anthologies, chiefly of Latin verse but with a fair amount of Greek poems and a few in further tongues, printed at the University presses and presented in a beautifully bound copy to the appropriate royal personage. At times an anthology was compiled for an important peer or notable benefactor: the deaths of Sidney, Bodley, and Camden were honoured by Oxford.

Cambridge produced fewer anthologies and was in general less adventurous in these matters of *pietas*. A proposed volume for Bacon was aborted by his disgrace. But in the years 1625–1632 it produced four volumes. Two came out in 1625: *Cantabrigiensium Dolor et Solamen* for the death of James and accession of Charles ("with an auspicious and a dropping eye," so to speak); and *Epithalamium* for the nuptials of Charles and Henrietta Maria. Then in 1631 a *Genethliacum* appeared for two royal births, the "illustrissimorum principum Caroli et Mariae." In 1632 the *Anthologia in regis Exanthemata* congratulated the king on his recovery from boils.

By 1631 Cambridge had got behind Oxford: Oxford honoured the birth of Prince Charles with *Britanniae Natalis* in 1630, so Cambridge caught up in the next year by marking not one but two royal births. It then got ahead with the boils volume, so Oxford caught up with a reply marking the King's return from a peregrination. This competitive motive may be minor, but should not be forgotten. As Milton's friend Diodati had contributed to the Oxford volume for Camden in 1624, the year before Milton matriculated, we can assume at least that Milton knew of the anthologies, and might envisage appearing in print of this sort.

That he did not may have resulted from anything between dislike of the subject-matter—the incessant contorted praise of royalty, since Cambridge did not succeed in honouring anyone but royals—to sheer circumstances, his not being invited or the timing of the volumes.

To take those points singly: though I believe the subject-matter had become uncongenial by 1631–1632, and hope to prove this in another chapter, there is no evidence for disaffection as early as his first year

---

[1] The most convenient round-up of publication details is now that of Money, *The English Horace*, 373–79. Many of the poems are discussed from a more technical standpoint in Binns, *Latin Writings*, esp. 60–75.

at Cambridge. He was having a tumultuous first year, including some clash with his first tutor and some disciplinary action against him by his college in 1625. Next year, he was voluntarily praising Cambridge worthies including two conformist bishops. So political awareness in 1625 is not established or even plausible.

The four anthologies themselves, when their front-matter and contents are examined, suggest a different line of thought. The editor of all four was Ralph Winterton, a Fellow of King's. (He was made Professor of Medicine, probably because of his classical attainments—he edited Greek medical texts.) A very energetic man, Winterton got his contributions in rapidly. Speed could be important, when a royal happening was not of a foreseeable kind, or when the aim was partly to outwit Oxford. How he could act so quickly was naturally by practice: the first 1625 anthology set up the channels of communication and response for the second one that year, and similarly with 1631 and 1632. Even more significant was the King's College connection. While it was vital for each such volume to contain contributions by the Vice-Chancellor, heads of houses, and undergraduates of high birth, the staple or makeweight of the volumes came from King's. It came, for example, from Winterton's own pupils, a quarter in which he could command or induce. He also supplied a number of items himself, possibly thus ensuring variety amongst the Latin metres employed and a fit proportioning of Greek to Latin poems. Correspondingly, however, the input by other colleges varied widely, some being only sparsely represented.

In truth, the volumes are not as representative as one might have expected. This is because of the King's College presence and (presumably) the accidents of Winterton's personal network round the colleges. Consequently we notice that for *Dolor et Solamen* King's contributes sixteen poems but Christ's only two, this notwithstanding Christ's being the larger college in 1625. In the *Epithalamium* again, King's scores thirty-four, Christ's only three. It does seem as if the young Milton, an embattled freshman, would have had trouble getting one of his poems into either collection, even if he had had the wish.

What can be inferred *per contra* is that in 1626 he sought a reputation of the same kind, as if to catch up, and to achieve what 1625 and Winterton had not allowed him to. Furthermore, though he had by 1630 achieved that reputation (as evidenced in general by the statement of the anonymous biographer, and in particular by the recruitment of his services by a Fellow of Christ's as ghost-writer), he again did not appear in the volumes of 1631 and 1632. This is a more surprising absence, since we know that by that time he had gained wide repute for his exercises and verses. It will be suggested from other evidence in Chapter Eight that by then his political awareness had become such that he would be unlikely to honour royal babies or royal boils.

Milton's Attitudes to Print and to Cambridge

What is the relation of the official University anthologies to other anthologies to which he did contribute? He contributed to the Shakespeare Second Folio published in 1630, and to the Hobson miscellanies in manuscript of early 1631. If we may judge by his overwhelming contribution of *Lycidas* to the Edward King *Justa* later, he liked to be asked and was willing to join in quite diverse medleys. Then how come he was not asked in 1631 and 1632, since by then he was reconciled and well-reputed? My thesis is that by then he was unwilling to praise royalty. Cambridge anthologies had failed to honour Bacon, or anyone but royalty. Though Milton was troubled by his own unripeness in his three-and-twentieth year (1631 or 1632), he may well have known what he did *not* want to do.[2]

The evidence supports the conclusions of Alberta T. Turner's study "Milton and the Convention of the Academic Miscellanies."[3] There is no particular reason to think Milton in 1625 avoided the anthologies or was excluded from them, and no great reason to have expected his presence there. 1631–1632 may be a different story. Turner's conclusions in any case refer to print publication, whereas prior to 1645 we are concerned rather with performance and manuscript publication.

Her conclusion (93) prompts further thought:

---

[2] The dating of his Sonnet VII could mean "in my twenty-third year of life," ergo before his birthday in December 1631, or else "my age being 23"; see Carey, 152.

[3] Alberta T. Turner, "Milton and the Convention of the Academic Miscellanies," *Yearbook of English Studies* 5 (1975): 86–93.

The importance of the miscellany convention to Milton is that it formed part of a larger educational convention . . .[4] A significant continuation of this education was the need and opportunity for university members to write occasional verse and the ability to display it on walls, recite it on public occasions, and publish it in university miscellanies. No matter how many or how few miscellanies they published in, the recurrent fact of miscellany publication must have stimulated active and conscious practitioners like Milton and [Edward] King. There they could see poetry taken seriously by administrators, teachers, and students alike.

Harold Love's monumental study of scribal publication makes the similar point that academic miscellanies "give us valuable insight into the shared culture that linked scholars of all ages and disciplines." Moreover,

> The don who might himself be called on to provide an elegy, an oration, a grace or a memorial inscription would be sure to have personal copies of work by admired practitioners. [Manuscript circulation is implied.] Writing of this kind was an advertisement for the wit of the donor community and the excellence of its Latinity, with rival authors competing in the display of their linguistic endowments.[5]

So let us turn to a relevant extended example of this culture, the community at its emulations. It is the ode in alcaics which his friend Diodati had contributed to Oxford's volume to honour the death of its benefactor, the historian Camden. The fact of friends writing obituary alcaics upon academic worthies makes a comparison relevant, despite one set reaching print, the other not.

Alcaics by Diodati (1623) and Milton (1626)

It may be worth reiterating that the Cambridge exercises and voluntaries were paralleled by those of Oxford, if not indeed overshadowed by them. Oxford put out more anthologies than Cambridge in this period, and was honouring more than royalty therein—worthies who would

---

[4] The words omitted, as tendentious, are "without which he would probably never have become a poet."

[5] Harold Love, *Scribal Publication in Seventeenth-Century England* (Oxford: Clarendon Press, 1993); here 223.

be worthy in anybody's esteem, like Sidney or Bodley or Camden. Milton's friend was joining in the emulative honouring of a notable historian, who only the year before had founded a lectureship in history.[6] As Diodati published no further verses, he may have been prompted by a special *pietas*, in that Camden had preceded Diodati and Milton at St Paul's School.

Because it is in the same slightly less usual metre, alcaics, Diodati's ode has been combed for signs of connection to Milton's. Estelle Haan argues persuasively, however, that the correspondences are only of a general nature—mythology, topoi, reflections on mortality.[7] In choosing nonetheless to compare the two friends' odes by reason of such *general* similarities, of genre, metre, and university occasion, I am heeding a different probability. Not only in general did colleagues or friends compose competitively within this culture: these two friends in particular joshed each other multilingually in letters, and exchanged verses in order to improve them.[8] So whilst not arguing that Milton took anything from the Camden poem into his own, I do think Milton saw it. An external or reading influence is more certain than any internal indebtedness, and so my form of comparison has a solid enough foundation for present purposes.

Diodati wrote:

> Sic furva coniunx Tartarei Iovis,
> Sic quae tremenda fila secat manu
> Mortalibus talem invidentes
> Aërias rapuere ad umbras?[9]

("Thus has the dusky wife of Tartarean Jove [i.e., Proserpine], thus has she who cuts with dreadful hand the thread [of life], being envious of

---

[6] See Donald C. Dorian, *The English Diodatis* (New Brunswick: Rutgers University Press, 1950), 107. Thus the professor of Roman history at Oxford is still the "Camden Professor."

[7] See E. Haan, "Milton and Two Italian Humanists: Some Hitherto Unnoticed Neo-Latin Echoes in *In Obitum Procancellarii* and *In Obitum Praesulis Eliensis*," *Notes and Queries* 44 (1997): 176–81.

[8] A letter of Diodati's to Milton in Greek survives, complete with its errors (Dorian, *English Diodatis*, 109–10, Hale, *ML* , 208, n. 7); at the end of *Elegia* VI Milton asks Diodati to be like a judge to him, "'iudicis instar."

[9] The text is that in Dorian, *English Diodatis*, 108, but modernized (because e.g., its use of u/v is irrational: "viuent" at line 20).

mortals, snatched away so distinguished a man to the places of mist and shadow?"[10])

The stanza is competent but not more. How is Proserpine "furva," dusky, and how are the shades "airy" (since *aerius*, of the *air*, refers us upward not downward)? Is it not a little confusing to call Pluto or Dis—even epithetized as "Tartarean"—by the name of another god, Jove, the chiefest god? It would still be forced if Dis is Jove because he is *a* Jove or chief god of his own domain. The sense of the stanza is not very picturable; it seems strained.

>   Crudele fatum, cui reverentia
>   Nulla est senectae, nec refugis caput
>   Carissimum Musis, virisque
>   Artibus et probitate sacrum.

("Merciless Death, you are without reverence for age, nor do you spare a man dearest to the Muses and to his fellow men, one sacred for his knowledge and uprightness.")

"Cruel" fate was cliché then as now, but the double negative "nec refugis" ("you do not shrink from, or spare") is stronger. Moreover, joining it with Camden's head locates by an agile synecdoche fate's attack upon his aged, sacred head, the intellectual and most vulnerable part of him.

>   A quo tenebris eruta squalidae
>   Oblivionis patria, debitis
>   Honoribus fulget, per orbem
>   Ingeniisque opibusque clara.

("His native land, plucked by him from the darkness of neglected oblivion, shines forth [now] with [its] deserved honors, manifest throughout the world for both its men of genius and its resources.")

The new stanza moves further from platitude, to honour Camden himself: his country owes him a debt for "rescuing" ("eruta") her past luminaries as antiquarian. A pleasing circularity of reciprocity makes the thought more lively and individual: Britain shines because

---

[10] The translation is Dorian's, *English Diodatis*, 254, n. 54, cited after each stanza of the Latin.

of Camden who records her past heroes, while the stanza implies his fame as being her benefactor.

> Sed nec brevis te Sarcophagus teget,
> Camdene, totum: multaque pars tui
>   Vitabit umbras, et superstes
>   Fama per omne vigebit aevum.

("But the narrow grave will not altogether hide you, Camden: rather, an important part of you will evade the shadows, and [your] surviving fame will flourish through every age.")

I am unsure about the word-order of the first line, and find the rest a tissue of allusion (Horace, Ovid, almost verbatim).[11]

> Donec Britannum spumeus alluet
> Neptunus oras, dumque erit Anglia
>   Ab omnibus divisa terris,
>   Magna tui monumenta vivent.

("As long as the foaming sea washes against the coasts of the Britons, and England is divided from all [other] lands, your great memorials [i.e., your books] will live.")

The thought continues traditional and unsurprising, and though "spumeus" is a good epithet for Neptune it is cancelled for me by the sea's inevitably "washing" the shores. England's state of apartness, equally inevitable, is awkwardly conveyed by the syntax and word-order of "erit . . . divisa." Let me not sound like Polonius condemning the wording of Hamlet's love-letters: Dorian rightly commends the deftness of allusion within the stanza to Camden's writings, the "magna tui monumenta" being his written memorials, of Britain first but then of himself also. Still, though deftly expressed and built into the stanza's ending, it is hardly a new idea; or rather (as that may be to ask too much of an alcaic ode) the idea is not given individuality of expression.

It is worth observing, too, that though the lines are not too end-stopped the stanzas are. One of the especial beauties of the alcaic stanza occurs when it runs on into the next. Timed correctly, so as to be expressive of urgency or momentum or controlled passion in the speaker,

---

[11] Horace, *Odes* 3. 30. 6–7; Ovid *Amores* 1. 15. 42 and *Tristia* 3. 7. 50.

this running-on gives special delight. Diodati does not provide this, a quintessential pleasure of ode;[12] but Milton does.

> Haec constituta est a Iove sedulis
> Merces laborum; hanc omnipotens pater
>   Tibi, atque virtutem secutis,
>   Et meliora dedit, dabitque.

("This reward of labors was established by Jupiter for the diligent; this and [still] better things [our] Almighty Father has given and will give to you and to [all] those who pursue virtue.")

This, though, is worthy of Horace! It catches his limpid economy of words, and his strength of thought. It expands the accolade, right through to the final word. And the simplicity of diction conceals the art of the envoi. Its close is less striking, because it leaves the individual Camden behind in favour of generality, an exhorting of all the pious to work hard and earn a heavenly reward like his.

By contrast, though Milton was even less connected with Gostlin than Diodati was with Camden, he manages a more personal vibrancy, and especially here at the ending. How does he do it? And how has Diodati's competence helped to uncover Milton's overgoing flair? In more practical terms, what has the present comparison uncovered that the earlier appraisal in Chapter 6 did not? Is this about anything more than my own contingent thought-processes?

Milton's ode cannot be addressed stanza by stanza as we did his friend's. It is more than twice as long. It runs on between stanzas. Besides, simple repetition of points made about it in Chapter Six should be avoided, though of course corroboration from a new perspective can be welcomed. Instead, we will compare the two poems first as wholes, then in the aspects which received most emphasis in our discussion of the Camden ode.

The impact of the Gostlin ode is of conviction, and control, to an effect of momentum and weight which increase through to the close. This effect is gained, first and foremost, by the wielding of the alcaic stanzas.

---

[12] It is well managed in Milton's "Rouse" ode, and materially persuades at the climax of *Lycidas*.

Schematically speaking, its twelve stanzas launch off with one declarative imperative stanza: "learn to obey the laws of Fate," we are all enjoined, with the word "obey" leading. Another like it tells us of the way we all *must* go: the journey over the dark river of death is one you must go, "ire certum est." Then a two-stanza sentence[13] lists the great worthies of the past who fell under the stern decree: Hercules and Hector, and Sarpedon "for whom even Jove wept." Five more stanzas build up the great list, till its last two include the dead Vice-Chancellor: a majestic, impressive *a fortiori* is being spelt out, such that if all those former great ones could not escape, neither can you—but the apostrophe, the tuque (line 29) is also praising the newly-dead addressee, by incorporating him among the glorious dead. Last and not least of these is his fellow-healer Asclepius (25–28).

"But No" ("At," line 37)! Your thread of life is broken, precisely because as healer you robbed death of so many: so now death has come for you. This peripeteia attracts Milton, just as in the companion funerary piece the marshal Ridding is "marshalled" to the underworld. Its medical counterpart, perhaps learnt from the gospels ("Physician, heal thyself"), will return—very poignantly too, in view of the present comparison with Diodati—when Milton's *Epitaphium Damonis* laments that his best friend died young because his own medicines could not avail him in his own need.[14]

> Ah pereant herbae, pereant artesque medentum
> Gramina, postquam ipsi nil profecere magistro! (153–54)

This poem knows what it is doing, both in the stanza and in the onward march of the stanzas. Look what it does next: a complete change

---

[13] The sentence-division is not always to be trusted in modern editions, because all too often they merely follow seventeenth-century printing-house practice and place a full stop at the close of every stanza, just because it is a stanza. They do the same with elegiac couplets, even when the sense manifestly and intentionally enjambs. See John K. Hale, "The Punctuation of Milton's Latin Verse: Some Prolegomena," *Milton Quarterly* 23 (1989): 7–19. In the present ode, stanzas which begin "Nec" or "que" or "et" require to be read in close conjunction with the preceding stanza, so as to follow how the poet is getting excited, thinking in units larger than the single stanza, massing the sense to gain the momentum and conviction I discern.

[14] Carey, 278.

of direction, address, and tone. Odes by nature do this, if we think of Pindar's, Wordsworth's, Hölderlin's. So this one does, breaking away from admonition or lament, and certainly from a procession of precedents. It breaks away to prayer, then to blessing, given one stanza apiece. The transition is sudden and daring, but felt to be right.

Milton's speech-act is longer, and more varied, than Diodati's. It is less uniform, both because its units are less predictably single-stanza-sized, and because it twists and turns more dramatically. The speaking persona, the mourner, impinges as far more involved in his subject, the dead scholar (not forgetting, either, that both the dead belonged to the Oxbridge Latin culture, and had turned out verses in their time for their own lost leaders). In fact, our comparison, far from reducing Milton's ode to an average of competent mediocrity, makes it look—and sound—passionate.

How does he manage it? Much of the effect is achieved by the stance and the persona Milton creates in the text for himself. He does not mention himself; but thus, like Spenser as bridegroom in the *Epithalamion*, he can be everywhere. He is the unseen but heard choregus, presenter, master of ceremonies, hierophant. He is directing the audience to think about death, including their own. He is reminding, enumerating, admonishing, grieving, consoling throughout the cataloguing of the legendary dead. He then praises the newly dead by placing him among legends. Then, therefore, he can change the mood which he has been creating through the sudden turn to prayer, the burial-place, the tomb and what may grow there: the lengthy past of the tribe, its sad present and more fragrant future. The "tribe" in question is the whole colossal evoked culture, Greece and Rome from the death of the demigod Hercules past the fall of Troy in Hector and on to him that died just now. Though to speak of a "tribe" is only metaphor since "culture" is meant, the perfervid evocator still speaks like a priest or psychopomp: he imagines himself, momentarily, as the voice of the tribe. By the pageant or literary procession the poet is seeing the dead man out of this life and into the next one, and doing it in two ways together—down across the Styx with the grim ferryman (35), and also into the tomb on earth. Life continues in the tomb, as flowers spring up there (42–44). Life may continue in the other world, too: may its judges judge you kindly, and then you can pace about in the spacious Elysian fields, among the other blest ("felices"). The poet has spoken on behalf of the *grex Palladius* (33), the academic community, imagining himself the unelected officiant and celebrant of the rite of passage.

To work the comparison through the aspects to which Diodati's poem alerted us—epithets, allusions, caesuras, diction and what not—is feasible. but perhaps superfluous. That is, although one could demonstrate how much better Milton wields these aspects, it would be superfluous because Milton so *integrates* them that only in analytical retrospect and slow motion do we pause on them at all. Thoughts of technique or competence have vanished. If we do go back to inspect detail, we find excellence there as well. To instance only one, the allusion to Taenarus (5). It is a virtual synonym for Hades or death; but since it names a promontory of the Peloponnese which had a cave believed to give entrance to the underworld (like Avernus for Virgil), the name becomes more than a handy cretic (—u—) or unusual metonymy. It pinpoints Milton's central conception, of the journey of the ship of death and of the rite of passage. Taenarus, like the dead Gostlin and the vates Milton, stands on the *limen*, between the two worlds. As with so many of the best moments of these Cambridge "exercises," this one apprehends liminality, both for the poet and for the body of which he speaks as a member.

Funerary Verses: Lennox, Topham, Milton

For a brief further comparison with Milton I have chosen two sets of verses from Cambridge's 1625 anthology, *Dolor et Solamen*. These were written to express the University's chorus of grief for the dead King James, that grief moderated, however, as the title states, by joy at his son Charles's succession. From Milton I have chosen Elegia II again, the poem for the bedellus Ridding, as a poem declaring an official, University grief in the same metre.

Lennox is James Stuart, fourth Duke of Lennox, a thirteen-year-old undergraduate at Trinity College. The dead King was his nearest male kinsman, hence by Scots law his uncle-guardian. His poem comes first in the anthology simply because he is the highest-ranking contributor, but thereby the collection begins well since the poem's grief is that towards a parent as much as a king. The poem's afterword declares this in prose, and the poem hinges on the point. It makes it four times over. The structure consists (after an opening modesty-topos) of three elegiac couplets capping the grief of all mere subjects with the more personal, filial grief of the writer. The short pentameter line of each couplet aims higher than the preceding hexameter line. A *pair* of couplets close it off, in which two lines, not one, of patriotic / ecclesiastical grief are matched and capped by two of individual sorrow.

In Obitum Augustissimi Regis
IACOBI

> Da tenui veniam Musae (Rex magne) parentis
>   Exequias lacrymis condecorare sui.
> Defunctum luget nunc moesta Britannia Regem,
>   Defunctum moestus lugeo at ipse Patrem.
> Extinctum queritur plorans Ecclesia Daphnim:
>   Heu! queror extinctum iam Decus esse Meum.
> Deflet & amissum pullata Academia Phoebum,
>   Amissum pullâ defleo veste Iovem.
> Lugeat ergo suum Patronum Ecclesia, Phoebum
>   Musae, IACOBVM Terra Britanna suum.
> Nulla queat nostro par esse querela dolori,
>   Funera quêis tria sunt tanta dolenda simul.

Hoc epicedium Iacobus Dux Lenoxiae Avunculi sui longe charissimi, & quem Parentis loco habuit defuncti Regis piis Manibus parentavit. e Coll. Trin.
("Permit, Great King, this slight muse to honour the death of his parent with tearful verse. Woeful Britain now mourns a dead King; but *I* am mourning a dead Father. The Church weeps and laments its extinguished Daphnis:[15] O alas, I lament that my Glory has now been extinguished.[16] The University is dressed all in black and bewails its lost Phoebus: in my own black garb I am bewailing my lost Jove. So let the

---

[15] Pastoral shepherd-singer, alluding to James as writer on ecclesiastical matters and as Defender of the Faith, head of the Church of England.

[16] Perhaps alluding to the biblical "Ichabod" = "the glory [of Israel] has departed" (1 Samuel 4:21); but the line is obscure, and shows signs of strain or metrical fill-up.

Church bewail its Patron, the Muses bewail Phoebus, and the land of Britain its JAMES: no lament can equal my grief, for I must grieve for three great deaths at once.[17]

This funeral song is offered as a sacrifice to the sacred departed spirit of his most beloved uncle, whom he held in the place of a parent, by James Duke of Lenox, of Trinity College.")[18]

Whether the young Duke invented and composed it all unaided is not material, as it was perfectly usual for those who could pay for it to commission an anthology poem. Competence and decorum were the thing. The prime consideration is that the ducal poem stands first on page 1, to launch the whole volume. A bound copy would have been presented to Charles by the University's top officials. Charles might thus notice the important presence of his kinsman. The dual note of sorrow, with the personal continually capping the patriotic, would stand out.

Aesthetically, however, the poem's repetitiveness ensures not only attention and the decorums, but a deserved oblivion. It shows a mechanical, lifeless competence. By the fourth variation, the *a fortiori* falls with a dull thud.

How, then, does Antony Topham tackle his task and how does he fare? Topham, who contributes two sets of elegiacs on page 7, was also from Trinity, a D.D. He propounds a striking conceit from the myth of Niobe. Niobe, who turned into marble after seeing all her children slain by Apollo, is declared to be lucky ("felix") compared with grieving Britain, because as marble she can be the tomb for her slaughtered progeny: all Britain wishes it could be the mausoleum for the dead James. And, because the legend went on to affirm that Niobe's marble (snatched by a whirlwind to the top of Mount Sipylus) stayed wet with tears, all Britain aspires to become a perpetual weeping marble.

> Diriguisse ferunt Nioben in marmora, natos
>   Cum iaculis fixos vidit Apollineis.

---

[17] Of his Father (line 4), his Glory (line 6) and his Jove or God (line 8). After each pentameter in Lennox's voice has answered a hexameter in the voice of some estate of the realm, the final couplet balances its predecessor in this summarizing way. The poem is a repeated *a fortiori*: if the nation or its parts mourn an unparalleled loss, how much more must *I* mourn *my* losses?

[18] The text is taken from the STC microfilm copy. My own translation.

Quam felix Niobe es marmor iam facta, peremptis
    Pignoribus tumulo cui licet esse tuis!
Invidet ecce tuo gemebunda Britannia fato,[19]
    Marmoreamque cupit se fieri statuam,
Ut Mausoleum possit decorare Iacobi
    Quem telis petiit saevus Apollo suis:
Et fato similis lacrimarum forte perennes
    Distillet vitreo marmoris instar aquas.

("They say that Niobe stiffened into marble when she saw her children pierced through with the darts of Apollo. How fortunate you are, Niobe, to be made marble, for that enables you to be the tomb for your slain children! Behold, grieving Britain envies your fate and yearns to be made a statue too, to decorate the Mausoleum of James whom cruel Apollo has sought out with his weapons: and like Niobe in fate so may this statue perchance distill in a glass the perennial waters of tears.")[20]

Whereas the sycophancy of courtiers to James was notorious and virtually de rigueur, Topham here rivals Shakespeare's Goneril and Regan in precarious overstatement. The striking conceit does not rescue the poem from spectacular bad taste. Where Lennox was competent, this is audacious; ludicrous where Lennox was dull.

Milton's poem for Ridding contrasts, being both competent and striking, and reconciling the two qualities through imaginative coherence. For a highly generic poem it achieves surprising particularity and vividness—for example by bestowing a local habitation and a name upon the dead functionary. The marshall, so often seen at graduations in his glory, is outmarshalled by Death. Let all the "schools" echo with laments: "Personet et totis naenia moesta scholis," where the "schools" means both the University teaching rooms (the Logic and Divinity schools, and so on), and the scholars who study there. Is there a hint that poems of condolement might receive a public *hearing* there? If so, this would be another motive for Milton in composing this and the

---

[19] Most unusual, and probably counterproductive, is the purely dactylic line to express grief.

[20] My translation. The sense is strained or at any rate cramped in the last line, if as taken here "vitreo" is a local ablative, "in a glass." A preposition would make it more idiomatic ("in" or "into" the glass receptacle); but such licence in verse is not uncommon, and certainly is found in Milton.

other elegies in 1626: to be heard as well as read at the University's rituals of acknowledgment to its dead worthies.

Though we have no funerary poem by Milton on James, he does at any rate praise him in elegiacs, the four "Gunpowder Plot" epigrams; and in the second of them he affirms that James has gone to heaven:

> Ille quidem sine te consortia serus adivit
>   Astra, nec inferni pulveris usus ope.

("James has now gone to join the starry brotherhood, at a ripe old age, without the help of you [the "Beast" of Rome] or your infernal gunpowder.")[21] Yet the praise of James is only the dry certainty, that he went to heaven much later, not expedited thither by terrorism. The elegiacs maintain an attack, as epigram, throughout the series: James is accessory or instrumental, to a more distinctive use of the sub-genre.

I conclude that when Milton wrote these elegiacs for a national occasion, probably the November 5 commemorations which become the subject of the next chapter, the thrust was political and religious, and the tone was sharp. His writing of four or five such would-be barbed epigrams shows his interest, but also its political, critical nature. The laments for Cambridge worthies, on the other hand, all tell a story: with or without an imagined presence for the poet's persona at the grave-side, they dramatize the obsequies of which they make a part. The stance is simple enough, and not at all new to the long Greco-Roman tradition. Yet when placed alongside the printed, official tributes I have been sampling, his funerary pieces sound natural and simple. These are virtues anywhere, but especially in a dirge.

---

[21] Carey, 35, his trans.

CHAPTER

8

In Quintum Novembris and the other Gunpowder Poems

Late 1626 was a remarkable time for Milton's Cambridge Latin. After a turbulent and not very productive first year, he put himself forward in that autumn by composing obituary poems—voluntaries, but of an orthodox Cambridge piety. At the same time he was composing four epigrams on the Gunpowder Plot, mainly mocking the Catholic conspirators; another epigram, on gunpowder itself; and the short epic, or satiric epic, "On the Fifth of November." The six poems lack any known Cambridge connection, or any local occasion, because although Cambridge observed the November 5 rituals, they were observed everywhere, as required to be done by act of Parliament. To see whether we can recover some occasion or prompting for these poems just then is one purpose of the chapter. More important, though, it seeks to trace how Latin, and the chosen Roman genres, helped express his mind on a political subject, in 1626. That year was the second of the new King's reign, so that while the poem has King James and 1605 as its point of reference it may also reflect or contemplate the beginnings of the new reign.

Composition and Grouping of the Six Poems

Several assumptions are being made in this questioning, and need to be explained. Should one assume that the six poems were all composed in autumn 1626? Should one think of them as all composed at one time, or indeed think of them as a group at all?

The most substantial poem of the six is in fact Milton's longest Latin poem, so that everyone has always connected the five Plot or gunpowder epigrams to it in the course of subordinating them to it. But that is still assumption, not evidence. The self-editing for *Poems 1645* affords no evidence, because the epigrams are placed together amongst Milton's other epigrams, well away from the little epic. The epic is in hexameters, whereas the five epigrams are printed as a sub-group of the poems in elegiac couplets: these comprise seven full-length "Elegiae" in a numbered series, then the short ones together.

Nonetheless, *In Quintum Novembris* itself has a clear enough dating in 1645 (and 1673): it is headed "Anno aetatis 17," which is confirmed from other occurrences of the idiom to mean "At age 17," not "in his seventeenth year."[1] Milton was seventeen from December 1625 to December 1626. Whether or not the poem was composed for an actual celebration, as will be argued, it strikes me as perverse to imagine Milton composing—and especially entitling—such a poem at any other time of the year. Title, occasion and subject cling together.

Similarly, we can ask whether the epigrams belong to another time, or are dispersed and not a group at all. There is no evidence for either of these rejections of the orthodox, natural assumption. We have just seen him tackle four poems of a similar type in a bunch that term. The first four epigrams read even more like a series of attempts at a single theme, with the same or similar wit; in fact they read to me as if he revised till he got the subject right—short and pithy, as an epigram ought to be—at the fourth attempt.

Only the fifth epigram sits more loosely, in subject and attitude, in the putative grouping. I am content, though, to regard it as a fresh attempt at epigram, as short as the successful fourth, but now taking the form in a more ambiguous direction. Does it praise gunpowder? Not if it does not first praise Prometheus. This it does not do: only "*blind* antiquity," "*caeca* vetustas," praised him (my emphases). So to praise the inventor of gunpowder is also to be "blind." After four straightforwardly caustic epigrams, of direct sarcastic attack, this one is more oblique, or uncertain. All five alike are practice pieces, in some way preparatory for the very major poem which Milton attempted in autumn 1626. It is likely enough, indeed characteristic of his known personality, that he would be competing for public recognition in one type of poem at the

---

[1] Carey, 37–38.

very same time as he composes poems with more of himself in them, and these on both a smaller and a larger scale.

Did it have no particular occasion, however? On the basis of the little evidence we have, I suggest that Milton performed it aloud, in Christ's, desirous to make a splash there in person to his confreres, after performing to University individual readers by paper on the hearsecloth.

The evidence is not direct, because it comes from later and from Oxford. At Christ Church, Oxford, after 1660 exceptional and prestigious pieces were performed to a gathering of a whole college upon a feastday or commemoration. At Pembroke College in Samuel Johnson's time November 5 was celebrated "with great solemnity, and exercises upon the subject of the day were required."[2] So Masson was not merely guessing when he opined that our poem was performed in Christ's because "There were probably opportunities in the colleges of Cambridge for the public reading of compositions on the subject by the more ambitious of the students."[3] *In Quintum Novembris* would fit the bill, as a notable piece of display and of ambitious scope, from a student whose muse was ambitious at that very time. (Masson points out that November 5, 1626 is only two weeks after the day of the Vice-Chancellor's death, which makes it likely that composition of the two poems overlapped.) The epigrams would be a somewhat earlier tuning of his lute for the "more ambitious" endeavour.[4]

The resultant poem is so manifestly ambitious that it possesses more of a critical tradition than the other Cambridge Latin pieces do. Accordingly, we shall take the opportunity to approach it through that tradition.

---

[2] MacKellar, *Latin Poems*, 46, n. 2, quoting Boswell.

[3] Masson, *Life*, 1: 148.

[4] See E. G. W. Bill, *Education at Christ Church Oxford 1660–1800* (Oxford: Clarendon Press, 1988), Chap. 5, e.g. 252; and cf. again Masson, *Life*, 1: 148; also MacKellar, *Latin Poems*, 46, n. 2, citing Boswell, and mentioning Thomas Gray when a student at Peterhouse, Cambridge. (Gray's "In Quintam [*sic*] Novembris," composed at Peterhouse, is rightly deemed a "mechanical exercise" by R. W. Ketton-Cramer, *Thomas Gray: A Biography* [Cambridge: Cambridge University Press, 1955], 21: too long for an epigram, too short for a worthwhile narrative, it is a poem without discovery or passion, hence quite the opposite of Milton's.)

Approaches to *In Quintum Novembris*

It was back in 1605 that King, royal family, and both houses of Parliament narrowly escaped being blown up together, by Guy Fawkes and other Catholic extremists. Whether or not a twenty-first anniversary had the inscrutable significance which that number of years holds today, readers of Milton have often asked what significance the choice and timing of the topic held for Milton. The number of the epigrams, and the length of the epic, both suggest a deliberate voluntary.

Some interpreters, it is true, have dismissed the poem as a mere undergraduate exercise. Others have put the focus on its chief villain, who is not Guy Fawkes but an airborne Satan, who wings his way round Europe stirring up evil and tempting the Pope to support the gunpowder-plotters. Later work has related Milton's poem to other contemporaries' Latin ones on his subject. Meanwhile, editorial scholarship has steadily accumulated notes on the Latin poems which have contributed to Milton's poem. The most recent approach emphasizes the poem's politics, anti-papal and Protestant.

The first two of the five approaches are misunderstandings, I believe; and the third is important but narrow. The last two approaches, however, offer a way forward. All five are now briefly passed in review.

The Cambridge exercises were not "mere" exercises for the practitioners, because—as we have been seeing—they were a means to reputation and preferment. Furthermore, this particular poem may have been performed (as Prolusion VI and also VII certainly were) to a throng of Milton's peers if not the whole of his college. The stakes, the risk of loss of face, increase in proportion as a college performance was an honour, and was used by Milton for a more personal agenda before his peers (as again he did with Prolusion VI).

Nor is the Satan of this poem much like Milton's later Satans: the relations of its overflying evil-doer to the epic character are almost wholly ones of difference, since this Latin Satan is allegorized pastiche, a caricaturing of *Schadenfreude*.[5]

---

[5] Links to the Satan of *Paradise Lost* are emphasized by (e.g.,) Macon P. Cheek, "Milton's *In Quintum Novembris*: An Epic Foreshadowing," *Studies in Philology*, 54 (1957): 172–84.

Connecting the poem with Gunpowder poems by other people, and especially Latin ones, is naturally much more relevant and fruitful than connecting up Satans by wrenching them out of context.[6] Accepting the detailed work of Estelle Haan and others, I seek to move forward, into a fuller sense of what Milton omits or avoids as he takes up this occasional genre at a time when its productions had slowed to a trickle.[7] Viewed in these terms, his silences may reveal as much, of difference or distancing, as his many congeneric words do of a shared theme.

Similarly with the many influences upon Milton's verbal texture from Roman or Neo-Latin poets, as accumulated by editors and commentators, I accept their collective influence as enormous, not least in respect of the Gunpowder poems (traced with precision by Estelle Haan).[8] Rather than repeating that influence, however, the chapter proposes a different emphasis within the influence, along with some further influences upon the poetic texture, but will indeed focus more upon ones of structure, so as to connect these to certain significant omissions or "speaking silences."

The present approach is most similar to the fifth group of responses, the political one of Stella Revard and others, who link the poem and its placing in *Poems, 1645* to Milton's increasingly articulate Protes-

---

[6] See esp. Estelle Haan, "Milton's *In Quintum Novembris* and the Anglo-Latin Gunpowder Epic," *Humanistica Lovaniensia* 41 (1992): 221–95; 42 (1993): 368–93. Haan has also edited Phineas Fletcher's *Locustae* (pub. 1627 but composed earlier) for *Humanistica Lovaniensia Supplementa* 9 (1996) (Leuven: Leuven University Press, 1996). Gunpowder Plot poems are listed in Binns, *Latin Writings*, 457 n. 31. Listed where possible by year of first printing, they are: Anonymous, Barclay, Goad (1605); Herring, Wallace (1606); Cooper (1607); Phineas Fletcher (pub. 1627, written c. 1611); Simson (1621); Campion (in MS only, till 1987); Milton, *In Quintum Novembris* (written 1626, pub. in *Poems, 1645*).

[7] As the previous note implies, it is uncertain whether Milton had seen the poems by Fletcher or Campion, which though reposing in Cambridge libraries in 1626 had not reached print. Haan argues temperately for this. The present chapter takes as proven that Milton's poem is "traversed" intertextually by the growing sequence of printed poems, without assuming any familiarity with Fletcher's or Campion's MSS. (He probably did hear talk about them.) My emphasis is placed on new suggestions, such as the "speaking silences" and sources outside the Gunpowder tradition.

[8] Haan, "Milton's *In Quintum Novembris*," 221–47.

tantism.[9] The approach extends the last two kinds of predecessor, by looking at some neglected contexts. For instance, Latin sources are examined which have been neglected, such as Ovid's *Fasti*, or interpreted in a limited lexical / textural way by the commentators, such as a satire by the Scottish Protestant poet George Buchanan. Examination also proceeds more fully than Revard's into such contexts as national, then Cambridge, politics in 1626; and the commemorations and their "vocabulary" between 1606 and 1626. The approach taken leads to a more precise hypothesis: that Milton's political awakening is found in this very poem, and indeed at its ending precisely because of the poem's act of thought, the realization which it enacts at a measurable moment.[10]

The chief arguments for these positions will come from contexts and from sources, and especially (to reiterate) from silences. Certain contexts and sources create an expectation which Milton does *not* fulfill; so when, and how far, may one infer that he *chooses* not to fulfill?

Within the challenge to consider where the argument from silence is applicable, there is implied a renewed modification of the accumulations of editorial scholarship. A Neo-Latin poem can become almost dissolved by zealous scholarship into verbal borrowings, because it is by nature an extreme of intertextuality. Yet the prior question remains, whether the cornucopia of allusion is mere pastiche, perhaps taken from a gradus or other compilation rather than from original texts, whether classical or Neo-Latin. Whereas some of the chief bodies of allusion in Milton's satiric epic do consist of diction (vocabulary to colour a detail or keep up the hexametric momentum), the ones to be emphasized now are a source of ideas, and of thought, regardless of whether they also emerge from scrutiny as absorbed for texturing. Furthermore, no single model of influence suffices for the appreciation of the whole poem: the focus will be less after all on intertextuality than on the poem's train of thought.

---

[9] Revard, *Milton and the Tangles of Neaera's Hair*; C. W. R. D. Moseley, *The Poetic Birth: Milton's Poems of 1645* (Aldershot: Scolar Press, 1991); Haan, *From* Academia *to* Amicitia, 26. The Protestant emphasis will be distinguished more for *In Quintum Novembris* here than by its predecessors, who are more royalist / Anglican.

[10] This is applying an approach formulated for different poems by J. Martin Evans, *The Miltonic Moment* (Lexington: University of Kentucky Press, 1998).

Speaking Silences

The obvious sources of Milton's poem lie in three types of material: in the events of 1605; in the rituals of commemoration 1605–1626; and in the bilingual tradition of Plot-poems as high culture's contributions to those rituals. None of these sources is used by Milton in the expected, precedented way.

First, Milton's poem gives almost no historical details, and nothing of the causality and cross-currents of the conspiracy itself.[11] Here in brief are the incidents of the Plot. In 1603 James VI of Scotland became James I of England too. Catholics hoped for relief from the punitive fines of Elizabeth's reign. By 1605 these hopes were waning: James liked the money and kept the Elizabethan balance. Catholic extremists planned to blow up the Parliament buildings, complete with members of both Houses and the royal family, all assembling there for a State opening of Parliament. But one of the conspirators warned a kinsman, Earl Mounteagle (also a Catholic, but a quiescent one), to stay away from the State Opening. Mounteagle gave the tip-off to the secret police. All the conspirators were killed or caught. The survivors were tortured; then came a show trial. King, royal family, peers, parliamentarians, all had been flabbergasted. Their joint escape was soon regarded as a divine intervention, a sign of God's special favour to England under its new dynasty.

Milton, on the contrary, mentions no names of actors in the melodrama except that of the King, and him briefly (twice by name and twice by epithets).[12] He says nothing about the divisions amongst Catholics,

---

[11] For this chapter I have relied on the narrative of Samuel R. Gardiner, *History of England from the Accession of James I to the Outbreak of the Civil War 1603–1642*, 10 vols. (London: Longmans, 1883), 1, 1603–7, especially Chaps 3 to 6. The recent popular work by Antonia Fraser, *The Gunpowder Plot: Terror and Faith in 1605* (London: Weidenfeld, 1996) valuably pays more attention to the Catholic side and to Catholic culture, together with the continuance of the Guy Fawkes cult into modern times.

[12] 1 and 203 for mention by name; for mention by epithets, 5 "pacificus . . . felix divesque" and 116 "rex magnus."

between quietists, Jesuits, and zealots; nothing about the tensions within the Church of England; nothing about the tortures nor the show trials; and nothing about why Catholics would go to such extremes just then. The poem contains only one historical character, and gives him no characterization whatever. It is not *about* James. He is not praised for things done, for it seems he did nothing. Unlike other Plot-poets Milton does not commend James for the King James Bible, nor unhistorically transfer to him the discovery of the plot and the clever sleuthing of its sequel.[13]

As against all that, Milton does stress agency. He dwells on the diabolic agency of the conspiracy, and the mysterious agency of the deliverance. Satan mounts the mischief, by tempting the Pope: God defuses it, through the actions of a personified Rumour.[14] Now although Milton was not the only poet to bring spirits and personifications into the story, no other Gunpowder poet I have read relies solely on their agency.[15] One could infer that Milton's poem simply aimed to be shorter than the cognate narrative poems (which tend to be circumstantial and correspondingly huge); and yet it is not all that short. What if Milton so relished the allegorization that he wanted to present the events as a myth of national deliverance—as that, and as nothing else? The dearth of historical narrative, the paucity of characters, the slight role for James, are to be seen not as mere devices to shorten the text—for it remains Milton's longest poem, and detail within it is by no means uncherished. The emphasis is religious. It falls upon the nation's deliverance. "Deliverance" here is meant in the biblical sense, of one of God's saving acts: the poem is ambitious, eschatological, politically alert. Its emphasis falls as much on the people, or the land or nation, as on the monarch.[16] The poem is moving from an opening emphasis on James and his accession

---

[13] See Haan, "Milton's *In Quintum Novembris*," 234, 236, etc. for details.

[14] Deriving from Virgil's Fama, as editors all comment. See below, n. 26.

[15] Known Gunpowder poems are listed above (n. 6). Of these, I have had opportunity to check Barclay, Herring, Wallace, Fletcher, and Campion.

[16] For references to James, see n. 12 above. For kingdom and people see 15–16, 31–34, 41, 95–96. For King then orders then populace, 115 then 116–28. People at 197, 202, the last a climax as the Lord speaks: "meque meosque Britannos" (" I, God, and my Britons"). Finally as the poem is closing, 211, 217–8 and 225.

in 1603, to the people, or rather to the people under God. "Under" God is exact, for God is the second personage alongside Satan, and he looks down upon the whole event, from a vantage-point higher still than Satan. Satan overflies Europe at about jumbo-jet height, looking down at cities where he can interfere, whereas God looks down from a heavenly citadel, a different downward-looking, done from another reality than Satan's worldly one.[17]

Secondly, the commemorations were not as fixed for all time as their sturdy survival into the present century might make one suppose.[18] At the court, already by 1609, the King had tired of hearing Protestant vituperations during the November 5 court sermon: he needed support from sundry Catholic monarchs for his foreign policy, and the balance of forces within the Church of England was under pressure. In fact, the tenor and tone of court sermons become a barometer of factional strength and royal thinking, from 1610 onwards.[19]

Much the same applied to the parish rituals. These were being damped down by officialdom from 1610. Contrariwise, they intensified when popular opinion (vaguely Protestant) saw the papacy as a renewed

---

[17] It may be significant that Satan "aspicit" at 32 but God "despicit" at 167, and cf. "ab alto / Aethereus" at 220–1.

[18] General official forms of the yearly commemoration from 1606 to 1626 included: (i) sermon to be preached before the King, at court; (ii) service of thanksgiving on November 5 in every parish; (iii) bells to be rung, with beer for the ringers at parish expense. General informal commemorations took the usual pattern of Protestant festivals: (iv) bonfires at cross-roads, and street-partying, with the special feature of (v) the burning of Guy Fawkes in effigy; also (vi) songs and nursery rhymes were composed for the event, like "Gunpowder, Treason and Plot."

At Cambridge University in particular, the rites of 1626 would have included: (vii) sermon in University Church, of Great St Mary's, in English; (viii) bells rung at St Mary's, as for (iii) above; (ix) Latin oration to University Senate, in King's College Chapel. In each college, too, something would have marked the day, but I know of nothing recorded. At night, street celebrations of the usual popular sort would have included bonfires, effigies, fireworks; perhaps also beer and food offered in the streets (rather like the street parties at the end of World War II in Britain). The question whether Latin poems formed a part of the day's doings in colleges is discussed below.

[19] See Peter McCullough, *Sermons at Court* (Cambridge: Cambridge University Press, 1998).

threat, or felt the King was going soft on Papists (usually those two feelings coincided).[20] By relating Milton's poem to these trends, then, we might glimpse him placing himself politically by his handling of the popular cults. The popular 5 November commemorations were becoming distasteful and embarrassing to the Stuarts: Milton, on the other hand, makes them the sole focus of his ending. King and courtiers fade out of the triumphant rescue and concluding jubilation of the poem, making way for a theophany, then a cadenza describing the people's November 5 cult practice. His omissions and emphases are alike unusual, tendentious, and hence to be read politically.

Thirdly, the tradition of poems celebrating the nation's survival follows a course similar to that of the folk-rites, of which it might be seen as a part or a high-culture counterpart. Printed poems abounded at first, then stopped till after 1626. Manuscript poems seem to have fallen to a trickle, as far as one can tell.[21] Two of the best poems remained (like Milton's) unpublished for years: did publishers fear the market had dried up, or was the censorship more actively discouraging the fiery Protestant ones?[22] There is much we do not and perhaps cannot know until new evidence is forthcoming.

National and Cambridge Politics in 1626

The chief contextual factor missing from standard accounts of the poem is the political climate of late 1626 in Cambridge. To put it summarily, the Commons were lining up against the new monarch, Charles I, and

---

[20] See David Cressy, *Bonfires and Bells: National Memory and the Protestant Calendar in Elizabethan and Stuart England* (London: Weidenfeld & Nicolson, 1989), esp. Chap. 9, 141–155, "Remembering the Fifth of November." Fluctuations in the amount of beer issued to the bellringers provide a bizarre criterion—a liquid measure—of the confidence of the authorities and of its agreement with the popular mood.

[21] This may seem an insecure inference, since Binns, *Latin Writings*, p. 457, lists sixteen such poems. However, the list includes Milton's one, two not published till modern times, and one published the year after Milton wrote. Some poems, too, are bunches of epigrams preceding a *prose* text, or are poems in Oxbridge anthologies.

[22] Since most of the poems were monarchist in emphasis (for example giving an unhistorical role to James in the detection of the Plot), reasons for their non-publication may have been simply commercial and personal. It is puzzling that Fletcher managed to publish his poem in 1627, a time of tension between King and Commons, yet Campion's never saw print at all.

his unpopular mentor the Duke of Buckingham. Buckingham had only just escaped impeachment in the Lords. Cambridge, or rather its dons, and above all its manipulative heads of colleges, chose *this* moment to elect him their Chancellor. The King had hinted a wish. So they contrived and connived to oblige him. Buckingham was elected by a margin of five votes: "[I]t was known that many had voted for him sorely against their wishes, and it was whispered [...] that [...] an impartial scrutiny would have converted [Buckingham's] victory into defeat."[23] There must have been extreme tension in Cambridge, and it must have been felt by the undergraduate body as they watched the manoeuverings of their teachers during the campaign and the election.[24]

Now, all this was going on in the summer when Milton was conceiving, or gestating, the poem. Its topic being political, one naturally looks for reflections of the tension. The tension being dangerous, one looks next for coded reflections. Such coding resides in the choice and use of particular literary sources, especially the following: the Bible; Buchanan's satire upon the Franciscans; and Ovid's *Fasti*. I consider them in turn.

The Bible

That the poem owes much of its verbal texture to earlier Latin poets, both ancient and Neo-Latin, is amply recorded in editions, especially those of MacKellar and Bush;[25] and particular, pervasive indebtedness to Virgil has been amply demonstrated.[26] Yet without discounting such

---

[23] S. R. Gardiner, *A History of England under the Duke of Buckingham and Charles I, 1624–1628*, 2 vols. (London: Longmans, 1875), 2: 67.

[24] Evidence is lacking, but it stands to reason that undergraduates would be aware of the national crisis of 1626, and would be agog when it led to a trial of strength locally. Any election for Chancellor is a trial of political strength when one of the contestants is a politician, which Oxbridge Chancellors tend to have been, right up to the present day. As an undergraduate, and not a very political one, I myself was well aware of the lobbying amongst the fellows of my college who were backing Harold Macmillan for Chancellor. Indeed, I had friends studying history who complained that they were not getting full tutorial attention from their tutors because the phone kept ringing, about the lobbying.

[25] MacKellar, *Latin Poems*; Bush, *Variorum*.

[26] Besides Cheek, "Milton's *In Quintum Novembris*," see Mason Tung, "Milton's Adaptation in In Quintum Novembris of Virgil's Fama," Milton Quarterly 12 (1975): 90–95.

textural debts, our understanding of the poem is better advanced at the present stage of debate if we dwell on a source which provides structure yet seldom texture, namely the Bible. The poem comprises the following materials, thus disposed: 1–47: Satan plans revenge on England's prosperity under James VI and I; 48–132: Satan flies to Rome, and disguised as a Franciscan tempts the Pope in a dream to instigate the Gunpowder Plot, timed for the State Opening of Parliament; 135–165: the Pope commissions personified Murder and Treachery to blow up Parliament; 166–215: God foils the Plot, through personified Rumour; 216–226: the commemorative cult of 5 November. But although the materials sound diverse, and have diverse origins, their structuring is biblical at the crises or turning-points.

The entire narrative is hung like a suspension bridge from three biblical moments. Its beginning consists of Satan "roving" the world, organizing temptation to evil (as at the beginning of the Book of Job):

> Iam pius extrema veniens Iacobus ab arcto
> Teucrigenas populos, lateque patentia regna
> Albionum tenuit, iamque inviolabile foedus
> Sceptra Caledoniis coniunxerat Anglica Scotis:
> Pacificusque novo felix divesque sedebat
> In solio, occultique doli securus et hostis:
> Cum ferus ignifluo regnans Acheronte tyrannus,
> Eumenidum pater, aethereo vagus exul Olympo,
> Forte *per immensum terrarum erraverat orbem*,
> Dinumerans sceleris socios, vernasque fideles,
> Participes regni post funera moesta futuros.

("Now came good King James from the far north and began his reign over that nation which traces its origins to Troy, and over the extensive domains of the English people. Now an inviolable treaty had united the Scots of Caledonia under English rule.[27] James, the peace-bearer, sat on his new throne. Wealth and good fortune were his: he was not worried

---

[27] Carey's rendering ("under English rule") would have seemed tendentious to Scots, since the line could simply mean that James had united English "sceptra" with Caledonian Scottish ones: he was literally king of both, without the two kingdoms being united. He just, so to speak, had two crowns on.

about any enemy or secret plot. It happened at that time that the fierce tyrant who controls Acheron's flaming currents, the tyrant who is father to the Furies and a wandering exile from heavenly Olympus, *had gone roaming over this huge globe*. He was counting up his companions in crime, his faithful slaves by birth, who, after their miserable deaths, were going to share his kingdom.") (lines 1–11, emphasis added)[28]

The entire verse-paragraph is quoted, to show exactly how it leads up to the crucial first action of the poem's plot, Satan's roaming. The sequence of tenses and moods in the Latin is unusual: "James [...] coming [...] held [...] and had united [...] and was sitting when [Satan] [...] had gone roaming." The syntax sets in parallel the twin pluperfects: James had done one key thing; Satan had begun doing another.[29]

That, then is the first pivot of the narration. There follows many a busy doing by Satan and his cohorts; but nonetheless, the second pivot or decisive intervention occurs when "the Lord looks down" at line 167. Soon afterwards, and now from the soteriological perspective, the Lord "takes pity on his people"—at which point we have come to the end of the Plot, and the plot, alike.

The action hinges on the moment when "the Lord looks down from the citadel of heaven and derides the vain attempts of the perverse crew" (167–168). This veritable theophany comes in the poem's shortest printed paragraph. Its very shortness makes it stand out. Thematically, it surely should do so:

> Interea longo flectens curvamine coelos
> Despicit aetherea dominus qui fulgurat arce,
> Vanaque perversae ridet conamina turbae,
> Atque sui causam populi volet ipse tueri.

("Meanwhile the Lord who sends the lightning from his skyey citadel and bends the heavens in their wide arc looks down and laughs at the vain attempts of the evil mob, intending to defend His people's cause

---

[28] Carey, 38, 47.

[29] The *cum inversum* construction here takes the indicative, as regularly when the verb governed by *cum* is really a new main verb: see E. C. Woodcock, *A New Latin Syntax* (London: Methuen, 1959), 193, § 237. Less regular, perhaps, is the pairing of pluperfects in this locution.

Himself.")[30] Whether or not it seems too abrupt to dismiss so many lines of menace by a single short divine intervention, or too reliant on hindsight or uncircumstantial or inaccurate, that is what Milton does.

His detail bears scrutiny also. The fact that the first line quoted is modeled on Ovid[31] may cause readers (and has certainly led editors) to notice Ovid at first for the rhythm and sound. Biblical modeling, nonetheless, is clearer and more important. To be exact, it *becomes* more important, as a first line of Ovidian coloration (God as a Jove-like lightning-sender) modulates into the Psalmist's thought, every detail of which is used and expanded. In Psalm 2 "He that sitteth in the heavens shall laugh: the Lord shall have them in derision."[32] It is almost a disservice to Milton to bury the crucial biblical source amongst the more copious Latin parallels, the many topoi of Jupiter looking down from Olympus. Milton's *ideas* are biblical. They precede, not follow, his wording.

A further unnoticed detail should alert the reader to the preeminence of the biblical, and to the poem's climax as an act of faith: God "sui causam populi volet ipse tueri." The verb is future, even though prosodically it could easily have been a further historic present, "vult." Instead, we are told he "will be willing" to protect his own people. He was, he is, and he will be: this is to make a fuller affirmation of God's providence toward the chosen people. Seen in this light, too, the line's syntax is hung upon its pronouns, "sui" then "ipse"—God's very own people, then "God himself." (It is repeated in reverse order at line 202, "Coniurata cohors in meque meosque Britannos," where for good measure the twofold *-que* binds God and Britain still more closely, syntactically become one entity.) Coming furthermore in the last line of the paragraph, the future tense makes a valuable new impact on the sequence of the tenses: hitherto, these have been historic presents (picturing the past in the present), but now the future tense stretches them both into the future. 1605 is making a statement about 1626, and about an indefinitely extended future time. A normal apocalyptic tactic in Milton's age, it comes from the gospels.

---

[30] Carey, 44, 49.
[31] Ovid, *Metamorphoses* 6. 64, "inficere ingenti longum curvamine caelum..."
[32] I quote from the "King James" version, as seems appropriate here.

At the close, similarly, once the Virgilian Rumour has leaked the Plot, "the father of heaven pities his people from on high" (220–21):

> Attamen interea populi miserescit ab alto
> Aethereus pater, et crudelibus obstitit ausis
> Papicolum; capti poenas raptantur ad acres;
> At pia thura Deo, et grati solvuntur honores;
> Compita laeta focis genialibus omnia fumant;
> Turba choros iuvenilis agit: quintoque Novembris
> Nulla dies toto occurrit celebratior anno.

("But meanwhile our Heavenly Father looked down on his people with pity and put a stop to the Papists' cruel venture. They are captured and hurried off to sharp punishments. Pious incense is burned and grateful honours paid to God. There is merrymaking at every crossroads and smoke rises from the festive bonfires: the young people dance in crowds: in all the year there is no day more celebrated than the fifth of November.") (220–226)[33]

Here again, notice the biblical governing idea. It governs, amongst other things in the finale, the Ovidian allusion and emphasis. It will be urged shortly that the last four lines are shaped by the Ovid of the *Fasti*; a debt to an unusual region of Ovid, and I think a new suggestion into the bargain. Nonetheless, Ovid appears as final voice only because of the primary biblical resonance, preceding and enabling it. Only after all of that can the Roman voice corroborate the biblical idea.

In the three biblical moments together, then, a biblical ideology is applied to the English people. They appear in postures of faith or supplication, much like the chosen race of old, the Children of Israel. Whereas the words are those of Latin poets, the meaning is biblical. Moreover, the paralleling of a would-be Protestant people with the Israelites of the Exodus and afterwards is a favourite trope with seventeenth-century religious radicals. The present poem, which centres on allegorical melodrama, may even be its first express appearance in Milton's writing.

---

[33] Carey, pp. 40–41, 50.

George Buchanan

The second vital source, Buchanan, is equally reformist-Protestant. Verbal indebtedness to him is widespread and well-documented by editors. Hence it might be that since Milton stands closer to the attitudes of Buchanan as well as to his Latin texture than to other sources in these respects, we have here the completest source of all for the poem. It might appear so; but doubts soon surface.

George Buchanan (1506–1582) was a founding father of Scottish Presbyterianism, and a historian, University Principal, royal tutor, and much else. His European reputation, though, was for his Latin poetry. For instance, he versified the Psalms.[34] Buchanan is a major quarry for Milton in the section where Satan reaches Rome and disguises himself as a Franciscan friar, to tempt the Pope into blessing an act of terrorism (lines 74–132). The quarrying for words, phrases, and imagery is well-attested.[35]

There is an attendant puzzle, however. Why should Satan adopt the disguise of a *Franciscan*? It was English *Jesuits* who knew the conspirators and were blamed for their plot. Did Milton know that Franciscans at Rome had the ear of the Pope of that time?[36] In graphic representations of the temptation of Christ Satan is sometimes shown in a Franciscan habit, but it seems more likely that Milton artlessly follows Buchanan, who had indeed fallen foul of the Franciscans and let the world know it by poems.[37]

---

[34] Hence there may be biblical echoes in Milton's poem which have come to him through Buchanan's Latin rather than from the Vulgate or the Protestant Latin Bible. On Buchanan's psalmody see Philip J. Ford, *George Buchanan: Prince of Poets* (Aberdeen: Aberdeen University Press, 1982) 6, 44, 77.

[35] See especially MacKellar, *Latin Poetry*, and Bush, *Variorum*, passim.

[36] As the year 1605 had no fewer than three Popes, I doubt that all were under the influence of the Franciscans, and that Milton in 1626 knew much about the matter. See Ludwig, Freiherr von Pastor, *The History of the Popes from the Close of the Middle Ages Drawn from the Secret Archives of the Vatican and Other Original Sources*, trans. Dom Ernest Graf, OSB, 40 vols. (London: Kegan Paul, 1891–1953), 25: *Leo XI and Paul V, 1605–1621* (1937). The three popes came from three different families, which suggests that in 1605 the Papacy was preoccupied more with Vatican politics than with terrorists at the far end of Europe. The chief threat and worry for the Vatican at the time was Venice.

[37] I. D. McFarlane, *Buchanan* (London: Duckworth, 1981), chap. 2.

The reliance on Buchanan is intermittent, episodic. For the middle of his action and its plot-machinery Milton absorbs the satirical scorn and Reformation stance of Buchanan, even to the notable idea of Satan breathing temptation into the Pope's ear as he falls asleep (91)[38]—with which we could compare Eve's dream in *Paradise Lost*. Yet satire upon the Franciscan order connects only with Milton's fourth paragraph (68–89). Buchanan's dream-poem, likewise, informs another episode (90–132, the poem's fifth paragraph). The indebtedness is verbal and local, yet not structural, and only questionably thematic.

So far, then, the poem relies on a naively millennarian ideology, and an artless, limited use of the reformist Buchanan. Yet although the poem is in some ways a naive pastiche, a clear personal, political significance continues to emerge: Milton wants to see the events of 1605 in a simple, stridently Protestant way, linking if not equating that providential escape with the providence of the Lord God (who "reveal[s] Himself to his servants, and as his manner is, first to His English-men").[39] Does Milton, toward his close, admonish the nation to see itself as Israel, because of this saving act? His passing over of the historical details[40] moves the reader's or listener's attention in that direction. Indeed, this omission of details is the greatest speaking silence of all. It makes Milton's poem unlike others of its type and occasion. It redirects the propagandist intention of this whole genre, away from monarchism and toward a Reformation Protestantism, more concerned with the people as a whole than with the particular dead monarch. Should we see the redirecting as the poem's discovery, its personal dynamic?

Ovid in the *Fasti*

My final new source-suggestion concerns the sense of an ending. The poem closes on the commemoration rituals, the November 5 street bonfires (the passage is quoted above). Whereas the poem had begun

---

[38] Not the *Franciscanus*, but the *Somnium*, where a Franciscan tempts Buchanan himself as he falls asleep.

[39] *Areopagitica* is quoted from *YPW* II (1959), ed. Ernest Sirluck: *YPW*, 2: 553.

[40] A detail which is especially well omitted is the fact that it was a *Catholic* lord, Mounteagle, who divulged the conspiracy to James's secret police.

by plunging into the events of 1605, it ends with the events of 1626. Whether or not Milton's Gunpowder poems were themselves a part of his college's commemorations in that year, he puts his closing emphasis on the present, not the past. His poem's title turns out to refer to the current November 5 as well as to the first one: the poem is "On" November 5, that date of any year.[41] Thus it ends calendrically, saying, "This date is the one most celebrated in all the year's festival days" ("Nulla dies toto occurrit celebratior anno"). If 5 November thus attracts greater celebration than Christmas, Carnival, and Easter, it is a sure sign that the Protestant festivals had captured the popular imagination.[42]

At this point Ovid and the *Fasti* come to mind, his voluminous ethnographic celebration. The *Fasti* record the greatest of Rome's festival days. They do so with a triple time-sense: of past origins, of how the rite is reenacted now, and often closing with a prayer for the future of Rome. Although Milton takes the last two matters at a fast pace, one may feel their presence at the close precisely because it is the close, Milton's last word on his subject.

Ovidian details and spirit cluster there, as indeed befits a Latin poem summarizing history by evoking community joy in its cult. The idea of a *dies fastus*—holy day and holiday, recorded in the people's calendar of red-letter-days – makes a decisive contribution to the poem's interpretation. It is an appropriation, declaring England the new chosen nation.

Where is Ovid to be seen, and how does Milton absorb and apply him? The whole poem is steeped in words, phrases, and rhythms from Ovid. If examples are needed, one is line 166, "longo flectens curvamine coelos": Ovid has "longum curvamine caelum," and "curvamen" is first used by him, and used often.[43] If Milton's Ovidian words are common ones, they naturally but not significantly occur in the *Fasti* too. At the close, nonetheless, the words used almost all appear in the *Fasti*, strongly thematic words like "fumare," "genialis," "compitum" ("smoking" and "festive" altars, at a "cross-roads"). The particu-

---

[41] Perhaps performed on it, and about it thematically.
[42] This is arguing from the closing lines: these describe the continuing November 5 festivities, and round off the poem by looking at its title, "In Quintum Novembris."
[43] Bush, *Variorum*, 193; the citation is Ovid *Met*. 6.64.

lar, and to my mind clinching, debt to the *Fasti* is the line "tura ferant placantque novom pia turba Quirinum" ("Let the devoted throng bring incense and appease the new Quirinus").[44] Compare this with Milton's cadenza:

> At <u>pia thura</u> Deo, et grati solvuntur honores;
> Compita laeta focis genialibus omnia fumant;
> <u>Turba</u> choros iuvenilis agit: <u>quintoque Novembris</u>
> Nulla dies toto occurrit celebratior anno. (223–226, my emphases)

Milton takes over words, idea, spectacle and meaning. Note that James VI and I does *not* take a posthumous bow as England's Romulus: "Deo," Israel's sole God, replaces him. Notice that even the *sound* of Ovid's celebration of Quirinus / Romulus reappears, when "novom Quirinum"[45] becomes "<u>q</u>uinto <u>No</u>vembris." We might even press the parallel, past sound to theme again, and urge that the sounds applied here to Rome's deified founder are transformed into the idea of the event, November 5, as foundational, constitutive for redeemed England.[46]

The relationship with Ovid may be negative as well. No less a scholar than Ronald Syme[47] had seen certain "instructive" omissions in Ovid's treatment of Roman festival cult. Ovid omits quite a number of the festivals, and these include several anniversaries of the cult of the Emperor, Augustus. True, his resulting explanation is painstakingly demolished or qualified by a later scholar.[48] But both argue from the contexts, the historical contexts, and both take the silences themselves most seriously. Similarly with the instructive omissions or speaking silences which I have been remarking: are they not to be

---

[44] *Fasti* 2. 507. Quirinus is the deified Romulus, so there are overtones of foundation and tutelary deity.

[45] "Novom" for "novum" is an archaism, helping to suggest an ancient, foundational affirmation.

[46] Milton takes this idea further than ever in his Greek version of Psalm 114 (1634), where line 4 declares that "Then Almighty God was King among the people." The detail is not in the original psalm nor in Milton's youthful paraphrase of it.

[47] Ronald Syme, *History in Ovid* (Oxford: Clarendon Press, 1978).

[48] Geraldine Herbert-Brown, *Ovid and the Fasti*. See also M. Pasco-Pranger, "Added Days: Calendrical Poetics and the Julio-Claudian Holidays," in *Ovid's* Fasti, ed. G. Herbert-Brown (Oxford: Oxford University Press, 2002), 251–274.

expected of *political* poetry, of an authoritarian and repressive society—just as they were in eighteenth-century France, or Soviet Russia? It is like using your franchise to abstain or spoil your voting paper, to register something by that means. The things that may not be said can be inferred by context and silence, a coded silence. Royalty's fading out from the climax and the ending of Milton's poem, and also his reliance there upon the Bible and Ovid, combine to become a candidate for a coded silence. While this emphasis could seem farfetched, or like a conspiracy-theory, it is more like Sherlock Holmes's case of the dog which *didn't* bark in the night, as a brief look at the mostly royalist effusions on the same occasion would confirm. They ooze compliments to the King; and some most unhistorically ascribe his escape to his own vigilance.

Milton's Own Work as Context

Milton wrote another five Gunpowder poems, probably at about this time. These are a sign, at the least, of repeated effort and interest in the theme. So is Milton's retention of the five in his work-box, and his publication of all in his collected poems, 1645. No other such set of works on a single topic exists.[49]

It is not that the epigrams deserve any higher acclaim by moderns as poems. Yet still Milton had not exhausted the subject, for he wrote a further epigram: equivocal praise for the inventor of gunpowder, as a greater than Prometheus. These facts are inscrutable individually. Collectively, however, they surely betoken a sustained attempt at political thought; a Protestant fervour, perhaps timed to the Plot's twenty-first anniversary in 1626.

It is being proposed, then, that the poems together convey a sense of the nation's passing through crisis and emerging into settled safety under the Lord. The 1626 crisis was indeed troubling to Protestant reformists, just as Charles' marriage to a French Catholic and his other policies were. But the look back to 1605, coming after the Buckingham crisis

---

[49] The nearest parallel might be Milton's two groups of Psalms, and these too have political (church-and-state) significance.

and upon the anniversary of the Plot, could lead to a timely, psalmodic reaffirmation.

"Let the people serve God, and be glad": that is what the poem's ending affirms. First the one thing, psalmodically; then the other, after the manner of Ovid and the *Fasti*. This is the main conclusion.

It leads to a stronger hypothesis, that Milton arrived at this view during and because of the poem. At its beginning, the nation has prosperity under its new king: the dynasty, and the uniting of the two kingdoms, are the means to this blessed state. But at the close, the king has faded out of the blessedness: the emphasis has shifted onto the Lord, and then to the people in their folk-rites. The crisis as narrated has changed the emphasis.[50]

Furthermore, the occasion of *In Quintum Novembris* was the first time Milton expressed this patriotic, zealot view of history. His earlier Psalm versions speak of the Exodus without mentioning England or forcing one to make that connection. Nor do the five epigrams.

If this view of Milton's poetic development is correct, an explanation is supplied for the six poems as a group. Milton's repeated treatment of the same subject suggests a preoccupation with church-state relations in the England of 1626. He worries at them, like a dog with a bone, until late in the sixth and longest poem he sees what the subject means for him.

Can we also connect these ideas to his original audience? If the poem was not performed aloud, this is the kind of bold voluntary which would please his second-year tutor, Tovey, and would have displeased his first-year tutor, Chappell.[51] If it was performed aloud, then its tone would please all (being patriotic: what Englishman of the time would object to hearing of England as the chosen people!) but would mean most to those who wished Reform to go further. The voluntary aspect is bolder still on this view, but he does not abuse the request.

---

[50] This view accords with other poems by Milton, for instance *Lycidas*, in which he begins by feeling unripe in his vocation but ends more than ready. See Evans, *The Miltonic Moment*.

[51] These two were of opposite churchmanship, and held opposed views about the election of Chancellor: the Fellows of Christ's, notoriously, were divided three ways.

We come to the last of all his Cambridge Latin genres, the undergraduate event called a salting. Whereas a bid for University reputation was discernible in the 1625 obituary foursome, and whereas the six Gunpowder poems embody an awakening to political and religious consciousness, the salting text shows further new sides of his emergent personality. It shows self-confidence in performance, and a capacity for clowning. The self-confidence continued, though life gave few if any further opportunities for oral performance. The clowning lapsed altogether: let us make the most of our one chance, in a lengthy final case-study.

PART THREE

For the College Community

In Part One we watched Milton responding and performing in exercises which were required of all. He did at times overgo the required, by doing new things or modifying a set genre or accepting an invitation to ghost-write in a set mode. At other times, equally, he does the required with an audibly minimal exertion. In Part Two the emphasis changed to what he volunteered to do, along with what he may have declined to do. The November 5 poems, however, fit less clearly into these categories of required and voluntary, because while their general occasion was a set feast and their topic was one which might lead to performance, the number of the satellite poems, and the length and ideological zest of *In Quintum Novembris*, look decidedly willed, hence voluntary. The categories of "required" and "voluntary" may overlap; as in the ghost-written verses, so in the November 5 poems. This is certainly so with our final case-study of a Cambridge performance by Milton, for which the circumstances and occasioning are somewhat clearer. Accordingly, Part Three presents it with especial fullness, including a new text and translation.

Milton's salting of the summer vacation 1628[1] was composed when he was "created its emergency leader" ("Dictator creatus").[2] The emergency in question was that the natural first choice as compere of the student rituals had been sent away for orchestrating Gownish vandalism against the Town. Milton waxes witty and modest about being chosen: "why me?" he says, which could mean he is not clever enough or not stupid enough, and possibly both. The *invitation* nonetheless suggests he was known to be a capable bilingual orator, and moreover in a crisis acceptable to students and authorities alike. His growing reputation in general and the diversity of the 1626 voluntaries in particular would be

---

[1] Though other datings are hard to rule out, I see most sense in the argument that the joke about Buckingham's 1627 failure at the Isle of Rhé would be fresher in 1628 than any later. The English verse portion of the salting is dated "age 19" in *Poems 1673*, which again means 1628.

[2] *BLN*, 80–81.

bringing him to notice. The variety of his invention and the sheer scale of the four-part performance demonstrate Milton's desire to rise to this opportunity (albeit fortuitous) for display.

It is our own opportunity, too. While the distinction between "required" and "voluntary" is not always clear or essential, Milton's transcendence of it here displays him as the centre and very voice of his community through Latin. His salting text gives our best perspective on what Latin did within these Cambridge communities, be they University or college, seniors or students. It illuminates how he stood toward his fellow-students, and they toward him.

Rites of Passage

At this point it needs to be made more explicit than hitherto that most if not all of Cambridge's Latin connects to some ritual occasion of the community. Latin is the sole or main medium, both of the University community and the college ones. The exercises were the ritualized performances in formal wit-combat of every member of the University, seniors as much as students (*seniores* and *iuventutes*). College versions of exercising were practice, or rehearsal, for the University tests, which in turn—being "exercises"—were battle-training for the speech-occasions of life, life in the tense early-modern world of lawyers or divines or courtiers. Funeral poems, placed on the University pall or printed in its anthologies, more obviously escort the dead person worthily through the greatest transition of all, out of life and into the afterworld. We noted that the Latin medium afforded the priest-like bards a choice of afterworld destinies with which to make surmises. The November 5 poems are even more aimed at a rite of passage, this time the rite of commemorating the deliverance of the entire nation, under God, but with a popular joy which in the long poem moved easily to a happy climax of Ovidianized bonfires.

The popular and ritual affinities of these Latin performances stand out in our final rite, the salting by which a year's intake of freshmen were inducted by means of a public ordeal and drama into seniority, in front of their older peers. As we shall see, the Cambridge versions of this universal custom are sanitized and sophisticated by comparison with the raw, sometimes brutal versions seen in other universities of Europe: the sanitizing and sophisticating come, precisely, from the combination of a more roomy Latin with a more developed element of show and drama. Milton as master of the ceremonies stands at the centre of the rite and its Cambridge version alike.

The Latin is the largest portion and comes first. Let us next see what sort, or rather sorts, of Latin he is using. Latin is not sanitizing in itself, not when its full range and history are exploited: as dignified as it can be, it can be equally coarse in its comedy or satire. Nor, whether elevating or wallowing by means of it, does Milton's Latin depart from the Cambridge norms. Cambridge had a Latin for *all* its occasions.[3] Correspondingly, by his wielding of Latin then English at the 1628 salting Milton was rising to one of its odder occasions.

Relaxation and Playing through Latin

All the Latin texts examined to this point have sought to be worthy of a certain idea of good style, linked to a measuring of Cambridge life as that of a "grex Palladius," or "gens togata." That is to say, Cambridge public performances have been conducted in a Latin which heeds ancient theory and practice, be it in style or diction or canons of decorum. The point is obvious for the verses and declamations; and though one might suspect of Milton's disputations that he is mocking scholastic jargon or at least putting it inside his equivalent of scare-quotes, the diction and aim remain within the official bounds. All so far comports to a general *gravitas*: Latin and the exercises give each other dignity. Thus it is not ridiculous for Milton to dub Cambridge an Athens ("Palladius"), and to reconfigure academic dress in the great processions as a wearing of Roman togas. The images capture what Cambridge, in its public life, is trying to be—an amalgam of Greece and Rome in dialectic with Christian orthodoxy and scholastic thought-forms.

It comes as a surprise, therefore, to discover that the University at its exercises, at the apex of its self-expression, should have listened to such Latin as these verses:

---

[3] Including its less official moments, such as playgoing, where *Latin* comedies or tragedies abounded (Binns, *Latin Writings*, 120–40).

Sileant Thomistae	Silent, Thomists!
Taceant Scotistae	Quiet, Scotists!
Scholastica turba	Mob scholastic
Nil dat nisi verba	Paraphrastic
Umbratiles quidditates	Words, nought else can proffer
Nec non et leves haecceitates	Wet and shady quiddities
Haecceitas grata	Empty, light haecceities
Est uxor parata	These alone can offer
Matrimonii per conjugata	The thisness which a student pleases
Hic est logica vera	Is a wife, not barren theses;
Et plusquam chimaera	This is logic true, not to fancy due.[4]

Classical Latin on the whole had an aversion to rhyme, as the "jingling sound of like endings";[5] yet here rhyme dominates; and indeed because of the shortness of the lines, it shouts. The frisky couplets are typical of medieval Latin, the Latin of the great hymns or the vulgar Vagantes; and yet medieval Latin, Latin which was spoken and still growing when the Renaissance impinged, was the Latin which humanism spurned. What, then, is going on, in this performance at a graduation?[6] An older, rejected Latin is enjoying (if that is the right word) a revival, for low and comic purposes.[7]

Here is another startling debasement of normal "correct" Latin, this one performed at another graduation by Thomas Randolph. Milton's wittiest contemporary perpetrated these licentious hexameters in his role as University "Praevaricator" in 1632:

---

[4] Costello, *Scholastic Curriculum*, 27–28, quoting and translating CUL, MS. Dd. 30. 39r. There are three more such stanzas, and "Et plusquam chimaera" comes in as refrain each time. As discussed shortly, the contents contrast the aridities of logic with the substantial realities of having a wife. The connection to the Quaestio, of the mind as a tabula rasa, is less clear.

[5] As Milton himself put it when explaining in 1668 why *Paradise Lost* was not written in couplets.

[6] Costello, *Scholastic Curriculum*, 27 and n. 63.

[7] IJsewijn, *Companion to Neo-Latin Studies*, 2: 12; "Apart from prayers, mediaeval versification was most of the time used for students' songs [like "Gaudeamus igitur"] and for lighter stuff such as humorous poems and parodies." Thus "In William Mewes' Cambridge tragicomedy *Pseudomagia* (Emmanuel College, c. 1625–27) the 'pseudomagus' Otho is using short rhyming rhythmic passages for his conjurations: 'Hinc spectra procul et inanes / Dirae, lemures et Manes . . .'" (ritual, apotropaic).

Iam sileat *Jack Drum*; taceat miracula *Tom Thumb*;
Nec se gigantem jactet *Garagantua*[8] tantum;
Nec ferat insanus sua praelia *Tamberlanus*,
Nec *Palmerinus*, nec strenuus *Albovinus*.
Se quondam ratus sapientem *Tom Coriatus*,
Et *Don Quichotte* dicit, sum nunc idiota! 5
Nunc metuit dia divortia *Technogamia*:
Insignis *Pericles* non audet tam celebres res.
Impiger *Orlando* iam non est tam *furioso*;
Non te, *Jeronyme*, cogemus surgere lecto.
Nemo dicat jam prudentes pascere *Gotham* 10
Namqu'est doctorum comoedia scripta virorum[9]
Quae superat cunctas (tanta est fiducia!) laudes
Et jam securum petiit post praelia prelum
Ignavum fucus pecus est, petit illico lucos;[10]
Et factus blancum non saltat prinkum prankum. 15
Dicunt hoc puerile *Odium* vicisse *Senile*,
Hic est sensus non, et possis ludere *checkstone*.[11]
    Jam peracta est Fabula—Plaudite.[12]

(This contains so many puns and tonguetwisters and topical jokes that one might say it comprised little else, and as a result is almost untranslatable. However—"Now let Jack Drum be silent, and let Tom Thumb

---

[8] "Garagantua" could be a simple mistake for the obvious and equally metrical "Gargantua," but in these slapstick surroundings I wonder instead whether Randolph is showing off. "Garagantua" makes the line more dactylic by the extra syllable, to show he can do a classy hexameter when he chooses to, and do it by expanding the giant's gigantic name.

[9] Hazlitt's text has a full stop after "virorum," which I have removed to enable the sense to run on—"a comedy *which* (quae . . .)"

[10] Tongue twister now, and next line.

[11] Delayed negative, as in colloquial parentheses like "I don't think" or "not." Checkstone ("chuckiestones") is a game and a play title, thus in similar vein to "prinkum prankum," a prank or a dance. Baby-words and popular, oral culture are being allowed in: high culture, more or less willingly, makes room for them because of the needs of the occasion.

[12] The text is taken from Thomas Randolph, *Poetical and Dramatic Works*, ed. W. C. Hazlitt, 2 vols. (London: Reeves & Turner, 1875; repr. New York: B. Blom, 1968), 2: 679–80. I have used his notes and those of Alan H. Nelson in *R.E.E.D.* "Cambridge," supplementing both with my own suggestions; but even so the allusions are too quicksilver to be completely codified. Randolph, at these crowded and boisterous occasions, surpassed himself.

keep quiet about his exploits! Nor let Gargantua boast about his gigantic size; nor crazy Tamburlaine brag of his battles, nor Palmerin, nor strenuous Albovinus! Tom Coryat used to think himself a sage, and Don Quixote declares 'Now I am an idiot!'[13] Now Technogamia fears divine divorce; famous Pericles dares no such celebrated deeds as ours! Energetic Orlando is not so Furioso now, and we shall not be compelling you, Jeronimo, to rise from your bed! Let nobody say that Gotham now nurtures wise men,[14] because a comedy of the learned has been written which (so great is my confidence!) surpasses all praises and now has sought print after propugnation [*praelia* / *prelum*]. Folk are a clueless crowd, they head straight for the woods [meaningless in English because the Latin is mainly a tongue-twister]; they become a blank and won't dance prinkum-prankum. They say this childish text of mine has beaten *Odium Senile*, [because] here there is no sense whatever, and you can play checkstone.

Now my play is finished: Applause, please.")

With sufficient wrenching and cheating the verses can be heard as Roman hexameters, but the primary impact is that of macaronic—a playful, low, and again medieval proclivity. A further low and medieval feature is the rhyming, which is incessant within lines, and sometimes crosses them: we do not have, here, the approved and limited rhyme of Ovid's "golden" line, but something close to schoolboy word-games. This "leonine" rhyming sounded comical to the humanist ear, much as the limerick stanza does to ours.[15] How else but comically could we respond to the gorgeously infantile melody in "Et factus blancum non sal-

---

[13] Joke obscure in these two lines.

[14] There is no need for wise men of Gotham (i.e., fools) because I have written learned fooling enough here (with puns on *commedia erudita* and learning being made fun of?). Randolph's tone is triumphal.

[15] Leonine hexameters rhyme the two halves of a line. The effect is so easy in a flexional language that the ancient world thought it more artistic to avoid than to use such rhymes, except as a special effect, Ijsewijn and Sacré, *Companion to Neo-Latin Studies*, 2: 431 and n. 1. They were limited to the pentameter line of an elegiac couplet or used as a rare special effect of assonance in the hexameter line. Medieval verse worked on the opposite principle. Randolph's practice here plays off the two attitudes against each other. See further D. S. Raven, *Latin Metre: An Introduction* (London:

tat prinkum prankum," which bulges with metrical licenses[16] tolerated for the sake of multiple exploding wordplay? The writer is pretending to be a fool ("blancum") to make the line dance like the silly dance called "prinkum prankum. " It is playing a prank on the audience.

This, the ending of the final line explains: Randolph wants the audience to "Plaudite," and "plaudite" ("Applause, please!") is the routine ending of a Roman comedy. Randolph's verses are to be received as comedy would be. Not that it should surprise us that Cambridge's Latin should incorporate comedy. For one thing, no one going up there could escape either writing or performing or watching its numerous neo-Plautine comedies. King James's addiction to Ruggle's *Ignoramus* (1615) makes the point.[17] What merits elaboration in the present context is that for comic Latin, for macaronic doggerel, for obsolete medieval genres and their different Latinity, Milton's Cambridge had a licensed, indeed a sacrosanct place.

We must describe and analyse that place next, because although Milton did not so far as is known perform in this genre to a University audience, he did to his college. There is an *a fortiori* about it. If a university graduation could so drop its rules about Latin and dignity, with all the worthies on view and notables visiting in the midst of maximal grandeur, what might the *iuventus* not get up to in its more private Latin frolics? And how did Milton respond, when called upon to be scriptwriter and master of the frolics?

To answer such questions will be central to the case-study which is our next chapter, and the whole of Part Four. Suffice it for now that Milton was following a Cambridge tradition, quite closely, and that the tradition's exercises—however they might be ridiculed and subverted—were

---

Faber, 1965), 39 n. 1; and A. G. Rigg, "Latin Meter: Rhyming Dactylic Verses," in *Dictionary of the Middle Ages*, ed. J. R. Strayer et al., 12 vols. (New York: Scribner, 1982), 7: 372–73.

[16] Chief being the totally spondaic line, unparalleled in the Latin exemplars, or tolerable there only as onomatopoeic plangency of *grief*; solemnity is so out of place here that it is funny (burlesque, bombast).

[17] The comedy was so popular that it enjoyed revival, with the King's manifest approval (Binns, *Latin Writings*, 140). See now Hilaire Kallendorf, "Exorcism and the Interstices of Language: Ruggle's *Ignoramus* and the Demonization of Renaissance English Neo-Latin," in *Acta Conventus Neo-Latini Cantabrigiensis*, 303–10.

here being followed. The verses excerpted above are both in support of a thesis, like yet unlike the act verses of Chapter Two. The verses on the superiority of love to logic support, or rather "vary," the Quaestio, "Whether the human mind is a tabula rasa."[18] Randolph's cacophonous hexameters conclude his farcical treatment of another inherently serious Quaestio, "Whether truth resides in intellection or in objective facts."[19]

Randolph is "praevaricating." He is "varying" the solemn thesis. Macaronic medley, childish word-games, perverse logic, and unofficial or dog Latin are in place on *his* lips, *ex officio*. Let us next go deeper into the Praevaricator's terms of existence within the high solemnities of the University, into his job description which has its counterpart in Milton's role at the Christ's salting. Both parody the disputations of a graduation, as all jokes about Fathers and Sons attest.

Praevaricating and Playing Socratically

"Praevaricator" is Latin for "shyster," shifty lawyer, colluding advocate. At graduations, even the most august, this functionary sat on a special stool, the Tripos, at the foot of the proctors. Whereas the main disputing entailed a thesis, its proponent and his opponent, so that every thesis was seen in two ways, adversarially, the *Praevaricator's* job was to address the thesis in a third, or fourth and fifth way; his other name was "the Varier." He had to do it amusingly – either stupidly, or by parody, or inversion, or in fast forward. In short, the philosophic jousting was punctuated by licensed folly.

Now the Praevaricator's parody and buffoonery had a lower-life counterpart in the college ceremonies by which undergraduates in their colleges inducted freshmen. This was like a "hazing," or whatever ritual

---

[18] "An anima hominis sit rasa tabula," Costello, *Scholastic Curriculum*, 27.

[19] "Veritas in intellectu fundatur et pendet in veritate rei?" ("Whether truth is grounded in intellection and inheres in the truth of data?"). Hazlitt prints "et" but I would read "aut," "or," so as to make the issue whether truth is a quality in the mind's activity *or* inherent in the things observed. This very issue was debated with lively heat at Oxford by the Philosophy Faculty when I was an undergraduate.

our own students inflict on each new intake. It was called a "salting," because nasty things involving salt were done to the freshmen. Milton was master of ceremonies at one such rite of passage in 1628.

Let us pause there, to reflect how intriguing it is to meet formalized, licensed foolery, obligatory parody, at a graduation ceremony. Which of our own universities would tolerate such a thing, let alone ordain it? Or is it part of the world we have lost, but which Milton possessed, and indeed appropriated as master of the revels? As I return into the *Latin* of this formalized mayhem, I shall risk case-studies, because the beauty is in the detail. Here is Thomas Randolph again, hot from his successes as a Latin comedian and playwright and hence promoted to Praevaricator. The scene is Great St Mary's; the date is July 1632.[20]

He opens by greeting the Praevaricator as if this person were not himself. "I love him as I love myself" [mild irony, silly miming, or gospel misapplication?],[21] then calls him "my alter ego." "Alter ego" in Latin means a friend so intimate as to be like a second self; but Randolph changes the metaphor, to hint that the Praevaricator is within his own self, inhabiting some parallel time and reality, where normal rules don't apply. Not even the rules of grammar apply: he farewells the Praevaricator by saying, "Didn't he give myself good advice there?" The Latin is, "mihi ded*it* ego." It breaks a prime rule of grammar, first person subject misjoined to third person verb. ("I gives me good advice.") It is a schoolboy joke, but it also blurs the clear lines of personality—as prevarication and salting both do.

After farewelling himself and then *not* departing, he begins his whole speech all over again, then urges the audience to "take the advice of a fool." This resembles "All Cretans are liars," said by a Cretan. We are entering a world apart, a world upside down, thanks to the Latin. It's enjoyably bewildering, and if the speaker does not speak literal truth nor the whole truth, that is because pleasure is paramount. We are crossing a frontier, into a liminal region where folly makes rules which have their own weird logic.

---

[20] *R.E.E.D., Cambridge*: 881.
[21] "Love thy neighbour as thyself," Matthew 19:19, etc.

Milton, likewise, takes his hearers into such regions in his salting, Prolusion VI, abusing the laws of fact and reason for the greater enjoyment of holiday. Playing is needful, folly is wise. He calls it "more Socratico ludere," playing in the manner of Socrates. This at once evokes ideas of Socratic *eironeia*, self-deprecation, claiming to know only that one knows nothing. Taken comically, this axiom is very releasing. To show how Milton exploits this freedom, we analyse his whole salting, then (after conclusions) present it in a new text and translation.[22]

---

[22] The need for a new text is explained as a preface to the text itself, below, initiating Part Four.

CHAPTER

9

Milton Plays the Fool: Prolusion VI and "At a Vacation Exercise"

Milton is often thought of as a lifelong sobersides, reading to midnight in his childhood, taking on a colossal reading programme of world history after leaving Cambridge, then fighting the good fight in public for numerous serious causes till muzzled at the Restoration, only to turn to a late frenzy of publishing on further serious topics (history, grammar, logic). Yet although these are the pursuits of a serious, even austere personality, the early biographers emphasize his companionability, his love of music, and his cheerfulness;[1] at which point one remembers the sonnets on those themes, and the fact that companionship is highly valued in his Eden.[2]

Unique, extended proof of this is found in his entertainment which we read—albeit incomplete and in pieces—as his Latin "Prolusion VI" and the English verses "At a Vacation Exercise."[3] This entertainment, with some English prose which has not survived, was delivered to a large audience of fellow-students in the long vacation of 1628. It was delivered at an occasion of licensed fooling, of a greater than usual freedom of speech, by Milton as the master of the ceremonies. My purpose here is to revivify, if I can, his exercise of his role, so as to show him in public performance, as a licensed jester, the life and soul of this special kind of party, a "salting." After summarizing the work done by others on saltings in general and on 1620s Cambridge saltings in particular, I sketch

---

[1] Helen Darbishire, ed., *The Early Lives of John Milton* (London: Constable, 1932).
[2] See esp. sonnets XIII (Carey, 294), XVII (Carey, 343) and XVIII (Carey, 345). For *Paradise Lost*, see e.g., Bks. IV, V, or IX. 235. The prolusion is cited from Part Four of the present work. Tillyard, xx, and Carey, 78, discuss the assemblage and dispersal of the Latin and English parts of the whole entertainment.
[3] A "prolusion" is a prelude or exercise, in general. More specific senses are discussed at an appropriate place later.

the genre's affinities in literature and anthropology, because such contextual aspects are needed if we are to understand and so enjoy Milton's many-splendoured performance, in a role exercising the combined talents of stand-up comedian and master of ceremonies. It is the Latin, especially, which releases this unsuspected persona and talent.

Saltings[4]

A salting was a feast of misrule for all present, and a rite of passage for some of them. Candidates for admission to some seniority or fuller membership of a sodality were put through a public test or ordeal. Like a hazing of freshmen, or the prolonged entrance rituals of Dutch universities such as Leiden, a salting combined performance and entertainment, with emphasis upon contestation, penalties and alcohol. Where the act of "salting" came into it was when each freshman in turn did some performance (typically a Latin speech), which if it pleased the audience won him a large beer; but if it displeased, won him a large salted beer.[5] The penalty was supposed to remedy his deficiencies by giving him more "salt" in the transferred sense of wit (Latin *sales*). Puns and jokes about salt are incessant, because the root idea is that speech, and social life as a whole, do not taste as good as they should unless they are "seasoned" with "salt," to bring out their full and proper flavour.[6] This metaphor is pervasive, almost obsessive. The immediate seniors, who have undergone this ordeal of initiation themselves, together act

---

[4] I am indebted in this account to work by Roslyn Richek, "Thomas Randolph's Salting (1627), Its Text, and John Milton's Sixth *Prolusion* as Another Salting," *English Literary Renaissance* 12 (1982): 102–31; by Alan H. Nelson in *R.E.E.D., Cambridge*; and especially by Elizabeth Ann Perryman Freidberg, "Certain Small Entertainments: The Texts and Contexts of Thomas Randolph's Poems and College Entertainments," 2 vols. (Ph.D. diss., Cambridge University, 1994), hereafter "Freidberg, 'Small Entertainments.'"

[5] These fundamentals are not often actually stated, being taken for granted in the fragmentary and allusive private memoirs which make up our record. I am relying here on the memoir of Anthony Wood (see note 7), because though it comes from another time and place its account is the clearest.

[6] Estelle Haan, *From* Academia *to* Amicitia, 87 and 97–98, argues for similar salt-punning in Milton's later poem, to his Italian friend Salsilli.

as judges. Clearly, the rite could get out of hand, and gave good scope to bullies, yet it lasted for centuries in one form or another, being common for example amongst apprentices.[7]

Coming nearer to Milton's Cambridge, I quote and give running commentary on the salting experience of Anthony Wood at Oxford in 1648:[8]

> ... every freshman, according to seniority, was to pluck off his gown and band, and if possible to make himself look like a scoundrel [*remove signs of existing status, enter a liminal or limbo zone, adopt a disguise*]. This done, they were conducted each after the other to the high table, and there made to stand on a form placed thereon [*place of prominence, threshold of new higher status in the sodality*]; from whence they were to speak their speech with an audible voice to the company [*do the set solo performance, an oration, at a site of contestation before their peers and seniors*]; which if well done, the person that spoke it was to have a cup of cawdle[9] and no salted drink [*get a reward, and pay no penalty, completing a ritual exchange betokening acceptance by fraternity*]; if indifferently, some cawdle and some salted drink [*reward and penalty, mixed*]; but if dull [*the worst offence, where the audience are judging and the sole criterion is their pleasure*], nothing was given him but salted drink or salt put in college beer [*so that the audience would receive pleasure anyhow, from the look on the face of the dullard drinking a disgusting drink; and as if that was not enough*] with tucks to boot [*where "tucks" are the slicing of the offender's face with fingernails (sharpened for the purpose)*]. Afterwards, when they were to be admitted into the fraternity, the senior cook [*experienced but a servant, hence nicely liminal in this rite of transition*] was to administer to them an oath over an old shoe [*oath as symbol of becoming bound to a new group, shoe as parody of the oaths required by the University*]. After which spoken with gravity [*absurd or parodic rituals are funniest when done solemnly*] the Freshman kissed the shoe, put on his gown, and took his place among the seniors.

At Cambridge in Milton's time the individual's ordeal receives scant mention. It seems to have been replaced by a corporate, semi-dramatic

---

[7] Richek ("Salting," 108, n. 22) mentions that salting crossed the Atlantic early and is recorded at Dartmouth College in 1890. Salting customs are recorded at Syracuse, NY, till 1919, in Robert Emery, "Salting Freshmen: An Old Academic Tradition," *Notes and Queries* 40 (1993): 351.

[8] See *The Life and Times of Anthony Wood, Antiquary, of Oxford, 1632–1695, Described by Himself*, ed. Andrew Clark, 5 vols. (Oxford: Oxford University Press, 1891–1900), 1:138–39.

[9] Or "caudle," thin gruel enhanced by beer or wine and spices.

entertainment, or subsumed into it. The Cambridge rite of passage required the initiands, or more probably some of them, to stand up on stage and be inducted to seniority by taking a small (possibly scripted) part in a much more lengthy scripted entertainment.

One can only guess at reasons for Cambridge's difference of practise, though perhaps the fact of the scripting would mean that authority could forestall trouble or that the allowed time was too heavily occupied with drama to admit much mayhem. There would have been little time for each freshman to do a solo. Indeed, some of them are doing a scripted solo. Presumably salt beer figured in the proceedings somewhere at a salting, but no record of where and when remains for Cambridge. For my present purpose, however, it is the Cambridge 1620s *differentia* which I wish to emphasize, because it alerts us to the parody and the wit of the scriptwriter as master of ceremonies. In other words, the important salt, the wit, was of the metaphorical kind, provided by someone chosen because held to be witty.

Can it be solely accident that most of the extant salting scripts come from Cambridge, and from Milton's time there? Or was scripting becoming the normal way of a Cambridge salting? The title "At a Vacation Exercise" reveals something: the event was an "exercise," hence involving bilingual speech-making, and its being in the vacation showed that the exercising was freer and more demotic than the regular, term-time, serious disputations and declamations. At all events, Milton's script (once reassembled from its separately published portions) can be understood more fully than before from comparison with other specimens of this kind of text, especially that of his coeval Thomas Randolph.[10]

As final preliminary, let us glance at some wider affinities of saltings, and the constitutive traditions of fooling. Rites of passage, separating off its adolescent males from a tribe until they pass an ordeal to reenter it as full members, are widespread if not universal. The rituals of students and other young-male groups are lovingly recorded by Hastings Rashdall.[11] Indeed, they still occur, because not only can one interpret de-

---

[10] Richek, "Saltings,"; Nelson, *R.E.E.D.*; Freidberg, "Small Entertainments."
[11] Hastings Rashdall, *The Universities of Europe in the Middle Ages*, ed. F. M. Powicke and A. B. Emden, 3 vols. (Oxford: Oxford University Press, 1895; rev. 1936), 3:367–85.

gree-study and the graduation itself as such rites, but undergraduates practice them still, in their cruder forms at least.[12] The vital thing in the present context, however, is to see that the salting rite belongs to the *immediate* seniors, not the tribal elders; and hence that those authorities may be parodied and pilloried.

This was in fact central: the master of these revels posed as a college tutor presenting his bunch of pupils for University examination or graduation (of which more in a moment). The Fellowship tolerated it because they had been young once and gone through it themselves, so it was maintaining the customary usages of the tribe. To put it another way, the allowed and ritualized parodying of hierarchy (in the name of safety-valve or equilibrium) upholds rather than subverts hierarchy, because it involves a parallel inverted hierarchy. Up to what point, however, can such carnival release be assumed to confirm rather than undermine the status quo? This question was often put into the mind of authority in early-modern times.[13] The details of the rites perpetually push the limits, as indeed is the nature of parody. Licenced release may have its licence revoked. Nonetheless, to push hard until that point seems to be part of the amusement, the delicious danger, by which distinctive age-groups test out one another in public once a year; to see what the other is made of, and in some unformulated way of the emotions and imagination together to learn about themselves by strenuous play—such actions as these constitute the heart of the saltings rite.

Metaphors, Structure, and Contents of a Cambridge Salting

At a "salting" in Cambridge of the 1620s the master of ceremonies was chosen to lead the revels with a long solo performance, followed by a semi-dramatic parodic pageant, in which the chosen person posed

---

[12] A freshman ritual involving the throwing of catfood made the headlines of our local newspaper, 25 February 2001. It is always the cruder or more violent or disastrous forms which make the headlines, as whenever a freshman dies as a result of overdoing some hazing "jape." Then there is talk of banning or suspending the rite, but the cycle resumes.

[13] Cf. Emmanuel Le Roy Ladurie, *Carnival in Romans*, trans. Mary Feeney (New York: Braziller, 1979).

as a "Father" to the freshmen as his "Sons." The metaphor of paternity was identical with that of the real-life University examinations and graduations. The chosen student would be playing the regular, familiar part—and wearing or aping the regalia—of the college tutors.

So usual and understood was this parodic metaphor that it would at once be topped by another, this time not recurrent but best if newly-invented for the unique present salting. The "Sons" might be presented to the audience "as" something else, a metaphor beyond the usual one; as assorted animals, or parts of the body, or meals of a dinner—almost anything absurd and derogatory, hence funny when applied to the *people* up on stage in a gaggle. It seems an inspired way (what with the sense of a licensed occasion and the lubrication of drink) to release the scriptwriter's comic imagination. It blends the recurring absurdity of one undergraduate claiming the paternity of numerous others, of all shapes and sizes, who may be about one year younger than himself or sometimes older, with bizarre comparisons of individuals to the birds or dishes or whatnot which they might in fancy (or by surnames or other in-joke) resemble. Milton does all of this, as do Thomas Randolph and the others whose scripts survive.[14]

Milton amusingly exploits the rhetorical figure of talking at length about what he will *not* be doing, the typical and very physical things he will not compare his group to. Whereas such a disclaimer was not without parallel, the sequence and contents and wit of the disclaimers provided a great chance for one salting script to distinguish itself from all predecessors. Milton's differs from all others so far discovered because his pageant compares the Sons to the "Predicaments" of Aristotle, the "Categories" of Substance, Quantity, Quality, Relation, Place, Time, Posture, State, Action, and Passivity.[15] Unsuitably abstract and

---

[14] Four saltings texts are recorded by Nelson in *R.E.E.D.* 2:996–97 (Appendix 12); another one, and a fuller text of Randolph's, are recorded by Freidberg, "Small Entertainments," 38.

[15] Carey, 81. Randolph mentions that his Trinity colleague "My brother Keys" called his Sons "Tropes & figures" (Richek, "Saltings," 110). "Brother" here keeps up the University familial metaphor. The "Categories" of Aristotle ("Praedicamenta" in Latin) are roughly the ten most general nameable qualities or ways in which assertions can be made ("predicated") of a subject. *OED* s.v. "category" summarizes the uncertainties in the term.

intellectual one might at first think, a wrong choice bound to bomb. Yet it was not necessarily so. Since the co-father at Randolph's ceremony had introduced his sons as various rhetorical figures, Milton's metaphor seems not unduly egregious, nor should it startle.[16] The Predicaments were a basic part of the scholastic curriculum. And being so hard to impersonate (or costume!), the choice of the Categories might make the pageant succeed by its own failure; the audience, no doubt well-primed in the *categoriae* and not all in love with them, would laugh at the inadequacy of the representation. Parodies can succeed in making us laugh by falling short as well as by excess.

Structure is less important, and less discernible, than the mixtures of metaphor. The performance as a whole left time for things unscripted, to judge by the shortness of some of the texts.[17] It was a medley by nature. Thus it was bilingual. It combined verse with prose. The verse might be doggerel or accomplished; the Latin might be good Latin or dog-Latin. This was in the choice of the scriptwriter-presenter while he was on his legs and doing the solo part of the whole thing. The main structural compulsion was to perform solo but to close by presenting the "Sons" in their roles in the semi-dramatic pageant.

Typical salting features, mainly motifs, included:[18]

1. Naming of the Sons.
2. Responses of the Sons (not necessarily scripted, nor even verbal).
3. Singling out of Freshmen Distinguished by Rank.
4. Anecdotes of Particular Sons.
5. Father-and-Sons metaphor, the commonest characteristic.
6. An occasion, once a year for each college but the actual date varying with the college, so that students might attend or gatecrash other colleges and get ideas from others' saltings.
7. Burlesque invocations.
8. Classical allusions, for instance to explain the birth of so many sons.

---

[16] Freidberg, "Small Entertainments," 41.

[17] Others, like Milton's, seem improbably long. Little is yet known about the relations between saltings texts and the actual performance. It is certain, though, that the writer had to choose between playing a text of the right length and having it run longer because of impromptu additions (endemic to this kind of show) and writing a short one on the expectation of such additions. Performances being unrecoverable, one can only work from analogous shows of today, using imagination and probability.

[18] Freidberg, "Small Entertainments," 38.

9. Prepared insults, and impromptu parries of audience's insults.
10. Puns, especially on "salt," paternity, and prodigality.
11. Jokes about the college or the University curriculum.
12. Jokes about bodily functions.
13. Satire on persons, or antagonistic groups (especially Gown-against-Town jokes).

Randolph and Milton Compared, including Textual Issues

It should be clear by now that much of what wrinkled the nostrils of Milton's biographers and editors in his salting text, for instance his jokes about farting, are (whether found offensive or not) just what the reader should *expect* in a salting text—expect, and enjoy for the pleasures of the way it is done, much as we approach the indecent in Shakespeare. If it works, or if it is appropriate in its place and occasion, or if it makes us laugh in performance, all is well. Consequently, although a performance of any salting is a tall order now, if only because of the bilingualism required and sense of the vanished curriculum, we should eke out the unperformed text with our own imagination, the theatre of the mind.[19] All this can be confirmed by looking across at Randolph's text;[20] and indeed the comparison will bring out the distinctiveness of Milton's own text.

Randolph is a fascinating term of comparison. He made a career of purveying comedy, whether in parodies or comedies, and whether to college or University or (ultimately) London audiences. He had a gift for comedy. It is his native element, his forte. With Milton, it is the opposite: his native element is gravity, not levity, and that (it will be argued) gives a distinctive strength to his fooling. At present we should take all the more notice when he does the same as Randolph, because that indicates needs and purposes of the genre. To watch him facing the same needs differently helps bring out his different response to the same sort of occasion. There may even be direct influence: Randolph's text (1627) comes the year before Milton's, and so Milton's appears to

---

[19] This is attempted in Hale, *BLN*, 93.
[20] Freidberg, "Small Entertainments," 75–80.

include echoes of Randolph's or sardonic reflections on it. In what follows next, we consider structure, then such detail as the echoes and reflections; making less of details which correspond in order to dwell on changes within the governing metaphors.

Randolph structures his performance thus: Latin prose, Latin verse, English verse. Milton structures his thus: Latin prose, of two distinct genres ("Oratio" then "Prolusio")[21]; English verses ("At a vacation Exercise"); then some English prose, now lost. The register of Randolph's Latin at first descends, for when he moves out of Latin prose into Latin verses the verses are in medieval, rhyming Latin (not classical, unrhyming Latin); and the descent is marked as well by the jolly tumbling accentual (not quantitative) rhythms:

> Si sumpto sale[22] probe sapiatis,
> Si consilia nostra teneatis,
> Nec unus vestrum erit contemnendus,
> Sic dixi Pater nondum reverendus.[23]

("If you take salt and become excellently wise, if you hold to our advice, none of you will be contemptible; thus have I spoken, as a Father but not yet venerable.")

His English couplets, however, are measured and rhythmic, the tumbling jollity being put aside as the native tongue gets its turn.

> No salting here these many years was seen,
> Salt hath with us long out of season[24] been.

Milton, likewise, moves from higher to lower, the *oratio* being on a small theme but in a high style, whereas the *prolusio*—a pastiche within a pastiche—scampers mercurially amongst high and very low; then invests the English couplets with fresh measure and majesty:

---

[21] These terms are hard to translate, because a "prolusio" occurs here *within* "Prolusio VI." The matter is discussed below.

[22] One of the usual abundant puns on the eponymous "salt = sense, wit."

[23] The rhyming style was not highly esteemed by humanists: correspondingly, it figures as a natural register of "praevaricators," university jesters up to their tricks (Costello, *Scholastic Curriculum*, chap.1).

[24] Another typical salt-pun, with side-glance at the biblical paradox of salt losing its savour (*raison d'être*), as Matthew 5:13, Luke 14:34.

> Hail native language, that by sinews weak
> Didst move my first endeavouring tongue to speak.

So both scriptwriters are moving from high to low then back higher, by a mixture of languages and genres. Milton's charivari seems to be unusual for its amount of prose, and for not including doggerel or other low-life verse.

Amongst Milton's echoes and backward looks to Randolph, two stand out. First, both writers refer prominently to the high-risk nature of their genre, with its history of cancellations; which might help to quieten an audience and catch its attention.[25] On the other hand, whereas Randolph the royalist refers to a likely victory of the English expedition to the Isle of Rhé (179–181), Milton refers sardonically to its appalling defeat: this is not solely the difference between the before and after of a topical political event, nor between the two colleges or audiences, but rather of a different self-expression through the license of the ritual event. Indeed, Milton's quip is blunt. In "nostros milites qui nuper ab Insula Reana *capessere fugam*" ("our soldiers who lately *took flight* from the Island of Rhé," italics mine), Milton's emerging political alienation peeps through, as suggested in Chapter Eight.[26]

Something of the momentum of the Cambridge version of salting can also be glimpsed. Some topics and laugh-lines are recycled: wordy

---

[25] Randolph glances several times at the gap in the office of salting-Father. See the English couplet just cited; also "sede iam diu vacante" (line 37, "this seat being long vacant") and "sterilitatem" (86, no Fathers with their Sons): Freidberg, "Small Entertainments," 26 and 27 respectively. Randolph's Latin allusions are termed "glancing" because they occur inside a secondary subject, respectively Popes ("Papa = Father") and the usual academic-exercise fathering trope. Milton tackles the awkward fact head-on, beginning the second part of his salting by saying "the republic of fools is tottering" because its natural leader has been sent down from Cambridge, and he himself is a replacement unsure of success. The words just quoted come from the beginning of the "Prolusio" or second part of the salting text. In Part IV below, it is paragraph 1. References henceforward will be abbreviated to the form "P¶1," the same for the English and Latin. The "Oratio" or first part of the salting will similarly be referred to as "O¶," with paragraph numbers again in roman and identical for the English and the Latin. P¶1 corresponds to *ColWks* 12:226 .

[26] P¶22, cf. *ColWks* 12:244..

mythological allusions (misuse or inappropriate use of the serious—Pythagoras, Romulus); the same Latin words ("nebulones," the "Sons" as "little rascals," in other words the master of revels can use his role to insult with impunity); references to previous saltings, to food and drink, to the Prodigal Son, to the scholastic curriculum and its syllabus (greeted with groans, presumably) . . . The routines of the generic repertoire are expected and hence supplied.

We notice equally the opposite tendency; how Milton not merely avoids the governing metaphors of Randolph's performance when he composes his own, but seems to promote Randolph's incidental jokes to his own governing metaphor. In Randolph, the Aristotelian Predicaments make several appearances (62, "Entia", and 112 or 165–166). He repudiates the comparison of his Sons to metals or to books (200–207); but his *governing* metaphor is of the sons as dishes of a banquet. Milton repudiates the dishes, but so lengthily does he pass over them that they become a sort of sideshow or riff anyway. He repudiates dishes and birds for his main metaphor, in favour of what had been incidental in Randolph's. Thereby the Categories give his salting its distinctive dotty solemnity. (Generic and contextual considerations dispose me to read the masque verses as less than stately, as will be argued later in the chapter.)

As a whole, then, the saltings by Randolph and others confirm that Milton worked hard and appropriately at his. For one thing, he tells us so: because the intended Presenter had been sent down after organizing vandalism against the townsfolk, a trustworthy substitute had to be found in a hurry.[27] But further, there are signs that he thought about other saltings, which presumably he had seen or heard about; that he took the generic chance to compose a bilingual medley, in a bizarre bunch of registers and modes—the potpourri of a variety show or undergraduate revue, but in his own way and on his own terms. He could name his terms because of the sudden removal of the intended presenter: this may be among the reasons why he worked in, as a personal statement amidst the flow of patter, his repudiation of the unwelcome nickname ("Domina," the "Lady" of Christ's.[28]) A personal statement

---

[27] See P¶1, as before.
[28] See P¶18.

is a similar sudden twist within Randolph's prattle; but *he* is letting the audience know that he has an uncertain future, and is open to offers of further employment. That is a different agenda for a different personality, whose personal situation was more circumscribed than Milton's though his comic talent was much less so. Milton, for his part, had further and more compelling reasons for voicing his thoughts on the nickname just at this event, and these will be examined in the Conclusions.

Milton's Awareness of the Festive and Salting Traditions

Milton's text is a medley, in another sense: it contains a mixture of genuine learning, mock-learning, exaggerated and misapplied learning. Which is which may be hard to establish; but recognition of the contextual must come first. For example, Milton opens his *oratio* with an allusion to the Ship of Fools ("navis stultifera") and his *prolusio* with mention of the "republic of fools" ("stultorum rei summae").[29] Both remarks put the speech which they launch into its generic and communal place, the traditions of licensed fooling; with the appropriate relaxed assumptions that humans are fools and fooling is fun. He shows awareness of his occasion, and eases himself into rapport with the festive audience. In 1628, however, the allusions would convey more than that. The first says, "There is no shortage of fools around: why ask *me* to lead the fooling?" He makes a joke out of the invitation to himself: it is a modesty topos, but also insinuates the question why he is thought to have the best qualifications for fooling. The second allusion raises the whole salting event to consciousness of its own nature, as a licensed and temporary "state" (*res summa*), governing society for a short time by its own foolish yet consistent rules: this is the axiom of the Saturnalia, the Boy Bishop, all feasts of misrule. For this one night, Milton is Lord of Misrule.

If we persist and ask why he, in particular, was chosen to preside, the answer can be inferred from what he says at once after mentioning the ship of fools. The most suitable person for the job has been sent down, for leading a Town-versus-Gown rampage. The rampage may have had an aspect of holiday license, since for one thing the London apprentic-

---

[29] O¶1 and P¶1, respectively, = *ColWks* 12:204 and 226 respectively.

es' misrule regularly involved the wrecking of brothels (licensed disapproval becoming hooligan violence) and in Cambridge there was persistent friction between City and University.[30] But that Lord of Misrule had overdone it, and a replacement must begin the new cycle of license more cautiously: Milton is a replacement who is acceptable to the Christ's College authorities and to the otherwise "headless" student body. He was acceptable to the Fellows because of his life-style and good Latin, and to the students because he could make prolusions entertaining. In terms of the present study, by 1628 he had a reputation for exercises and voluntaries, such that he was starting to receive invitations.

As for the awareness of the occasion as specifically a salting, this becomes manifest whenever the *prolusio* mentions salt—along with puns on Latin words of similar sound, like *saltare* (leap, dance). *Salio*, to salt, is a distinct Latin word from *salio*, to leap, or *saltare*, to dance.[31] Milton is not neglecting the difference but (like others before him) punning by means of it.[32] He makes his *prolusio* come to its crescendo by a fusillade of such puns. Some would make the audience groan, some are genuinely funny, but the clustering would enable him to hold the audience in his hand. Such puns were expected, but not the clustering and placing. They come right at the point of transition, just when the performance is ceasing to be a solo and beginning to involve the waiting freshmen on stage.

The Oratio (Portion One of the Extant Three)

We now consider each of the three extant parts of Milton's performance script — Oratio, Prolusio, and the Verses at a Vacation Exercise.

The Oratio is a *declamatio*, urging its one-sided proposition in the usual one-sided but polished way: "*That* sometimes sportive exercises do not obstruct the study of philosophy." It proceeds by a lengthy lead-

---

[30] See Rowland Parker, *Town and Gown: The 700 Years' War in Cambridge* (Cambridge: Patrick Stephens, 1983).

[31] *Salio, salire*, to salt; *salio, salire* or *salere* to leap; NB also *salto, saltare* (connected with *salio* = leap), to dance. The verbs are so close in form as virtually to invite confusion, and in a salting verbal confusions are grist to the mill.

[32] Mention of "saltare" in Oxbridge MSS of the period is one of the clues to a salting text, because it may mean not strictly "dancing" but larger shows including dancing or leaping at an undergraduate revel. (Information from Felicity Henderson).

in, about himself and his relation to the audience and the occasion; followed by an invocation; then the thesis is stated, after which it is upheld by a proliferation of *exempla*. To conclude, the speaker takes his thesis to have been proved, so that "freed from the laws of oratory" (and hoping that he has not "spun out the thread of the oration too long") he will "break forth into comic licence." Accordingly, "I ask as I begin my comedy for that which the comic actors beg as they finish: that you 'Plaudite, et ridete,' Clap your hands and laugh." Either he urges them to get in some practice at clapping and laughing now, in order to be ready for doing it louder later; or else he solicits both for his Oratio. The former might be amusing, but the latter looks more likely. So what is there to amuse or please in the "Oratio," Part One, before we reach the more blatant buffoonery of Part Two, the "Prolusio"?

It has been remarked that when a speaker says "I can't imagine why you picked me to play the fool" and "Aren't there plenty of bigger fools around?" it is quite easy to make this funny to a packed audience of relaxed (if not already well-lubricated) undergraduates.[33] More structurally, the speaker has given himself the easiest possible thesis to prove, to this audience. It is axiomatic, to them there then. So the laborious proving of the obvious is one source of the fun. Risky by itself, perhaps, it is enhanced for this audience by being done in the full *declamatio* manner; Milton gives his needless thesis the full works. The fun lies in the deliberate disproportion; in the exaggeration (like the torrent of allusions to witticisms or clownings of revered ancients); in the ridiculing of the University exercises. For example, as Freidberg ("Small Entertainments," 51) points out, he gives the obligatory invocation, only to turn it into an invocation of the audience itself: "why invoke the celestial, absent Muses when I have so many inspired intellects in front of me?" (O¶7, = *ColWks* 12:212, *YPW* 1:270). He sets up a contrast between the exercise of expounding the *Prior Analytics* of Aristotle and "today's exercise," as if to say which would *you* rather be doing . . .[34] Though hardly a Shakespearean comic sublime, it does tease, and should accordingly please.

---

[33] Beer is integral to a salting, food not. Richek, "Saltings," 105, quotes a historian of Pembroke College saltings to the effect that "a great deal of beer, as at all such meetings, was drunk." Naturally so, because beer was second only to salt as the centre of things.

[34] "Et loco Priorum Aristotelis ab initiatis recens baccalauriis [recently graduated BAs] exponendorum" in contrast with "scommata et inanes nugas inverecunde et intempestive iactari," (O¶16, = *ColWks* 12:222.)

Bearing in mind that other saltings make fun of the University exercises but as local effects in a less demarcated flow of wit,[35] I suggest that Milton's *oratio* is of the same origin and to the same effect but he has decided to make of it an extended set-piece. The corollary is that when he advances to the expected stand-up comedy routines, he splits this off, as a *prolusio*. Correspondingly later, when he reaches his English masque, he begins it by giving it too its own heading, genre, and identity. A similar clarity is seen as each portion closes, in its transition to the next mode, which it systematically signals.

Two questions arise, however. First, is this clarity part of the performance, rather than just of the texts, which after all might have differed from the performance and indeed have been titivated and expanded or reduced for publication much later? Secondly, if "Oratio" means a pompous parody of a regular *oratio*, what does "Prolusio" mean?

We do not know, and we have no way to know, the relation between any salting text and its performance. Speakers may well compose a full polished text in the study, only to perform it differently, under the influence of nerves, timing, or audience response (favourable and otherwise). We do know that Milton kept his text of this salting until his life's end, and published the English verses in 1673, the two Latin portions the next year. He might have revised any of them at any time, yet there is no evidence for that view, and it seems unlikely. In editing his *1645* poems he added titles or headings to some; so he may have done this in 1673–1674. However, being blind by then he was less likely to intervene much. The need for some helper to bring him the English verses for inclusion in the revised poems of 1673 seems to have left the Latin papers in some disarray: the publisher, Brabazon Aylmer, speaks of "haec iuvenilia hic illic disiecta" ("these works of his youth scattered about").[36] That would be the natural effect of a 1673 rummaging by intermediaries amongst Milton's old manuscripts, and especially of detaching the "Vacation" English verses from the accompanying Latin prose portions of the salting manuscript. The unlikelihood of major revision of the

---

[35] e.g., Randolph, line 122: "hinc vos tam suaves estis & a priore & a posteriore" ("you are sweet *a priori* and *a posteriori* / smell sweet in front and behind"): Freidberg, "Small Entertainments," 78.

[36] "Typographus Lectori" ("The Printer to the Reader"), at the beginning of *Epistolarum Familiarium Liber* (1674).

blind author's Latin prose pieces in those circumstances is of course increased. Consequently, pending any evidence to the contrary, we should think of the manuscript as essentially what he wrote in the 1628 long vacation, when he found himself unexpectedly chosen for the salting assignment and had to give that his whole attention.[37] That is to say, we should expect that the performed text was not much different from the written and at long last published portions. After all, this had been Milton's first attempt at a new genre, in front of a large audience of his intimates, before whom he must not lose face. One would expect him to script it fully, and then in view of its success to keep it intact.

As to the question why "Prolusio VI" of the whole set includes a section called "Prolusio," it seems to be a new question. Here are two suggestions, of which the second matters more. The second portion of the whole salting script is the "Prolusio" proper, the foolery to which the Oratio leads, that which is *expected* by the audience on this sort of occasion. The ending of the Oratio, examined earlier, is entirely consonant with this reading.

"Prolusio" was in any case a fairly vague term in the seventeenth century, rather like "prelude" in music. It could mean anything from a minor or playful piece, through to an "exercise," strenuous and public, like those of Famiano Strada. To my mind, in the present case, the root-sense of "ludere" is uppermost. In a salting, playing was uppermost. The second portion of the whole text is a "playing before." Both the morphemes matter. It is all a "playing-about," and it comes "before" the initiation drama itself.

The "Prolusio" (Portion Two of the Three)

In this portion of the whole the genre is most completely itself — most sportive and abusive. Not despite but because of this, Milton's handling of it is at its most distinctive. The paradox strikes most forcibly at two moments: first, when he exploits his privileged position to insult the different component groups of the audience in turn, and secondly when he moves out of straight comedy and turns to his Sons, who have been

---

[37] O¶1, = *ColWks* 12:204.

standing in a bunch on the stage to one side while he has been orating from the other, on the dais at the upper end of the Christ's College dining hall.

In the first excerpt, Milton exploits the licence to amuse all by abusing each in turn, first as individuals, then in their groups (covering all the possible groupings), then back to individuals. This is the classic device of comic divide-and-rule.

To get his listeners laughing he gives them lessons in laughing: how to laugh; then says what it means if they don't, or can't. "Smooth out your furrowed brow; let your nose curve with laughing . . ." He accuses the non-laughers of having bad breath, or being afraid of farting—further scope for visual or sound effects.[38] One of them might then "give us a duet, from two orifices! He might express some gastric riddles to us, not from his Sphinx but from his sphincter; his Posterior Anal-ytics." ("Praecinenti ori succinat, et aenigmata quaedam nolens effutiat sua non Sphinx sed sphincter anus . . .") The strident, heavy-handed puns are well-tried ways of getting the audience on your side, and silencing any wilful opposition as humourless, hence dreadful and beyond the pale.

"I return to you, my listeners. . ." Milton begins a new set of jokes, a new piece of his comic routine. "They do say, eight whole boars were set before Antony and Cleopatra at a banquet; but lo and behold, for you in your first course alone see *fifty* fatted boars!—pickled in beer for three years, and still so tough that they can tire out even dogs' teeth." Milton is enumerating the groups of the resident students: senior B.A. students have been "pickled in beer" for their three years at Cambridge. "Here are another fifty calves' heads, quite fat and meaty, but so short of brain that there is not enough for seasoning." Are these the third-years who will not complete the B.A.? Obvious jokes of back-handed compliment abound hereabouts. "Then young goats, a hundred of them (give or take): they are much too thin, I think it must be from too much rutting." These are the second-year students, who have no doubt enjoyed the abusing of the previous groups, not to mention the freshmen (their own immediate predecessors); but now they get *their* turn. "We expected some rams, with fine spreading horns, but our cooks have not yet

---

[38] O¶3, = *ColWks* 12:228–229. Hale, *BLN*, 83.

brought them in from town." The Fellows of Christ's have diplomatically gone into town for dinner while the undergraduates fooled around at the salting.

"If anyone prefers to eat birds . . ." Having lampooned everybody in their groups as kinds of red meat, Milton changes his metaphor slightly and lampoons individuals as improbable forms of white meat: "we have any number of them, all fattened up a long time with dough and flour and powdered cheese, as follows." An elaborate ridiculous list of bird-dishes follows, like the inflated descriptions which feature on menus in pretentious restaurants. Since the bird-dishes lampoon individuals, Milton has now lampooned everyone; all the possible groups, and some as individuals into the bargain.

Abuse is licensed by the festive occasion, and Milton exploits the licence to the fullest.

In the second excerpt, Milton as "Father" talks about his Sons, then to them. To gain immediacy, I give some paragraphs in my own translation, adding editorial stage directions and citing the Latin parenthetically when it is needed to explain a verbal joke. The paragraphs are key ones, in the sense that they come near the climax of the *prolusio*, and so the salt-jokes proliferate and with them the baiting of the audience as a whole, the vulgar festive licence.

"And so in my role as 'Father' I turn to my sons, and I look at the glorious number of them; I can see the fine rascals acknowledge me as their father by a sly nod. [*Presenter turns to the freshmen, presumably ten of them since that is the number of the Predicaments.*]

"Do you ask about their names?[39] [*Turning back to the audience now*] I refuse to name my sons after dishes: this would be handing them over to you to be eaten, like barbarous Tantalus and Lycaon serving up their sons for dinner! [*Here the sons could pull faces?*] And I refuse to name them after parts of the body,[40] in case you should think I have been fathering mere limbs or fragments. [*Here, he could mime disapproval of the resulting progeny.*] Nor do I enjoy naming them after vin-

---

[39] This was a set feature of saltings.
[40] As is recorded of one St John's College salting; was it becoming old hat, a cliché of the genre?

tages: you will say I can drink, not think.⁴¹ [*The pun arises from the fact that "Dionysus," inspirer of wit, is the same god as "Bacchus" inspirer of hangovers.*] No: my categorical imperative is to name them after the ten Aristotelian Categories, so as to express their noble birth and liberal way of life. [*Ambiguous*] I shall make sure that they all advance to some degree before I die. [*Joke about the chances of the Sons ever graduating: ad aliquem gradum = "to some small extent" or "to some academic degree-status."*]

"As to the salt of my wit, I don't want you to call it toothless and ancient, the sort of thing some coughing crone would spit up. [*Sound-effects?*] I don't think anyone will find fault with my wit as having been too biting either—and I don't care if some toothless nitwit complains of my teeth because they are not like his own. [*Does toothy grin? mimes bad breath?*] For sure, I wish I had Horace's luck, born the son of a fish-wife, for then I would have salt wit to perfection; yes, and I should send you off so well seasoned that you would regret asking for salt—like our army who got salt put on their tails as they fled from the Salt Islands. [*First salt-joke elicits groan, second is better, third is really sharp and contentious*]: "tunc enim sales mihi essent ad unguem, vos etiam sale ita pulchre defricatos [*unusual, flamboyant verb*] dimitterem, ut nostros milites qui nuper ab Insula Reana [*sudden hush, this is topical and risky*] capessere fugam [*ignominious, but for once English has a bonus, as fleeing = having salt put on your tail*] non magis paeniteret salis petiti" [*as if they went to those Salt Islands to look for salt . . .*]

"My sons, your father has no wish to press heavy advice on you. After all, why should I spend more effort in educating you than I spent in fathering you? [*Obvious bawdy joke.*] But take care to be my sons, not the Prodigal Son. [*Usual salting joke about prodigal sons, bringing the Sons more and more into the field of reference and audience gaze.*] If you devote your wills to cups, I shall cut you out of my will ("liberique mei ne colant Liberum", a name of Bacchus.⁴²). [*The pun-words come closer*

---

⁴¹ Miscellaneous puns follow thicker and faster than ever in this paragraph, changing to specifically "salt/ salting" puns in the next.

⁴² "Liber" was the old Italian wine-god, brother of Libera / Proserpina. The name connects with words for freedom and pouring.

together now, to make the audience slightly dizzy (Touchstone-fashion) in the run-up to the close of the solo.]"

While the jokes are often puns, and some of them indecent, such verbal joking is only a part of a total stage spectacle. Milton is tickling his audience's ribs by a panoply of arts, as indeed saltings would have to. Unless I am forgetting something elsewhere in his life, this part of his salting text gives us our only chance to witness Milton himself in public performance, in visible audible rapport with actors beside him and an audience around him. Whilst it may not have the grandeur of imagining him (say) delivering *Areopagitica* to Parliament, it has the advantage that it did actually happen.

He is fulfilling the requirements of the stand-up comedian in general, and the president of a salting in particular—to provide the kind of jokes which are expected, but also the delight of surprise as to the individual quips or miming or mimicry (and their sequencing). Many jokes are a kind of insolent imagery, seeing one thing "as" another. This image-making is paramount, and structural, in a salting. It is never to be forgotten, since the jokes are being handed down from a "Father" to his numerous "Sons."

The English Verses "At a Vacation Exercise" as Part of the Salting

Because the verses have been read since 1673 independently of their original, salting context, most readers take them primarily as praise of the English language, though a notable exception is Mary Ann Radzinowicz,[43] to be discussed in a moment. *Within* their original three-part context, however, a different reading is possible, if not requisite. For example, when Milton says "Here I salute thee and thy pardon ask, / That now I use thee in my latter task"[44] he is playfully apologizing to a personified mother tongue for using her after Latin. But that this

---

[43] Mary Ann Radzinowicz, "'To Play in the Socratic Manner': Oxymoron in Milton's *At a Vacation Exercise in the College*," *University of Hartford Studies in Literature* 17 (1985) 1–11.

[44] Lines 7–8, Carey, 79.

was the *expected* order, is the natural inference from Randolph's parallel practice. Playfulness (not solemnity) is uppermost, along with a continuing witty commentary on his own changes of medium or register. Again, when he goes on, "Thou need'st not be ambitious to be first, / Believe me I have thither packed the worst," (lines 11–12) he is also playful and explicit, that the least modest of his matter is placed in the second Latin portion. Just so, he had apologized for it in advance, when the first Latin portion closed. The main thrust is to come next, namely the witty compliment he pays to English: "The daintiest dishes shall be served up last." (Note that this continues the metaphor of "dishes" of a long banquet, but applies it no longer to members of the audience but to his own offering.) The touch is *light*, and not least because the changes of register are made overt to us, and provide a witty point for the presenter Milton.

Sonorities now ensue ("Such where the deep transported mind may soar / Above the wheeling poles . . ."), only to receive a mock apology and truncation: "But fie my wandering Muse how dost thou stray!" (52)

Radzinowicz has argued that throughout the verses the central figure is oxymoron. She means oxymoron both in its paradigm sense and in an extended one. The paradigm case is of course that figure of speech which combines two ostensible contradictories — such as Horace's "jarring harmony" (*concordia discors*) or "*splendide mendax*" ("wondrously untruthful," because the lie saved a life), or Milton's own "stupidly good" or indeed "oxymoron" itself, "pointedly foolish." Of this nature is the fine line where Demodocus held his audience rapt, "In willing chains and sweet captivity" (52). The tone and register here seek to attract the mind and give a mental pleasure, no longer the rumbustious laughing of the Prolusion nor the earnest parody of the Oratio. Milton is perhaps pleasing himself in apostrophizing his mother tongue, but the impact on the audience is more important to consider. He is ringing the changes, raising the register, before he lowers it again.

Radzinowicz's other, much more extended sense of oxymoron is "the expression of a compulsion to fuse experience into a unity without suppressing its paradoxical sense of literal variety" (1). She locates this in the thinking of Socrates, to argue that throughout the English verses Milton is out to "play in the Socratic manner," "more Socratico ludere solemus."[45] He is out to do this because it is the custom "at this time," at a salting in the vacation, at festival time. I find this still a long way from Socrates the philosopher, though it is in keeping with Socrates the tease, and with Socrates the parts-player if we think of his *eironeia* as a persona. But the idea that Milton is playing, toying, with philosophy at points within the verses I do find enlightening.

So Milton comes by way of more puns—the double sense of "predicament" at 56—to the long-awaited pageant of the ten categories, presented by Milton himself again, but now in the role of "Ens [Entity, Existence]... represented as Father of the predicaments his ten Sons" (58, Stage Direction).[46] Exactness is felt: he is not only "Father" of sons as any salting must pretend, but the sons are the ten particular sons of his chosen new ruling metaphor. Still another register, and idiom and fancy, begin.

Wit and play continue, but perhaps more important to the present argument is the impact of the transition itself. We are in a medley or farrago; and here the range and tone again innovate. Furthermore, if we had the English prose of the last six of the Predicaments, the medley would become more extensive still. The prose might even have included things said—or done—in reply by the six, and whatever was the ending of the entire performance. That is to say, Milton's concluding note "The rest was prose" need not be read as dismissive, but simply as saying—from the standpoint of the reviser of his *poems*, in 1673—that the script of the vacation exercise contained no further verse. From the standpoint of the reader of the reassembled pieces of the salting, at any rate, the omission of "the rest" is a major loss. Let us at least credit

---

[45] P¶15, =*ColWks* 12:238.13.
[46] The stage direction does not declare that Milton himself played Ens the presenter. Radzinowicz ("Oxymoron," 3) thinks that "the boyish Father then leaves the stage," at the words "That to the next I may resign my room" (line 58). From other salting texts I would expect the presenter to stay presenting throughout. Yet Milton, if it were he playing Ens, might have to put on some costume in order to be "represented as Ens." This is not impossible, though we know nothing about any costuming for a salting. I explain the English from the preceding Latin, the "prolusio" in which Milton calls his ten sons the Aristotelian categories or predicaments and himself their father (*ColWks* X12: 242). If the father of the ten is Ens, and if Milton is their father, then Milton is Ens. Tillyard, 142, arrives at this conclusion more briefly.

Milton *ex silentio* with some suitable English prose, which in conjunction with the two opening portions in Latin prose would have set the English verses—always charming, and digressively noble—in a frame of prose; exactly one hundred lines of couplets amongst perhaps fifty pages of variegated, bilingual prose.

Conclusions

To take first the verses "At a Vacation Exercise," they make a different impact when read in their original context from that which they have made standing alone amongst the English poems since 1673. Their Marlovian splendours have been often admired. For that matter, Milton himself must have admired them when he took them out of his salting-papers and inserted them into his revised *Poems*, in 1673.

> Hail native language, that by sinews weak
> Didst move my first endeavouring tongue to speak . . .

or

> Such where the deep transported mind may soar
> Above the wheeling poles, and at heaven's door
> Look in, and see each blissful deity
> How he before the thunderous throne doth lie . . .[47]

In their original context, nonetheless, such lines make a different, greater impact, for two reasons. We soar higher because of the contrast with the immediately preceding clowning. Thus we can recognise their wit and fantasy more clearly because they carry forward by a different motion the preceding flow of wit and fantasy. That is to say, their conceit of English as a gateway to intellectual space-travel can be enjoyed (in explicit digression, note) as a splendid new variation on the helter-skelter of saltings' conceit-making. There is equally a continuity in method, and most of all at the heart of the *inventio*, in the wordplay and metaphors by both of which one thing is seen "as" a surprising other thing, for the sake of pleasure: to compare an Irish bird with an Irish student

---

[47] Lines 1–2 and 33–36, from Carey, 79–80.

in the Latin is the same activity as in the English to imagine someone called "Rivers" as the "son"[48] of this or that actual English river.

Response to the verses must stay in touch with the *generic* fact that Randolph's script turned from a clowning Latin prose to accomplished English couplets at the same point as Milton's, namely when the core of the salting ritual—the actual presenting and metaphorizing induction of freshmen—impended. In terms of register, both writers' verses elevate the tone way above the preceding Latin clowning, so as to settle to the pageant itself at a level somewhere mid-way. The varying pleases the audience. The change gives the presenter liberty to present the pageant itself ensuing at whatever intermediate level he chooses. So everybody (including any nervous authorities) was made happy.[49]

Comparison with other saltings texts not only illuminates Milton's, but his illuminates theirs. In particular, his eloquence and range would have held the attention of an audience trained on rhetoric and eloquence: they would have known they were getting something beyond the average. He may or may not have set new standards, but he must have extended the range and idea of salting.

Milton had turned aside to do a job because he was asked; and sometimes he does rather grind out the conceits or obscenities, or overdo the classical allusion; indeed, the *oratio* and *prolusio* could perform better with cuts. On the other hand, a better metaphor may be *imitatio*, or better still *aemulatio*: the work as a whole, as well as in each part, exemplifies the humanist ideals of *serio ludere*, serious and strenuous play,[50] as well as of *spoudaiogeloion* (the blend of jest with earnest), all of

---

[48] Rivers thus becomes the "Son" of Milton as Father-Presenter, in four simultaneous metaphors: academic paternity; the ongoing saltings parody of this; Relation the Predicament is son of Ens; and Rivers is son of Trent or whatever. Milton is giving Fancy, if not Imagination, a lively workout.

[49] Were any fellows present? One imagines not, by the nature of the frolic and because they have no prescribed role. The feast is more itself in their absence. It may be significant that Milton's name-jokes swing towards the servants and cooks, yet not the Fellows. At Anthony Wood's salting there was a prominent role for the chief cook. All of this suggests that a salting is a parody ceremony belonging to the underclasses together, and more fulfilling of its peculiar holiday catharsis the more it is kept free of the everyday hierarchy.

[50] The humanist slogan is often felt, and Erasmus' *Praise of Folly* is named at O¶12, = *ColWks* 12:220.

them mixed modes which can disconcert the modern reader. The mixing is *meant* to please by disconcerting: that is the pleasure of surprise, and surprise in a fiction is itself a source of laughter, pleasure, delight (Bottom in the embrace of Titania). The *oratio* is a parody, succeeding by excess. The *prolusio* is a playful low-life voluntary. The verses are a higher-flying voluntary, modulating into the pageant proper.[51] "*The rest was prose*," declares *Poems, 1673*, to explain why there is no more verse and why that prose is not given.[52] ("Poems" in the title here at least means "Verse.") If only we had the whole thing!—to see, for example, why only the first and fourth of the Categories (Substance and Relation) were addressed in verse.

Milton is not slumming it, so much as doing his emulation thoroughly, responsibly, and in a fashion responsive to the needs of the occasion. His mind and fancy are engaged. Indeed, the Fancy is at times transmuted under the comic pressure into Imagination. For example, he calls the freshmen "Saltaturientes," "those who desire to leap up [to higher status]." He lets fly with this imposing new Latin word to glance simultaneously at increase of status, at possible hubris ("jumped-up"), at the "dancing" or antics by which they acquire tribal seniority; and then, down at the bottom of the pile of puns, "sal-" (*and* "salt-" for the monolinguals present) give to the central salting idea a sudden and surprising new embodiment.

Thus when Milton plays the fool in his salting presidency, and keeps and eventually prints the text, we get a serious playing; a praise of folly; a whimsical peep at celestial beings; a bizarre embodiment of the least dramatizable of abstractions; parody, bawdry, and mercurial changes of register; an embryonic anthropology; a whistlestop medley of undergraduate wit which pushes license to its limits. We get a whole which is youthfully overlong, but equally has youth's energy.

---

[51] Radzinowicz calls the tonal transition among the three parts "serio-comic," "mockery," then "oxymoron." I have found an even wider variety, and hence prefer a pervasive metaphor of "playing," Socratic or otherwise.

[52] Carey, 83.

CHAPTER 10

FURTHER PERSPECTIVES

What was the value for Milton of sharing in the Cambridge Latin performances?

Extrinsically, he gained reputation at Cambridge itself, and it is being argued that he sought it. Later, it is true, he does not explicitly assign great value to his Cambridge Latin. The best implicit testimony is his inclusion of Cambridge-occasioned poems in the Latin half of *Poems, 1645*. His having kept his undergraduate prolusions, and his agreeing to have them brought out of cold storage in 1674, mean he was not ashamed of them, nor disgusted with their kinds.

Intrinsically, however, value may be found in the spirit of the doing, as evidenced by mental or imaginative engagement. "Joy's soul lies in the doing." This is the value emphasized in the present work, case-study by case-study through the genres. In this finale I seek to show the intrinsic value by adducing perspectives either new in the study or emerging more clearly because of it. The new perspectives comprise Milton's Latin writings which come from the Cambridge years but lack Cambridge, together with his inferred personal life of that time. A previous perspective now becoming clearer is that of a Milton steeped in the genres of Cambridge who participates in its rites of passage, and experiments with personae which it releases.

The centred self is trying out masks. Our study is ultimately a study of the Many and the One, within Milton as a student. In these genres we watch a personality both imitative and emulative, bold and empathetic, joining in things and weighing up their human worth. The two opposites may achieve reconciliation by adapting the anthropological concept of participant observation.

Milton's Other Latin Writings 1625–1632

To any dismissal of our view that *In Quintum Novembris* moves into a voluntary Protestant soteriology, and to any replacement of that reading by one which sees the poem as an orthodox, commissioned patriotic set-piece, I would reply by adducing Milton's verse epistle to Thomas Young. *Elegia Quarta* is only slightly later, dating to early 1627;[1] by late 1626, the year of *In Quintum Novembris*, the danger of the Thirty Years War to Young in Hamburg was considerable. Milton consoles his old tutor by urging that the Lord will protect true believers, as happened in two crises of the Book of Kings (Sennacherib and ben-Hadad). The sense of God's nearness to his people is developed into a higher drama now, but is continuous with that which took over centre stage in the earlier poem.

Another point to notice is that in the verse-letter Milton has to begin by apology for owing a letter and not writing sooner. Why, then, does he write just now? It may have been through realization of the danger, together with his own being preoccupied hitherto; for we can view that preoccupation as his 1626 "campaign" to win a Cambridge reputation, and take a further aspect of that campaign to be poems which look at England's confusing variant of the continental wars of religion. Having made up his mind on the former struggle, with its Cambridge convolutions, Milton in his Elegy could write more sonorously on the latter, starker struggle.

The Elegy is consonant with my view of the Cambridge genres in a further way. His writing to Young is again constrained and voluntary. He owes the letter, and it is late, and Young needs moral support. Milton writes it, nonetheless, *when* he sees how to make a full, varied, Romano-Christian performance. He writes it when he himself is ready to. On this view, he is ready thanks to his immediately prior Cambridge excogitation and versification. Perhaps he wrote the poem after going home for Christmas 1626, but this particular speculation is unimportant, since it is extrinsic to the poems and the value found in them.

Alongside this linear development, this deepening of a tactful public politics into a private fervour, it is important to place for contrast *Elegia Quinta*, of early 1629.[2] Politics and religion are *not* Milton's subject here: instead he writes a celebration of the coming of spring. Pagan as it may be called, it is more of a universal rapturing. He keeps things beautifully simple here, led along by a natural joy in the warming of

---

[1] Carey, 55–56.
[2] *Elegia Prima* and the prose letters of 1625–32 have been touched upon earlier.

the weather. (After all, Milton is not seldom apologetic about England's cold climate, and for that matter he lived his whole life in the "Little Ice Age."[3]) Yet under the flow of this simplicity he revels in some surprising things—not just the earth and its dwellers, but the gods who dwell in both. There are gods who dwell on earth (Sylvanus or satyrs)[4] and others who prefer to leave heaven and come visiting earth (lines 131–132). There are gods in every grove—and let them be there. To be alive at this moment is like being back in the golden age:

> Dii quoque non dubitant caelo praeponere sylvas,
>   Et sua quisque sibi numina lucus habet.
> *Et sua quisque diu sibi numina lucus habeto*
>   Nec vos arborea dii precor ite domo.

("The gods, too, unhesitatingly prefer these woods to their heavens, and each grove has its own particular deities. Long may each grove have its own particular deities: do not leave your homes among the trees, you gods, I beseech you.")

The words I have emphasized register by their ecstatic repetition, by the incremental repetition of "diu" added in the repeated line, Milton's momentary concurrence and desire, his going all the way with this joy in immanence. Is it just an exaggeration, a going with the mood? Or is there a part of Milton and his sense of God in this Latinate moment, if it later feeds the portrayal of unfallen joy in God's immanence within Paradise (*Paradise Lost*, Book IV)?

In these examples, at any rate, we see emerging by way of Latin a poet of the conscientious, egotistical sublime and a poet of the empathetic, of negative capability; and not the latter despite the former, as a kind of holiday from it, but the two together and because of each other. Similarly, the combined need and desire to perform the Cambridge Latin genres has clarified some aspects of spirituality and conscience for Milton, and encouraged him to play with some less moral perspectives on human life. Most genres, in fact, did both things for him. In principle,

---

[3] H. H. Lamb, *Climate History and the Modern World* (London: Methuen, 1982), e.g., 63.

[4] Lines 119–122, Carey, 88, his trans.

the medium of Neo-Latin was fundamentally both Roman and Christian, and in varying proportions and combinations. Latin gave the way of talking, faith gave the vision to express; yet also faith gave the security, and Latin the means, to "entertain" alternative possibilities. "Entertain," here, is used in the sense of giving them a chance to be heard, unthreatened because unthreatening; to enjoy them while making them enjoyable. If Milton is at his most "entertaining" in a pure voluntary like *Elegia Quinta*, it may have been Cambridge as much as inclination which kept most of his performances more staid. On the other hand, the Companion Pieces are voluntaries which start from an oppositional view of things in terms of large abstractions, very like the Cambridge binarism. At all events, the poem to Ely has an equivalent full-throated ease, using a surprising Latin metre to express a space-travel or dream-vision that is loosely orthodox.

The Latin Performances in Milton's Personal Life

Many of us make enduring friendships at university, possibly lifelong ones. We grow up there together, we grow into the friendship, and it goes on growing. Milton appears to have had no such experience. His closest friend was Charles Diodati, a friend made at school, who went to the Other Place, and died young. No second particular friend is known of, certainly not from Cambridge. Like Wordsworth in so many ways, Milton is unlike him in this: he met no Beaupuis to look up to, he had no Jones to walk hills with. Was he lonely, then, or self-sufficient, or a bit of both?

To judge by the *Epitaphium Damonis*, and by some later letters, he did get lonely. His late marriage, and career as a much-married man, will not have eclipsed that, but rather suggest he found the closest relations of life somewhat difficult. "Nos durum genus, et diris exercita fatis / Gens, homines, aliena animis et pectore discors, / Vix sibi quisque parem de millibus invenit unum, / Aut si sors dederit tandem non aspera votis, / Illum inopina dies qua non speraveris hora / Surripit..."[5] When

---

[5] Hale, *BLN*, 126–27, lines 106–11 of the poem. Here is Masson's version, preserving the Latin rhythms, "*We* are the hard race, we, the battered children of fortune,/ We of the breed of men, strange-minded and different-moulded!/ Scarcely does any discover his one true mate among thousands;/ Or, if kindlier chance shall have given the singular blessing,/ Comes a dark day on the creep, and comes the hour unexpected,/ Snatching away the gift..."

we look at his Cambridge years in this light, some inferences about the Latin performances suggest themselves. A troubled first year, though assuaged by his continuing contact with Diodati, usually by letters in Latin or Greek, is not mitigated by any other known companionship. It looks more like the opposite, if we can rely on the adversarial way he alludes to his contemporaries in some of the prolusions. Unless the tone is purely ironic, he sounds unpopular, or at least an outsider. But he overcomes this mild alienation, just as his row with the college about tutoring is overcome. A change of tutor repairs the latter relationship, in 1625–1626; the former seems to have taken longer. Still, any true hostility is mitigated by the presence and acknowledgement of some few fellow-spirits.

If we now reckon the Latin performances into this speculation, it seems that he sought and won a reputation from his teachers by a concerted effort in the approved genres—and some others—during 1626. Reputation is not necessarily respect, however, let alone affection. His fellow-students seem to have felt a wary respect some terms later than the teachers did. He has won recognition from both groups of his community, nonetheless, by the time of the salting. Trusted as a stop-gap by officialdom, he is by now able to tease, and genially insult, all sorts and groups at Christ's. He does this as a part of his performance to them all. True, real closeness is given, not won. But we have the signs of increasing rapport, and therewith self-confidence, as a performer of the rites.

If there is any solidity in these inferences, then, it was partly the Latin—the Latin performances and genres—which were instrumental in rescuing his time at Cambridge from being hideous and lonely. This is not to say, as for instance David Daiches[6] has argued, that his early Latin writings are closer to his personal life than his English ones are. They may have been, though in some ways the impersonal grief of *Lycidas* is more of an intimate anxiety than the personal grief of the *Epitaphium* for Diodati. Rather, the Latin genres of Cambridge enable a *sidelong* rapprochement with the place, the college elders and contemporaries.

This is not accidental, but by the nature of the tribe and its customs—its festivals, its rites of transition, its self-expression by the vocabulary of these. All involved Latin, performed. By rising to one after another of these occasions, Milton and his Latin created a name for themselves, a name and a niche.

---

[6] David Daiches, *Milton* (London: Hutchinson, 1957).

I am not speaking only of the required genres here, since the required intermingled with the voluntary. To repeat, he volunteered to do performances which were required of somebody, but not necessarily him in particular. He was asked from on high to oblige with another performance. His greatest performance, that of the salting, was yet another mingling of accident, pressure, and choice. Others he did choose; and he chose how much effort to expend on each. In all, he found some value; in some, manifestly he found a great deal, and especially a new voice.

All alike required of him, and intrinsically not extrinsically, the adoption of a persona, one given not optional, but helped, in fact empowered, by the tradition of the rite and its Latin. So any loneliness, or anxiety of metaphorical exile, was—by about 1628 at least—well and truly modified into being the occasional voice of his time and place and community. That is why these case-studies have persisted in joining the vocabulary of the Latin with that of the rituals. This was a world of ritualized life, indeed a time when ritualizing was on the upsurge. The theatricalizing of court life, and the imposition of the beauty of holiness on liturgical life, doubtless left him cold. Nonetheless, a similar thing was happening in the saltings, since Cambridge was transmogrifying a crude student rite into a scripted liturgy; and so he entered on his greatest social glory, as salting-presenter. Rising to occasion depends on choosing the right occasion. Most of the Cambridge occasions on which he performed were the right ones for him; right for his powers and his role-playing; right for the self-expression and self-extension which these apparently pointless communal activities entail.

Participation in rites of passage, experimentation with personae

We will pass in review all of the rites of transition into which Latin entered and in which Milton through his Latin participated. This will prepare for a concluding new perspective on his exercising of the genres.

Of Milton's participation in his first rite of passage at Cambridge we know nothing: his matriculation was like anyone else's; speech and performance were not required of him.

In his college, next, he disputed and declaimed, as all had to do. This was practice for the same exercises in the University Schools—a sterner, less cooperative contest. In falling foul of his first tutor, Milton may have been telling Chappell that disputation was a waste of everyone's time, whereas disputation was Chappell's forte. But that Milton came to accept the usual compromises is shown by his two disputation-texts—by their lengthy undisputative prologuing, and their perfunctory derivative exegesis once the thesis itself was reached. Thus, then, he fulfilled the requirements, without conviction. Thereby, all the same, he could graduate; rising to higher status in the academic community by upholding one side of a fictional contest. It was the upholding, not the thesis, let alone conviction, which the step up required. The upholding might later be a means to a serious end, even life-and-death matters in that long crisis of church and state. For the student, nevertheless, the means was itself the end. In this, disputation corresponded exactly to fencing with the foils protected, and to any form of military training, and ultimately to the Roman "exercises," these being how the army or *exercitus* prepared itself for real warfare. (To reiterate, although the originary military sense will have lapsed from English "exercise," in the Latin of students drilled in a linguistic philology *exercitatio* sounded much closer to *exercitus*.)

To interpret the disputations in terms of simulation or war-training is thus entirely fitting: for these latterday Roman *iuvenes* to dispute is to enter the ranks of an adult Roman war-readiness. Ritual, accordingly, expresses and heightens these meanings.

Declamations were also adversarial and combative, but less extreme. Declaimers prepared their speech, and the speech was all; no unprepared phase of combat, no hand-to-hand fighting of interrogations and improvisations followed. The prepared performance could be solemn, and was unbroken, monolithic.

The third prose kind, the salting, allowed greater variety, not least through being built on a base of parody, entailing an alternative perspective on the solemnities, if not several such perspectives. The element of contestation is not absent, but that of play is central now. The presenter must play about, play the fool, put on masks, indeed—in the Cambridge scripted medley—put on a series of masks. The mask of crude buffoonery (of the *bomolochos*) is one of them, another is that of the comic pedant, another the clever slave, and so on through the comic masks, which are familiar from Roman comedy but correspond to immemorial folk traditions.

Quite why such masks are needed to celebrate an age-group changing status is hard to say. It is also needless, because it is universally social and irreducibly human. The same can be said for such graduations being attended with food, drink, speech, and a lot of noise. The pointlessness seems to be part of the point. Why do it if you had to, or if it was productive work? It is a heeding of more obscure compulsions we obey when we celebrate a time in nature or a time in our lives. Is it the paradox that we find so much meaning in what (despite a vivid vocabulary) has a very obscure significance, because thus *we* put the significance in? This indeed, I shall argue in a moment, is what Milton is doing in his moment-to-moment wielding of the Latin of his Cambridge tribe.

Act verses are a part of disputation, and a smaller part than the opening speeches. They are intriguing in the present context because they were not spoken, but instead printed. To that extent they are not performance. To the extent that Milton ghost-wrote some, though, they *are* a performance of sorts, a commission for an influential senior of his college. The oral aspect of his two specimens is so strong that I would speculate he either did perform them, but to his college, or that his two are extensions of the little genre itself, beyond the perfunctory summative into pugnacious and even dramatic orality. *De Idea* in particular, despite or because of its jettisoning the set forms, epitomizes Cambridge chop-logic.

With funeral verses the genre is self-evidently to be explained by rites of passage. And here, more clearly, Milton assigns himself a role and position and stance at the fictionalized ceremonies, be they of mourning or interment or anything else. The body must be worthily laid to rest; the soul must be conducted appropriately into the afterlife. Sharing in the first is in principle a physical action, of standing or walking or witnessing or casting flowers on the remains. Sharing in the second must be a movement of empathy, an act of the imagination—a journey of one's own soul, by vision or dream or reiteration of shared myths, into a temporary renewed communion with the soul of the deceased. The two souls may commune together, one last time. Milton sees himself helping to build each ship of death and, like a shaman, going a little way on its voyage. Milton's art in imagining all of this activity, corporeal or spiritual, in different but apt ways four times over, should not be found artificial. Funerals themselves vary the thing said and done, to demonstrate that where the rite is the same the individual is different.

Whether or not it is correct to infer anything political about his absence from the University anthologies of 1625, in his very productive next year he prolongs a contemplation of the nation's escape in 1605. The four epigrams and his longest Latin poem amount to a prolonged meditation on a national rite of passage. From more caustic interpretations in the epigrams he moves to a theophany, a providential vision of the Lord watching over his new Israel. Royalty fades out of the vision; the people themselves take over the ending. He embraces a Protestant as well as patriotic interpretation of the crisis, by dwelling on its continuing meaning as the newest and also greatest of the Protestant festivals. It is an exodus, an escape from the Red Sea: Milton blows his Latin shawm loud and long.

To bring in the salting's vernacular verses may seem illicit; but to leave them out of this survey of rituals which Milton conducted would be worse, since it would continue the regrettable sundering of the third part of his salting text from the first two. Accordingly, let me be brief. The verses aim at wit, as a pleasing variety to follow the coarser clowning of the "Prolusio." The wit itself varies, from majestic conceit to wry humour, to the implicit absurdity (parodic certainty) of staging such abstractions as "Ens" or "Relation." We must accept in its essence Mary Ann Radzinowicz's suggestion that the key trope is oxymoron, and that oxymoron is a Socratic playing, and that it is a concealed but committed way to examine human life—because "the unexamined life is unlivable."[7] Without following or even grasping all her suggested instances of that troping, I find the idea fundamentally sound, in fact profound. We should use it as a lever, to lift some further weights.

Socrates was both *bomolochos* and *eiron*: he played a persona lifelong, and (said Plato, who should know) his outside belied the inside, like a Silenus-doll. If all of his life was playing, then his playfulness was profoundly varied. The profundity of variety is that it tolerates difference, it entertains alternative views of life. A community — a university or a club, or a church or a college — must do this or perish. Over time and place, stable and continuous communities have evolved forms and rituals and vocabularies to ensure exactly this tolerance.

My contention is that Milton revelled in the chance to be the spokesman of these forms, and that at times he glimpsed their inner meaning.

---

[7] "ὁ δε ἀνεξέταστος βίος οὐ βιωτὸς ἀνθρώπῳ," in Plato's *Apology* 38 a.

While it does not become the paramount code of his life, it does receive expression in later years—for example in those poems where he commends sociability, and in the references by early biographers to his companionability (and his making and hearing of music). It is also to be seen in a continuing intellectual passion which I can only call anthropological. The thing without the name, I mean: he does not use the name, which was rare till the next century; but as for the passion or mind-set, it flows into his salting text and thence with increase into all those times when he comments about human customs and rituals, whether in his Euripides marginalia or in the course of some polemic or when writing a gloss into his greatest poems. He always wants to describe a custom *aright*, and to probe what it means for the community that created it.

Participant Observation

Two final ways of appreciating Milton's student Latin performances are to connect them with the anthropological notion of participant observation, and to think of Cambridge's Latin as the rites of a notional "tribe."

For participant observation we should more strictly say observant participation. If the fieldworking anthropologists of our own time try to share in the cults and rites they wish to understand without influencing them, or changing them only to the least possible extent, then Milton's position is not identical. He stood within, not apart.

Yet something of the field anthropologist's combination of sympathy or empathy with detachment can be seen in Milton's conduct of all his roles. He draws upon the extraordinarily rich bank of available data from classical antiquity and beyond, to interpret the rites of his own small community.

Let the Palilia explain festival fooling! Let it explain the salting to the salting-participants! Let him interpret his own role, as master of ceremonies, lord of misrule, gubernator of the ship or "republic" of fools (itself a cunning metaphor for understanding the ship of state in its dafter moments). If these moments are not to disgust or depress us, let us laugh them off. He does that. What of the appalling catastrophe of the Isle de Ré, a national humiliation? Down goes that disaster, as Buckingham getting salt put on his tail. Every act of history is attended by a laughing chorus, as Bakhtin put it. If only he were right! Rituals ensure that the if-only gets a fair hearing.

It is the same with the other rituals of his Latin community. One and all, they are a trying-out of alternative views. It is the most anthropologically rich of them, though, which mentions "playing in the Socratic manner." If "the unexamined life is not worth living for humans," Milton's Cambridge genres and his emulative perfomance of them are his examinations of life through the different ancient lenses.

The emphasis on observant participation accords with my psychobiographical speculation. Loneliness encourages detachment, and observation of the seemingly happier majority of a group (like those "more timely-happy spirits" of Sonnet VII).[8] The outsider has a special view of the insiders, and may think about that distinction itself to special effect.

Though it might seem more economical to ascribe this "observant participation" to the simple needs of occasion, or to the poet's need to make conceits and the extensive allusion-making so adored by Neo-Latinists (all of which indeed have their place in his overall performance), I persist in commending anthropological matrices alongside. They are new to the examination of this body of Milton's work. They defamiliarize works which languish in the dust of an older philological scholarship which could presuppose Latin literacy. To read the works in their Latin is to stand at the heart of the rite, semantically and ritually alike. Since we have considered the particulars till now, a more theoretical foray concludes our whole undertaking.

Tribal Latin: *Communitas* in Action

Before speaking of "tribal" Latin, the limitations of the metaphor must be conceded: Cambridge was more literate than oral, its members were not (even ancestrally) kindred, and so forth. Still, it behaved at its *most* tribal when performing its rites in Latin. These were his community's rites of passage in varying degrees, as the case-studies have shown.[9] The

---

[8] Carey, 153, line 8: a wistful coinage, expressing the pang of the outsider.
[9] See further Walter J. Ong, S. J., "Latin Language Study As a Renaissance Puberty Rite," *Studies in Philology* 56 (1959): 103–24.

"tribal" aspect is most visible in the University's own governing metaphor for what took place at its exercises. When disputaturient students walked from their college to the Schools in a gaggle led by their tutor, he was the "Father" of all these "Sons," who accordingly were each other's "Brothers." Now this does look tribal, because a tribe is a kinship-group, like Benjamites or the Clan Cameron. At set points during the disputation the Father would speak, and in various ways help each Son to survive his ordeal on the big, University stage. Similarities with tribal initiation procedures will suggest themselves, such as the separation of the group of the initiands, their bonding together by common risk (of loss of face), the liminal space (threshold) between states, or the party afterwards.

The tribal aspect of a graduation reappears in the figure of the Praevaricator, from his appointed stool — lowly but prominent, right at the feet of authority — ensuring that the philosophic jousting is punctuated by licensed folly. The Praevaricator's parody and buffoonery have their cruder counterpart in the salting ceremonies, unmistakably a rite of passage for each year's intake of freshmen. These tribally sanctioned rituals incorporate license into high seriousness, through some intuition that social well-being is thereby served. Archbishop Laud legislated for Oxford that the Terrae Filius,[10] its equivalent of the Praevaricator, must, despite incessant lapses of taste, continue.

In view of all this, it is proper to ask concerning Milton at a Cambridge Latin rite such simple anthropological questions as, "What is he doing? What does he think he is doing? Who does he imagine he is? Who and what and where does he think the participants are?" Let us review some of Milton's Cambridge Latin genres to show this emphasis and its pay-off. In a funeral poem for a University official he acts as an unseen, implied master of ceremonies, calling attention to the gleaming silver of the University's mace, or bidding the Schools resound with mourning. His Latin ululates paganly. For another dirge, he speaks in the role of a Roman priest, directing the soul downwards across the River Styx, the body into the grassy tomb. In the salting, he discourses upon Roman festivals, for their similarity to the salting itself. A special debt is to the *Fasti* of Ovid, for rites which are strange and fantastical (like the shepherds' festival of the Parilia, at which young men did

---

[10] "Son of the Earth": meanings include "Mr Bastard," "Mr Dolt."

fantastic high leaps over burning straw). Calendrical details take over as the close of his poem on November 5 rituals, again like Ovid. Is he doing his anthropology out of the *Fasti*, as did James "Golden-Bough" Frazer?

Be that as it may, the signs accumulate, to more than a literary Latin sheen upon an autonomous Cambridge event. The event brings out a Roman and medieval ancestry in Cambridge's Latin rites; a Latinity of continuity.[11] We should not think of Rome as a grave secular society, with a dignified culture and purified language. Rome was also a place of incessant rituals, of vulgar comedy, celebrating gross appetites. Evidence abounds of its enduring *communitas*. "Communitas," very frequent in Cicero, means a or the community, then community-feeling, within guilds and trades or across all Rome. "Communitas" embraces both the outward social forms and their ethos or spirituality. It can be located in Milton's Cambridge, if we look in appropriate places.

These range from the most august, graduations, to the most rumbustious, saltings. The two will be my points of reference.

I was in fact impelled to these speculations by finding that the anthropologist Victor Turner employs the Latin term *communitas* for the key moments in the varied rites of passage which he studies.[12] He finds an "equalizing" experience within the liminal space of ritual, whether it be among the procession of the initiands going to Eleusis, or on medieval pilgrimages, or among his fieldwork tribe, the Ndembe. It can be found in Milton's Cambridge, too, with Milton its shaman or hierophant.

We turn to graduations. Turner's theory argues that rites of passage by their nature suspend status in favour of *communitas*, and not although but because the rites are carrying out a change of status. Near the close of my own university's graduations the Chancellor—a very remote figure to students, whose event a graduation nevertheless is—welcomes the new graduates to the large body of full members of the University, and asks them to show loyalty to it, lifelong. There is a note of friendly equality in the proceedings at this point, which has been sub-

---

[11] Thus the rites incorporate some dog-Latin and medieval (rhyming) Latin, absent from the solemn genres, as a pleasing special effect inside more demotic happenings.

[12] Victor Turner, *The Ritual Process: Structure and Anti-Structure* (London: Routledge, 1969).

merged within the hieratic before. Equality, community and our links across the ages to the medieval universities are then paraded in a singing of "Gaudeamus igitur": "soon the earth will hold us all," we sing in jolly fashion to that great tune, "therefore long may the *University* flourish." As for Turner, he draws upon diverse "graduations." He draws on the practice of the Ndembu of Zambia when a chief is elected: the rituals include even insults in the exhortation to the elect one, not to get above himself or forget he is moved by the same motives as the lowest of the low. He instances also that a Pope promises to be *servus servorum*, and gives diverse instances from societies of every degree of sophistication.

All this moves to the summation, that rites of passage are "giving recognition to an essential and generic human bond, without which there could be *no* society. Liminality implies that the high could not be high unless the low existed, and he who is high must experience what it is like to be low" (*Ritual Process*, 97). This thought is present in everyone's mind at the close of a graduation, where after all the most important participants are the youngest ones, on the brink of a new life elsewhere, and we all think about the meaning of the graduating, in the same way that death is in everyone's thoughts at a funeral.

The key points so far are three. First, contemporary secular universities carry out their rituals of initiation in ways which depend emotionally and ontologically upon the links with human practice across time and space. Secondly, the rites are expressing a number of larger-than-personal values, such as celebration of origins, of continuity, of membership of a *communitas* which embraces past and future membership. Thirdly, somewhere lurks a temporary but felt equality in the bondedness, as if the alma mater "nourishes" all of us alike.

As for saltings, the tribal affinities are more blatant. Liminal features include these: (i) the induction of freshmen by their immediate seniors to a new standing; (ii) a liminal time of year, the vacation; (iii) postulants forming a separate group, an age-group; (iv) who undergo a stylized, symbolic ordeal, shepherded and shielded by a benevolent immediate senior of the tribe. Moreover, (v) that functionary rubs everyone's nose in the ritual by turns, lambasting the foibles of groups and individuals alike: they have to endure it, and laugh with the rest at themselves; (vi) one and all are in a "liminal space," betwixt and between their institution's normal categories of experience; and (vii) a parody of the normal helps to register the abnormality sharply, so that when we hear of "fathers" and "sons," "orations" and "prolusions," these terms are being stretched or stood on their heads.

Thus it is in a liminal space and time that Milton talks about his nickname, Domina. The ritual is moving to the transition between its monologuing and its more dramatic part, just at the moment when as "Father" he turns to his "Sons" and their moment of elevation. He can look at himself through others' eyes (the nickname) in order to make them hear how he views his name and himself, and them. This is about being a society, individuals but incorporated. Milton accepts the nickname, on the way to saying, "Better to look feminine in my way than to be masculine in your way, some of you . . ."[13] The personal statement looks both ways; it is a Janus-moment, when we hear his voice as celebrant on the threshold.

Clifford Geertz says, "The culture of a people is an ensemble of texts . . . which the anthropologist strains to read over the shoulders of those to whom they belong."[14] Milton's Cambridge Latin allows, or encourages, or at times demands that we do this. The literary genres depend on their cultic *Sitz im Leben*, the life-situations of the people present and what they are present to do. As a result, Milton's Cambridge Latin situations are remote because of the Latin and their vanished thought-forms, and yet—when anthropological imagination is brought into play—close enough to their current counterparts.

---

[13] Egghead and philistine look at each other's stereotypes, at the partial truth of each.
[14] Clifford Geertz, "Deep Play: Notes on the Balinese Cockfight," chap. 15 of *The Interpretation of Cultures* (London: Hutchinson, 1975), 452.

PART FOUR

Milton's Salting (editio princeps)

Text and Translation

Milton's Salting:

Text History and Problems of the Texts

As already explained, the bilingual text comes to us in a sundered and partial form. No manuscript survives. The English verses, "At a Vacation Exercise," may have been taken out from it to serve as copy when they were being included in the revised and extended *Poems*, of 1673. The English prose was not printed then ("The rest was prose," says the concluding note in 1673).[1] Probably it got lost in the process of being excluded, either at the printing-house or back among Milton's papers. The Latin prose portions became number VI among the Prolusions which were added at a late stage to Milton's personal letters (*Epistolarium Familiarum Liber*), in 1674. The publisher mentions that the papers were in disarray ("haec . . . iuvenilia hic illic disiecta"). As Milton had been tidy and retentive with his manuscripts lifelong, we can infer that because his blindness meant he could visit and extract his papers solely through intermediaries, successive proxy-visits left increasing disarray behind for the next visitor.

At all events, the three surviving pieces of his salting stayed separated for 248 years until the Tillyards reassembled them. They were translating the Latin, however: their text does not give the Latin itself. The Columbia edition (1936) kept the original English poem separated from the original Latin prose. The Yale edition (volume I, 1953) dealt only with the prose, and gives no Latin either, "to save space for annotations."[2] Columbia does include collations (12: 389). So does Yale, in the sense that it reprints Phyllis Tillyard's notes about the Latin text, which is nonetheless absent save in those vestigial glimpses.

As a consequence of this checkered history, both text and editorial matter are awkward or even incomplete to follow in the existing scholarship. The present version prints the extant text together, in its original tongues, for the reader to read as a whole and consecutive experience of what Milton did as the master of those 1628 ceremonies. It tries to add to the annotations of earlier editors such as the Tillyards and Yale,

---

[1] Carey, 83.
[2] *YPW* 1: ix.

emphasizing any details left obscure before the nature of the text as a salting was recognised, by Richek in 1982. In a peculiar and limited way, we are presenting an *editio princeps*.

Its presentation of the poem "At a Vacation Exercise" could not be anything but humble, for the work has been edited often and excellently. There is little to add, and most of it is said in Chapter 9 above. But the Latin "Oratio" and "Prolusio" do need some spadework. They reached their first printer in some disarray, and in 1674 the text was poorly printed, and even the printer's Errata miss much, whilst perpetrating some new errors.[3] These matters receive valuable attention in Columbia, but not nearly enough. The punctuation, in particular, is left in its confusing original form. The confusion is partly that it is rhetorical not logical, but more that it is not consistently or intelligently handled by the printer.[4] Columbia does not complete the job of giving a consistent and accurate punctuation.

The present text, accordingly, aims to improve both clarity and consistency. Corrections will not receive comment in the apparatus criticus unless they materially affect the sense, but readers are assured that they will be reading a modernized text, comparable with modernized texts of other Neo-Latin authors and of the classical authors on whom those authors modelled themselves. The benefit of this procedure is that readers can confront the text at an appropriate speed, without the distraction caused by following the vagaries of a slapdash printing in an older, excessively pausing punctuation. (Clear support for this claim is provided by the very first sentence, where Columbia's pointing is still actively misleading.)

The rationale of this edition continues my practice in editing some of the salting text for a Milton volume in the series Bibliotheca Latini-

---

[3] Here are the fierce but accurate comments of the Tillyards, 144: "The edition of 1674 contains a long list of *errata*, which, however, is far from complete. The following list contains further obvious corrections. In addition to these, the quotations from Greek authors invariably contain mistakes, which are however not enumerated here ... No attempt has been made to indicate changes in the punctuation, since these are too numerous, the punctuation throughout being completely at random and frequently obscuring the sense."

[4] See Tillyard, in preceding note.

[5] See Edwin Rabbie, "Editing Neo-Latin Texts." *Editio* 10 (1996): 25-48.

tatis Novae. The recommendations of Edwin Rabbie[5] are followed in the main, with emphasis on modernizing and standardizing for the reader's convenience. This is done not simply for punctuation, but involves the division of paragraphs, the practice with uppercasing, and the regularizing of u/v and i/j.[6] Spellings of words correspond to those in *A Latin Dictionary*, ed. Charlton T. Lewis and Charles Short (Oxford, 1879 and often reprinted; abbreviated here to *LS*), to make it simpler for readers to find words there.[7] The justification and detail of these procedures can be seen in Hale, *BLN*, 30-33.

Two further points should be borne in mind: accentuation and paragraph-numbering. Neo-Latin authors, or their printers, tend to add accents. These if reproduced give a pleasant period flavouring to a text, and clarify some inflexions or functions.[8] Yet since they were never systematically included, they give a casual or cavalier impression which after all may *not* help the modern reader.

Where the modern reader does need help, indeed active guidance, is in the paragraphing. Milton's hypotactic periodic sentences roll forth, and on the 1674 pages no paragraphs whatsoever give the eye relief. I have added paragraphing throughout, much as Columbia did in printing and Tillyard in translating. The new paragraphs are, as Rabbie advocates, "based upon a careful analysis of . . . structure and contents." Furthermore, my paragraphs are numbered, so that the eye and mind can move swiftly from text to translation or in the other direction.

Milton's Salting: The Translation

The problems of translation in general and of this text in particular are discussed in Hale, *BLN*, 33-35 and 81 respectively. For the first part, the Oratio, I have set out to give a literal, therefore oratorically florid rendering, in order that the reader can work freely between the Latin and

---

[6] /u/ for vowel, /v/ for consonant, but /i/ for both vowel and palatal semi-vowel.

[7] *LS* is used in preference to dictionaries which though newer cover later Latin less well.

[8] E.g., respectively, circumflexed /a/ for ablative singular as distinct from unaccented nominative, and grave to distinguish indeclinable adverb from inflected adjective (mensâ: mensa, fortè : forte). See *BLN*, 33.

English. The paragraphing and its numbering will facilitate this. I have been less literal within the Prolusion wherever the Latin becomes excitable or punning is rife, and especially towards its close where the puns come thick and fast. It seemed better to communicate something of the stylistic register at these points. If that does communicate, the reader is made aware of the still more startling gear-change when the English verses, majestic or charming, supervene on this coarser or corybantic Latin. In any case, it seemed better to supply some pun, however feeble, since otherwise the reader might not know that the Latin was punning, and be distracted by an *unmeaning* feebleness.[9]

---

[9] If I offend, it is in good company, because the Tillyards do not flinch from providing some English pun. Slowly but surely, a tradition of translations solves these problems.

Oratio.

(113)

In Feriis æstivis Collegii, sed concurrente, ut solet, tota fere Academiæ juventute.

Oratio.

Exercitationes nonnunquam Ludicras Philosophi studiis non obesse.

Cum ex ea Urbe quæ caput urbium est, huc nuper me reciperem, Academici,

"In Feriis . . . juventute" is a general heading, for the first two (Latin) portions of the salting text. "[Delivered] during the summer Holidays of the College, but with the customary convergence of almost the entire youth of the University. Oration. That at times Playful exercises do not obstruct Philosophical studies. When, Members of the University, I recently returned from that City which is chief of cities, . . ." The uppercasings seem to single out chief thematic and occasional words. In any case an emphasis emerges from the sequence "Collegii . . . Academiae . . . Academici. . ." on the festive licence allowed to an august, ancient, Latin-speaking *communitas*.

In Feriis aestivis Collegii, sed concurrente (ut solet)
tota fere Academiae iuventute.[p. 113] [1]

ORATIO.

Exercitationes nonnunquam Ludicras
Philosophi[2] *studiis non obesse.*[3]

1. Cum ex ea urbe quae caput urbium est huc nuper me reciperem, Academici, deliciarum omnium quibus is locus supra modum affluit usque ad saginam prope dixerim satur,[4] sperabam mihi iterum aliquando otium illud litterarium quo ego vitae genere etiam caelestes animas gaudere opinor, eratque penitus in animo iam tandem abdere me in litteras et iucundissimae Philosophiae[5] perdius et pernox assidere; ita semper assolet laboris et voluptatis vicissitudo amovere satietatis taedium et efficere ut intermissa repetantur [p. 114] alacrius.[6] Cum his me incalentem studiis repente avocavit atque abstraxit pervetusti moris fere annua celebritas, iussusque ego sum eam operam quam acquiren-

---

[1] In the original printing (hereafter cited as *"1674"*) the first two portions of the salting script run from pages 113 to 134, and here its page-numbers are given in square brackets. *"1674 Errata"* cites its list of corrections on its page 135.

[2] Philosophi] Columbia *Philosophiae*, unnecessarily: Columbia misreads the *Errata*.

[3] The uppercasing of /L/ and /P/ is kept from *1674* in case it reflects authorial emphasis.

[4] *satur* goes with *deliciarum*, "full of all the delights," and *prope dixerim* with the whole hyperbole, "so to speak filled to bursting."

[5] Philosophiae *1674*. Uppercase initial might indicate personification. *Errata 1674* makes a muddle here, "correcting" *Philosophiae* to *Philosophiae* (sic) and miscounting the line-number.

[6] In the course of modernizing I have expunged many of the commas which in *1674* break up the ambitiously periodic opening sentence, and I have done so throughout. To verify the full misleading hesitancy of the printinghouse accidentals see Columbia's text (12: 204): in the opening sentence, for example, there are further commas after *est, omnium, dixerim, litterarium, litteras, taedium,* and *efficere*. The one after *omnium* illustrates how definitive and non-definitive relative clauses are persistently rendered indistinguishable by the profusion of commas. Though other commas do mark some pause in the syntax and speaking, so bringing us closer to the composer, many more have no such oral or performative value, and delay or bewilder the modern reader.

Delivered in the summer vacation of the College, but[1] with almost the whole Academy assembled, as is the custom.

(I) Oration:

"That on occasion sportive exercises do not jeopardise philosophical studies."

1. Members of the University: when I returned here recently from that city which is the topmost city,[2] I was so to speak crammed full of the pleasures with which it overflows, and was hoping to have once more a time of literary leisure, as the mode of life which I believe heavenly spirits rejoice in. Deep in my mind was the intent to bury myself in literature, and to devote myself day and night to sweetest Philosophy; for thus always the alternation of work with pleasure tends to banish the boredom of satiety, and to cause interrupted tasks to be resumed the more eagerly. I was kindling to my studies, when all of a sudden I received a summons! I was dragged away by this almost annual[3] observance of our most ancient custom![4] I was commanded to transfer all that zest which I had destined for acquiring

---

[1] Does "but" oppose "Feriis" to "concurrente" or "Collegii" to "Academiae"? Since the college would not be empty in the summer holidays in Milton's era but indeed the reverse, since a salting was not held till a whole year's intake of freshmen had dribbled in, I take the second option: Milton performed to a full hall, including students from the other colleges, along for the fun.

[2] Since "caput urbium" is a traditional epithet for Rome, Milton may be making an in-joke about London.

[3] Why "almost" annual? The qualification spoils the flow, but may be mentioning that saltings averaged less than one per annum because very liable to be cancelled when they got out of hand—perhaps a calming device, or apotropaic.

[4] The exclamations and broken-up vivacity seek to catch the exaggerations, mock-solemnity perhaps, of the Latin. Milton is not grumbling, but painting a picture of himself as the swot pitchforked into sociability. "Why me?" he asks, like a minor Isaiah.

dae sapientiae primo destinaram[7] ad nugas transferre et novas ineptias excogitandas—quasi iam nunc non essent omnia stultorum plena, quasi egregia illa et non minus Argo decantata navis stultifera fecisset[8] naufragium, plane denique ac si ipsi Democrito materia[9] iam ridendi deesset![10]

2. Verum date quaeso veniam, Auditores; hic enim hodiernus mos, utut ego liberius paulo sum locutus, sane quidem non est ineptus, sed impense potius laudabilis, quod quidem ego iam mihi proposui statim luculentius patefacere. Quod si Iunius Brutus, secundus ille rei Romanae conditor, magnus ille ultor regiae libidinis, animum prope dis[11] immortalibus parem et mirificam indolem simulatione vecordiae supprimere sustinuit, certe nihil est cur me pudeat aliquantisper μωροσοφῶς nugari, eius praesertim iussu cuius interest tanquam aedilis[12] hos quasi sollemnes ludos curare. Tum nec mediocriter me pellexit et invitavit ad has partes subeundas vestra (vos qui eiusdem estis mecum collegii)[13] in me nuperrime comperta facilitas; cum enim ante praeteritos

---

[7] destinaram] (destinâram *1674*,) The contracted form of the pluperfect tense, -aram for -averam is commonly preferred in Neo-Latin.

[8] fecisset] misread from *1674* by Columbia as *secisset*: long /s/ and small /f/ are often barely distinguishable, or indeed wrong, in *1674*, as two lines later when giving "si"'as "fi."

[9] Democritus was known as the "laughing" philosopher because he found so much folly in the world to laugh at (while Heraclitus the "weeping" one found so much to weep at). Folly so abounds that Milton can't see why *he* is being called upon to do the jokes; anyone could. The tone is sardonically self-deprecating.

[10] From the first *quasi* the construction is an appositional exclamation. The exclamation is triple: *quasi, quasi, denique ac si*.

[11] dis] Diis *1674*. *LS* thinks the double /ii/ in MSS is only to indicate long vowel. Uppercase /d/ seems not to indicate authorial emphasis either.

[12] Aediles at Rome "exhibited public spectacles," and furthermore "inspected the plays" before performance and "rewarded or punished the actors according to their deserts" (*LS*, s.v.). If all of this applies to Christ's salting, Milton is speaking of a Fellow. *Sollemnes ludos*, following, compares (*quasi*) the salting to Rome's "customary games": Columbia's "presumably solemn diversions" is off target, because they were "customary" but emphatically not "solemn."

[13] Another sign that a college salting audience would include people from other colleges.

knowledge to trifles, to the inventing of new forms of fooling—as if the world were not already filled with fools! as if that famous Ship of Fools (as much sung about as the Argonauts') had met with shipwreck! and as if there was a sudden shortage of matter for Democritus himself to laugh at.[5]

2. But I ask your pardon, listeners; for though I have spoken somewhat too freely about it, this custom we celebrate today is certainly not a foolish one. No, it is extremely commendable, as I intend to demonstrate forthwith.[6] Surely if Junius Brutus, that second founder of Rome, that great punisher of royal lust,[7] could endure to suppress his godlike mind and wondrous genius and pretend to be a simpleton, why should I feel shame to play the wise fool for a while—especially at the bidding of the person whose job it is, like the Roman aediles', to organize these customary shows? I was further allured[8] into undertaking this role[9] by your new-found friendliness towards me, you who are fellow-students of Christ's College. I say "new-found" because when some months ago

---

[5] Democritus "himself" because the least thing is enough to get him laughing: the "laughing philosopher" did not weep at human folly but laughed at it.

[6] The clause illustrates a difficulty facing the translator in much of the oration. The Latin is overemphatic and redundant: literally, "which indeed I now have decided at once to open up more clearly." Why both "now" and "at once"? Why not just "open it up," without the "more clearly"? Columbia works literally and gives equivalents for each phrase, with consequent hesitancy and overlap ("which fact indeed I have proposed to myself at this time to set forth at once more clearly"). Tillyard is brisk, "as I intend to make plain forthwith." The content being so self-evident here, I have followed Tillyard; but yet it would be misrepresenting the author and his Latin to opt for briskness every time.

[7] Royal lust: royal lust was not yet an issue in Stuart England, but there might be a dig at royalty here in a broader way.

[8] Literally, "I was to no small extent allured and invited. . ." See note 6 above.

[9] sc. as MC for the salting.

menses aliquam multos[14] oratorio apud vos munere perfuncturus essem, putaremque lucubrationes meas qualescunque etiam ingratas propemodum [p. 115] futuras, et mitiores habituras iudices Aeacum et Minoa quam e vobis fere quemlibet,[15] sane[16] praeter opinionem meam, praeter meam si quid erat speculae,[17] non vulgari (sicuti ego accepi, imo ipse sensi)[18] omnium plausu exceptae sunt, immo eorum qui in me alias propter studiorum dissidia essent prorsus infenso et inimico animo—generosum utique simultatis exercendae genus, et regio pectore non indignum, siquidem cum ipsa amicitia plerumque multa inculpate facta detorquere soleat: tunc profecto acris et infesta inimicitia errata forsitan multa, et haud pauca sine dubio indiserte dicta, leniter et clementius quam meum erat meritum interpretari non gravabatur.[19] Iam semel unico hoc exemplo vel ipsa demens ira mentis compos fuisse videbatur, et hoc facto furoris infamiam abluisse.

---

[14] aliquam multos [menses] = "a considerable number of months before" (*LS* 89); awkward phrasing, post-classical usage.

[15] He expected from his peers even less mercy than from the legendarily harsh underworld judges.

[16] *sane* helps to send the sentence into reverse: "in fact," his misgiving proved unfounded.

[17] *specula*, a slight hope (diminutive of *spes*).

[18] Round brackets are used as showing more clearly than paired commas can do the exact duration of a parenthesis. *1674* punctuates more confusingly than usual hereabouts: between *futuras* and *qui* it prints nine commas, and only commas.

[19] The enormous sentence (142 words) is not untypical of Cambridge orations. In fact, what with vocal inflection and gestures, it would be easier to follow through performance than in a silent reading. It is not split up here because it is all a single thought, though the translation does make this accommodation. The period is in fact winding its ponderous litotic way to a handsome apology by Milton, for his "many errors" and "clumsy words." Even though this paragraph and the next might be classified as merely the usual *captatio benevolentiae*, Milton makes this personal, for he alludes to a previous oration to this audience which went badly wrong. He seeks reconciliation, as in key with the ritual occasion.

I was to perform an academic oration in your presence I thought that my excogitations would get a cold reception from you, and in fact that Aeacus and Minos would judge me less harshly than would any one of you. And yet, against my expectation, against any slight hope I had, I perceived instead—no, I felt it—that my efforts were accepted with unusual applause from everyone; even including those who at other times showed me nothing but hostility and dislike because of disagreement with me about our studies. What a generous way of showing rivalry! A way not unworthy of a king's generosity, seeing that though even friendship is accustomed to misinterpret things done mainly without bad intent, on this occasion a keen hostility proved willing to interpret my many mistakes and infelicities in a gentle and lenient spirit, more than I deserved. For then, in this unparalleled instance, mad fury itself was seen to be sound of mind: by this action it had washed away the disgrace of madness.

3. At vero summopere oblector et mirum in modum voluptate perfundor cum videam tanta doctissimorum hominum frequentia circumfusum me et undique stipatum; et rursus tamen cum in me descendo et quasi flexis introrsum oculis meam tenuitatem[20] secretus intueor, equidem saepius mihimet soli conscius erubesco et repentina quaedam ingruens maestitia subsilientem deprimit et iugulat laetitiam. Sed nolite, Academici, sic me iacentem et consternatum et acie oculorum vestrorum tanquam de caelo tactum, nolite quaeso sic deserere; erigat me [p. 116] semianimum, quod potest, et refocillet vestri favoris aura: ita fiet ut vobis auctoribus[21] non admodum grave sit hoc malum; at remedium mali vobis exhibentibus, eo iucundius et acceptius; adeo ut mihi fuerit perquam gratum sic saepius exanimari, modo liceat a vobis recreari me[22] toties et refici. At O interim singularem in vobis vim atque eximiam virtutem, quae tanquam hasta illa Achillea, Vulcani munus, vulnerat et medicatur![23]

4. Ceterum nec miretur quispiam si ego tot eruditione insignes viros totumque pene Academiae florem huc confluxisse tanquam inter astra positus triumphem; vix etenim opinor plures olim Athenas adventasse ad audiendum duos oratores summos Demosthenem et Aeschinem de principatu eloquentiae certantes nec eam unquam felicitatem contigisse peroranti Hortensio nec tot tam egregie litteratos viros condecorasse orantem Ciceronem; adeo ut quamvis ego hoc opus minus feliciter absolvero, erit tamen mihi honori non aspernando in tanto concursu conventuque praestantissimorum hominum vel verba fecisse.

---

[20] Literally, "my insignificance"; modesty-formula for "me," cf. "this unworthy person."

[21] auctoribus] authoribus *1674*. The classical /ct/ is given as /th/ in most Neo-Latin, though *LS* strongly advocates the more etymological spelling (√augeo, au<u>ct</u>um). Here, besides the desire to follow *LS* as single guide rather than individual vagaries, the text directs readers straight to the entries in *LS*.

[22] recreari me] recrearime, undivided in Columbia, ambiguous in *1674*.

[23] medicatur!] *1674*, on this occasion punctuating helpfully.

3. To tell the truth, I am highly delighted, in fact overcome with pleasure, to see myself surrounded on every side by so large a throng[10] of the most learned! But then again, when I descend into myself and with my eyes turned inward look secretly at my own weak powers, I blush from consciousness of what I alone know about myself. A sudden irruption of sadness depresses and throttles my mounting joy. But do not, fellow-students of mine, O do not, I beg of you, desert me as I lie here dismayed, struck by the keen sight of your eyes as if struck by lightning! Let the soft breeze of your goodwill erect me, faint as I am, for I know it can; let it warm me back to life. So, thanks to you, my incapacitation will not prove serious; and its remedy, since it is you who apply it, will be all the more pleasant and acceptable—so much so, indeed, that to faint like this more often will be most agreeable to me, for the sake of being brought back to life each time by you.[11] But think, meanwhile, what matchless power you possess, what amazing virtue, that like Achilles' spear (gift of Vulcan) can both wound and heal!

4. Besides, let nobody marvel if I triumph, and feel raised to the stars, because so many outstanding talents have foregathered here—almost the whole flower of the University! Indeed, I think hardly any more flocked to Athens in the old days to hear the two supreme orators, Demosthenes and Aeschines, contending for the crown of oratory: no such felicity ever befell Hortensius pleading a case; nor did so large and extraordinary a throng of literati ever honour the orating Cicero.[12] So true is this that no matter how unsuccessfully I complete my task, it will still be no small honour to have spoken at such a huge concourse, this assemblage of outstanding beings!

---

[10] Another allusion to the crowded hall, even if "the most learned" is flattering or mocking.

[11] The final paired infinitives *recreari . . . refici* are the climax of a theme running through the sentence, about fainting (Milton's) and his revival (by the audience): *erigat me semianimum . . . refocillet . . . remedium . . .* and so to *exanimari*, last of the "death" series, thrust back with finality by the final twofold infinitives. The style, despite wordiness in the less important positions of a clause, has pronounced rhetorical shaping at the important places (starting, pausing, ending). This example uncovers one way in which the whole is held together, and would have been *heard*.

[12] The hyperboles cut both ways, putting speaker and audience on even better terms with each other.

5. Atque hercle non possum ego nunc quin mihi blandiuscule plaudam qui vel Orpheo vel Amphione multo sim meo iudicio fortunatior; hi enim chordulis suavi concentu assonantibus digitos tantum docte et perite admovebant, eratque in ipsis fidibus et in apto dextroque manuum motu aequalis utrinque [p. 117] pars dulcedinis; atqui ego si quid hodie laudis hinc reportavero, ea sane et tota erit et vere mea, tantoque nobilior quanto ingenii opus vincit ac praestat manuum artificium. Deinde hi saxa et feras silvasque ad se trahebant, et si quos homines, rudes illos et agrestes; at ego doctissimas mihi deditas aures et ab ore meo pendentes video. Novissime agrestes illi et ferae iam satis notam et compluriens exauditam sequebantur nervorum harmoniam; vos vero huc rapuit et iam detinet sola exspectatio.

6. Sed tamen, Academici, hic vos imprimis commonefactos volo me non haec gloriosius crepuisse; utinam enim mihi vel in praesentia concederetur melleum illud seu verius nectareum eloquentiae flumen quicquid unquam Attica vel Romana ingenia imbuebat olim, et quasi caelitus irrorabat, utinam mihi liceret omnem penitus Suadae medullam exsugere, et ipsius etiam Mercurii scrinia suffurari, omnesque elegantiarum loculos funditus exinanire, quo possim aliquid tanta exspectatione, tam praeclaro coetu, tam denique tersis et delicatis auribus dignum afferre.

5. Nor, by Hercules, can I help congratulating myself, somewhat flatteringly,[13] on having much better luck than Orpheus did, or Amphion; for they only applied their fingers with skill to strings sounding out a sweet harmony—an equal part of the sweetness lay in the instruments themselves as lay in their hands' apt and dexterous playing. But I, if I win any praise here today, will have it wholly and truly for my own, and the more gloriously so in proportion as the creation of the mind excels manual skill. Then further, Orpheus and Amphion attracted an audience merely of rocks and beasts and woods, and if there were humans too they were untutored rustics; but what *I* behold is the most learned of ears, engrossed in my words and hanging on my lips![14] Last of all, whereas those rustics and all those beasts were following a stringed music which they knew well and had often heard before, it is expectation alone which has hailed you along and now holds you fast.[15]

6. Be that as it may, my Fellow-Academicians, I want you to be very clear indeed at this point, that I have not been vaingloriously prating; for I wish that this once I might be granted a stream of honeyed eloquence, or better still a divine nectared[16] one, such as formerly steeped and bedewed the great intellects of Attica and Rome. Oh, would that I might suck out the whole innermost marrow of the goddess Persuasion; oh, might I pilfer the bookboxes of Mercury, and empty to the bottom all the caskets of elegancies; so that I could produce something worthy of such eager anticipation, such a distinguished assembly, so polished and discriminating an audience!

---

[13] *blandiuscule*, diminutive of the comparative adverb, may be a coinage: the effect is coy in context, which suits the cheeky comparison of his speaking with Orpheus' musicianship, to his own advantage. By offering precarious virtuosity not high seriousness, Milton is fulfilling his promise to entertain, and supporting his thesis that playing has its place in the life of study.

[14] The absurdity is more palpable and amusing now, as Milton turns Orpheus' magical achievement inside out: Milton outstrips Orpheus, who drew even rocks to listen to him, because he has a fitter audience.

[15] They do not know what Milton will be doing at the salting, but their expectations are high. Gossip, or leaks from rehearsals, would fill the role of advertising in this close-knit community.

[16] Honey is an emblem of sweetness, but nectar is the liquid sustenance of gods.

7. Ecce, Auditores, quo me raptat[24] et impellit vehementissimus ardor et prolubium placendi vobis, quippe de improviso me provectum sentio in ambitionem quandam, sed eam sane piam, et honestum (si hoc fieri potest) sacrilegium! Et certe existimo haudquaquam mihi opus esse [p. 118] Musarum auxilium implorare et exposcere; iis enim me circumsaeptum puto qui Musas omnes spirant et Gratias, totumque reor Helicona et quaecunque sunt alia Musarum delubra ad hunc diem celebrandum omnes suos effudisse alumnos, adeo ut credibile[25] sit iam nunc propter eorum absentiam lugere et deflorescere Parnassi lauros; unde profecto frustra erit Musas et Charites et Libentias[26] usquam terrarum quaeritare quam in hoc loco; quod si ita sit, necesse est protinus ipsam Barbariem, Errorem, Ignorantiam,[27] et omne illud Musis invisum genus quam celerrime aufugere ad aspectum vestrum[28] et sub diverso longe caelo abscondere sese; atque deinde quidem quid obstat quo minus quicquid est barbarae, incultae et obsoletae locutionis abigatur extemplo ab oratione mea, atque ego afflatu vestro et arcano instinctu disertus et politus subito evadam![29]

8. Utcunque tamen vos, Auditores, obtestor ne quem vestrum paeniteat meis paulisper vacasse nugis; ipsi enim di omnes, caelestis politiae cura ad tempus deposita,[30] depugnantium homunculorum spectaculo saepius interfuisse perhibentur;

---

[24] Echo of Horace, Odes 3. 25. 1-2 ("Quo me ... rapis?") Cf. end of paragraph 5.

[25] credibile] *1674* credible

[26] Libentias] *1674*, Libertias *Errata*. libentias

[27] Uppercased initials in *1674* represent personifications, opposed to *Musis*.

[28] "At" (not "to") the sight of you.

[29] The audience will help him to speak good Latin! A strained compliment, it does emphasize the importance in this culture of polished, urbane speech. Exclamation mark added, to emphasize the hyperbole.

[30] At last the speaker comes towards the announced thesis. Although the length of the preamble or wooing of the audience is not unusual for a Cambridge declamation or disputation-speech, it is more surprising to find it even at the student parody. Randolph as Praevaricator is brisker, and cracks jokes from the very first.

7. See then, my listeners, whither I am being hurried and driven, by the sheer vehemence of my desire to please you! All unexpectedly I feel myself swept along by ambition—but it is surely an honourable one, and (if such a thing can exist) a virtuous sacrilege.[17] Certainly I do not see any need to beg and beseech the help of the Muses, because I find myself surrounded by men who breathe with the breath of the Muses and Graces:[18] I reckon that Helicon and the other shrines of the Muses have poured forth all their nurslings to celebrate this day, so much so that one could believe their absence makes the laurels of Parnassus mourn and drop their flowers. It will be vain, accordingly, for the Muses and Graces and goddesses of Delight to seek them out,[19] anywhere on earth but here. If so, then at once Barbarism and Error, Ignorance and all that tribe which the Muses loathe, must flee away at the sight of you, to hide far away under a different sky. And then nothing can stop my oration become purged of every barbarous, inelegant or trite expression. By your inspiration and secret impelling, I might emerge all at once as a paragon of polished elegance.[20]

8. Howsoever that may be, my hearers, I solemnly entreat you not to repent of sparing some moments for my fooling; for all the gods of heaven themselves are said to have put aside for a time the cares of the commonwealth of heaven[21] and to have attended the spectacle of petty human wars.

---

[17] What exactly is the "sacrilege" in this overheated sentence: stealing from Persuasion or Mercury, the "ambition" of eloquence (just mentioned) or the conceit which follows, of not needing the Muses?

[18] spirant Muses et Gratias: they "breathe" or "are full of" these deities.

[19] quaeritare] As often, Milton likes the frequentative form of the verb, as denoting a more energetic activity than the root-form (in this instance, *quaerere*) .

[20] Notice the assumption that eloquence resides in word-choice, especially in the negative form of shedding whatever word-choices are to be deemed inelegant. This seemingly shallow view is frequent in the writers on oratory: it explains Milton's virtuoso display of vocabulary, throughout the Oratio and on into the Prolusio; for it is playing which it is his thesis to defend.

[21] Phyllis Tillyard's superb English phrase for *caelestis politiae cura* (89). What that was, who can say? Milton, however, imagines the gods having weighty portfolios and full engagement diaries, anthropomorphizing with an offhand exuberance of empathy.

aliquoties etiam humiles non dedignati casas[31] et paupere hospitio excepti fabas et holera narrantur esitasse.[32] Obsecro itidem ego vos atque oro, Auditores optimi, ut hoc meum quale quale[33] conviviolum ad subtile vestrum et sagax palatum faciat[34] [p. 119].

9. Verum etiamsi ego permultos noverim sciolos quibus usitatissimum est si quid ignorarunt id superbe et inscite apud alios contemnere, tanquam indignum cui operam impendant suam—quemadmodum hic dialecticam insulse vellicat quam nunquam assequi potuerit,[35] ille philosophiam nihili facit quia scilicet formosissima[36] dearum Natura[37] nunquam illum tali dignata est honore ut se nudam illi praebuerit intuendam—ego[38] tamen Festivitates et Sales,[39] in quibus quoque perexiguam agnosco facultatem meam, non gravabor ut potero laudare[40]; si prius hoc unum addidero, quod sane arduum videtur et minime proclive,

---

[31] casas] casus *1674*. The word looks like *casus* ("incidents," "state," "condition") altered by Masson to *casas* ("huts"). The latter is more exact and learned, for it brings into view such Ovidian myths of the gods deigning to visit lowly mortals as that of Philemon and Baucis. Phyllis Tillyard (139) comments, "There is no absolute need to change the text," but then in *YPW* 1: 271 she opines that Masson was probably right, as "chances" do not make good sense with "humble." (In the copy used here someone has given the /u/ a cross-piece to make it /a/.)

[32] Eating *holera* may recall Proverbs 15:12 as well as the obvious classical myth of Philemon and Baucis.

[33] deprecatory, like "so so" in English (so Columbia also, *ColWks* 12: 215).

[34] faciat + ad: "be good for," *LS* s.v. *facio*, II.D.

[35] potuerit] *1674* potuit *1674 Errata* "leg. *potuerit.*"

[36] formosissima] *1674* formossima

[37] *Natura* is personified, not dialectic and philosophy preceding: though all three receive uppercase initials in *1674* it is Nature alone who reveals herself naked, to the philosopher.

[38] —ego] : Ego *1674*, strong pause and uppercasing to indicate that the long opening concessive ("etiamsi . . .") is now ended, and the countervailing main clause has been reached. The heavier punctuation and initial capital /E/ steer the reader through, though I have instead used em-dashes to distinguish the latter half of the concessive.

[39] Sales] = "wit," comes later in the paragraph without its uppercase /S/. Does the uppercasing of "Festivitates" and "Sales" signify emphasis or personification, because either would be appropriate to the crescendo of this paragraph (see next note)? The uppercasing may, however, be merely erratic, like other accidentals in *1674*. In any case, note the first of a stream of "salt"-references, at once repeated. This pun was *de rigueur* in any salting, apparently the more times the better. Nearby, in sound and sense and positioning, we have "insulse," "unsaltedly" = insipidly / tastelessly.

[40] *ut potero* goes with *laudare*, not with *non gravabor.*

Sometimes, too, the record tells us, they did not disdain humble dwellings, but accepted to be guests of the poor, eating their fill of beans and herbs.[22] So I beg and beseech you, most noble listeners, accept my own little feast which I offer to your superacutest of palates.[23]

9. But though I know many sciolists whose ignorant, arrogant habit is to belittle in other people whatever they themselves know nothing of, as if it must not be worth spending time on — as for instance one fellow carps witlessly against dialectic, which he could never grasp, or another rates philosophy as worthless because the most beautiful of goddesses, Dame Nature, has never so honoured him as to show herself naked to his eyes;[24]—despite all of this, I shall not make a burden of praising festivity and wit as well as I am able, despite recognising my limited powers in this regard. But I do first add that today my task is an arduous,

---

[22] As in the story of Philemon and Baucis. The pagan gods are seen most attractively here, first as above human pettiness and cruelty, then as sharing in the life of the lowest of the low. Milton's imagination is now engaged, in support of his preceding fluency, and both in support of his thesis.

[23] Clever how he swoops without warning back from the gods' geniality and their leisure amusements, to special pleading.

[24] Tillyard's phrasing again cannot be bettered (89).

me iocos hodie serio laudaturum.⁴¹ ⁴² Atque id non immerito quidem; quid enim est quod citius conciliet diutiusque retineat amicitias, quam amoenum et festivum ingenium? Et profecto cui desunt sales et lepores et politulae facetiae, haud temere invenietis cui sit gratus et acceptus.

10. Nobis autem, Academici, si quotidiani moris esset indormire et quasi immori philosophiae et inter dumos et spinas logicae consenescere citra ullam †enim†⁴³ relaxationem, et nunquam concesso respirandi loco, quid quaeso aliud esset philosophari quam in Trophonii antro vaticinari et Catonis plus nimio rigidi sectam sectari?—immo dicerent vel ipsi rusticani sinapi nos victitare!

11. Adde quod, quemadmodum qui luctae et campestri ludo [p. 120] assuescunt se multo ceteris valentiores redduntur et ad omne opus paratiores, ita pariter usu venit⁴⁴ ut per hanc ingenii palaestram corroboretur nervus animi et quasi melior sanguis et sucus comparetur, utque ipsa indoles limatior fiat acutiorque, et ad omnia sequax et versatilis. Quod si quis urbanus et lepidus haberi nolit, ne sit⁴⁵ hoc illi stomacho si paganus et subrusticus appelletur; et probe novimus illiberale quoddam genus hominum qui cum ipsi prorsus insulsi sint et infestivi,⁴⁶ suam tacite secum aestimantes vilitatem et inscitiam, quicquid forte urbanius dictitatum audiunt id statim in se dici putant; digni sane quibus id vere eveniat quod iniuria suspicantur, ut scilicet omnium dicteriis everberentur, paene usquedum suspendium cogitent. Sed non valent istae hominum quisquiliae urbanitatis elegantulae licentiam inhibere.

---

⁴¹ This is the heart of the Erasmic intention, to "praise foolery seriously." Having done this to his own satisfaction in the present Oratio, the first of the three extant portions of the salting text, Milton offers the Prolusio or second portion as his best effort at foolery itself, his actual festive wit.

⁴² Paragraph begins here in Tillyard (89); not in Columbia.

⁴³ enim] superfluous and disruptive to sense; misreading for some word / suffix meaning "whatsoever"?

⁴⁴ usu venit] *1674* usu-venit

⁴⁵ sit] *1674* sis Corrected by Tillyard, uncorrected in Columbia.

⁴⁶ The third pairing of wit (salt) and holiday-making, this time in the negative.

uphill one: I am to praise jocularity seriously. Such praising is merited too! What can make friendships more quickly or keep them longer than an agreeable, merry disposition? And likewise those who lack wit and humour and elegant pleasantries will scarcely be accepted as good company by anyone.

10. Take our own case, my fellow-students: if it were our daily custom to go to sleep and (so to say) die in philosophy, to grow grey among the thorns and brambles of logic without any relaxation or breathing-space being allowed us, how would the philosophizing life be anything more than a prophesying in the cave of Trophonius, and following the over-rigid sect of Cato?[25] Even yokels would say we were on a diet of mustard![26]

11. What is more, just as people who accustom themselves to wrestling and athletics become far stronger than others, and ready for any emergency, so equally it happens that by this "witwrestling" the muscles of the mind are made stronger; better blood and energy are gained, and the intellect becomes sharper and finer, flexible and versatile for every situation. But if someone does not want to be thought cultured and witty, he must not get annoyed when he is called clownish and a boor. We all know the sort who being incapable of wit and jollity secretly prize their own cheap ignorance; so whatever witty remarks are made in their hearing they imagine to be directed against them. It would serve them right if what they suspect without reason were to happen to them indeed, and they were to become the butt of everyone's wit, till they almost contemplate suicide. But these dregs of humanity have not the power to prevent the free play of well-mannered wit.[27]

---

[25] The first reductive equivalence is to prophesy obscurely in a far-off cave of Boeotia, referring to Stoicism (though in addition Boeotians were a byword for stupidity.) The second may mean "going to extremes," or perhaps losing the wood behind the trees, if it does not merely make the same point as the final quip about mustard — one-track-mindedness is a bad thing, variety is the spice of life. The successive metaphors seem better taken to mean different things than all the same one, in that difference would better support the praise of variety within life, levity leavening gravity. *Victitare* = to subsist on any thing is yet another frequentative verb.

[26] "Even yokels" etc.: even dimwits could see our one-eyed foolishness.

[27] Milton waxes quite fierce here, as he aligns himself with the wits (like some character in a Restoration comedy!). But he is setting up a war, between wit or good sense and the unhealthy opposite extreme.

12. Vultis itaque me, Auditores, rationis fundamento fidem exemplorum superstruere? Ea utique mihi abunde suppetunt. Primus omnium occurrit Homerus, ille oriens et Lucifer cultioris litteraturae, cum quo omnis eruditio tanquam gemella nata est; ille enim interdum a deorum consiliis et rebus in caelo gestis divinum revocans animum et ad facetias divertens, murium et ranarum pugnam lepidissime descripsit. Quinetiam Socrates, teste Pythio, sapientissimus ille mortalium, iurgiosam uxoris morositatem [p. 121] saepenumero quam urbane[47] perstrinxisse fertur. Omnia deinde veterum philosophorum diverbia sale sparsa[48] et lepore venusto passim legimus referta; et certe hoc unum erat quod antiquos omnes comoediarum et epigrammatum scriptores, et Graecanicos et Latinos, aeternitate nominis donavit. Quin immo accepimus Ciceronis iocos et facetias tres libros a Tirone conscriptos implevisse. Et cuique iam in manibus est ingeniosissimum illud Moriae Encomium, non infimi scriptoris opus, multaeque aliae clarissimorum huius memoriae oratorum de rebus ridiculis exstant haud infacetae prolusiones.[49]

13. Vultis summos imperatores et reges et fortes viros? Accipite Periclem Epaminondam Agesilaum et Philippum Macedonem, quos (ut Gelliano more loquar) festivitatum[50] et salse dictorum scatuisse memorant historici; ad hos Gaium Laelium Pub. Cor. Scipionem Gneum Pompeium C. Iulium et Octavium Caesares, quos in hoc genere omnibus praestitisse coaetaneis auctor est M. Tullius.

14. Vultis adhuc maiora nomina? Ipsum etiam Iovem reliquosque caelites inter epulas et pocula[51] iucunditati se dantes inducunt poetae, sagacissimi veritatis adumbratores.[52]

---

[47] quam urbane] should this read *quam urbanissime*? It is a choice between "How wittily he bridled her" and "he bridled her in the wittiest way possible." If *1674* is to be kept, add "!" after *fertur*.

[48] sale sparsa] "*besprinkled* with salt / wit" keeps the root meaning "salt" in view, as does the singular of the noun.

[49] The word reminds readers that we are in "Prolusio" VI of *1674*, but originally hinted that the present Oratio would lead to the salting *prolusio*; as "playfight," or "game-playing before" the scripted pageant.

[50] festivitatum] *1674* festivivitatum

[51] inter epulas et pocula] found in the Vulgate of Judges 9:27, oddly.

[52] New paragraph as at Columbia translation (12: 221.20); not in Tillyard.

12. And so, my hearers, do you want me to build a superstructure of convincing examples upon this foundation of reason? Examples indeed come to my mind in abundance. First of all appears Homer, the rising sun and morning star of good literature, he with whom all learning was born as a twin sister.[28] He, from time to time recalling his divine mind from the counsels of the gods and the deeds done in heaven, would turn aside to drolleries, and so most wittily he described the battle of the frogs and mice. How wittily, moreover, Socrates, declared wisest of all mortals by the Delphic oracle, no less, is said to have blunted the nagging shrewishness of his wife![29] And then all the dialogues of the old philosophers were sprinkled with wit, and everywhere crammed with charming humour. Certainly this was the one thing which gave an eternal fame to all the comedians and epigrammatists of antiquity, both Greek and Roman. We are told, furthermore, that Cicero's jokes and witticisms filled three books, collected by Tiro. And everyone now has in their hands that most talented *Praise of Folly*, work of a first-rate writer; and many other memoirs survive of this kind, on comic subjects by outstanding orators; very witty prolusions they are.[30]

13. Or do you want me to name great generals, kings and heroes? Take Pericles and Epaminondas, Agesilaus and Philip of Macedon: they were all (to speak in the manner of Aulus Gellius) brim-full of wit and humour, according to the historians. Take also Caius Laelius, Publius Cornelius Scipio, Gnaeus Pompeius; take the two Caesars, Julius and Octavius: we have it on Cicero's authority that all these excelled their contemporaries for wit.

14. Do you want even bigger names? Jupiter himself and the other heaven-dwellers are represented by the poets, who are our wisest witnesses, as giving themselves fully to mirth amidst their feasting and carousing.

---

[28] Homer indeed stands as the fountainhead of western literature. One of the poems ascribed to him was the *Batrachomyomachia* (Frogs-and-mice-battling), humorously polysyllabic name for the warring of puny combatants. Wisdom was born with Homer for the Greeks, to whom his epics were foundation-myths and sources of revealed religion or cult.

[29] I suspect the text here. The Latin words as printed do not mean what Columbia or Tillyard give as their English. A word or phrase is needed which says *how* Socrates blunted Xanthippe's nagging: "quam urbane" as an exclamation is not well placed in the sentence to have the meaning and emphasis needed.

[30] But the list and the sentence sputter out after the mention of Erasmus.

15. Vestra[53] demum, Academici, utar tutela et patrocinio,[54] quod mihi erit omnium ad instar, quippe quam non displiceant vobis sales et ioculi: indicat satis tantus hodie vestrum factus concursus, et [p. 122] hoc sane unumquodque caput mihi annuere videtur; nec mirum est mehercle festam hanc et mundulam urbanitatem omnes probos simulque claros viros sic oblectare, cum et ipsa inter splendidos virtutum Aristotelicarum ordines sublimis sedeat[55] et velut in Pantheo[56] quodam Diva cum Divis Sororibus colluceat.[57]

16. Sed forte non desunt quidam barbati Magistri[58] taetrici oppido et difficiles qui se magnos Catones, nedum Catunculos[59] putantes, vultu ad severitatem Stoicam composito, obstipo nutantes capite, anxie querantur "omnia nunc dierum commisceri et in deterius perverti, et loco Priorum Aristotelis ab initiatis recens baccalaureis[60] exponendorum scommata et inanes nugas inverecunde et intempestive iactari; hodiernum quoque exercitium, a maioribus nostris sine dubio recte et fideliter institutum ob insignem aliquem sive in rhetorica sive in philosophia fructum inde percipiendum, nunc nuper in insipidos sales[61] perperam immutari."

---

[53] Milton is deploying authorities grouped by anaphora, then alliteration: *Vultis, Vultis*, and now lastly *Vestra demum*. His address to his audience is becoming more animated.

[54] The fellow-students are Milton's "guardians and patrons" as he tries to be witty, in so far as they enjoy "sales & joculi," wit and jokes, or perhaps (hendiadys) witty jokes or merry wit. Yet again, Milton appeals for sympathy as he leads the revels by invoking the eponymous spirit of salt wit.

[55] *YPW* cites the moral and intellectual virtues (1: 275), without however coming near one relevant here. What about *eutrapelia* ="lively wit" (*Rhetoric*, 1389b11, *Nicomachean Ethics*, 1108a24)?

[56] Pantheo] *1674* (and Columbia) Panthaeo, incorrectly (the Greek is Panth<u>ei</u>on).

[57] Uppercasing kept as it may suit the humorously florid clausula.

[58] Magistri] uppercase kept, to signify or insinuate University "Masters," MAs.

[59] There may be a pun here on *catulus*, a puppy.

[60] Notice the language of ritual here.

[61] i.e., the salt has lost its savour; but a battle is going on concerning the true denotation of wit.

15. Lastly, my fellow-students, I shall employ your own tutelage and patronage, which will be my pattern for everything! For it is proof enough that wit and jollification do please you, that you are here in such a crowd today. Yes, I see every head nodding agreement. Nor, by Hercules, need we be amazed that this festive and cultured urbanity delights all worthy and outstanding people: it has a place of high honour in the splendid ranks of Aristotle's virtues; as though in some Pantheon, Urbanity shines out in her splendour, among the goddesses her sisters.[31]

16. Yet possibly there may be some bearded Masters;[32] crabbed and curmudgeonly, who esteem themselves great Catos (but are not even petty Cato-kins). *They* can arrange their faces into a Stoic severity; they can shake their perverse heads. They can complain querulously how "everything these days is mixed up and going to the dogs. To think that, instead of recent BAs expounding Aristotle's Priorums,[33] taunts and silly jokes are being bandied about — shamelessly, tastelessly! To think that this feastday's exercising, which without a doubt was rightly set up by our forefathers for the end of gathering preeminent fruits, be they of rhetoric or philosophy, has now of late been distorted into feeble witticisms!"

---

[31] Like earlier translations this one has to move amongst virtual synonyms like "humour," "wit," "pleasantry," and still occasionally runs out of worthwhile alternatives. Urbanity, however, *urbanitas*, remains a fundamental criterion; being "of the *urbs* or city," it embraces wit and culture and all civilised exchange through Latin. "Urbane Milton" was the apt title for the *Milton Studies* volume devoted to Milton's entire Latin poetry. Milton's clausula here attempts a theophany of urbanity, Aristotle assisting.

[32] At an undergraduates' (Bachelors') festival there are not likely to be many Masters present; that they are older is emphasized by their beards, *Barbati*.

[33] priorums: oral examination on Aristotle's "Prior" Analytics (Costello, *Scholastic Curriculum*, 34).

17. At vero his quod respondeatur ad manum mihi est et in procinctu; sciant enim illi, si nesciant, litteras cum leges reipublicae nostrae litterariae primum essent latae ab exteris regionibus vix has in oras fuisse advectas: idcirco cum Graecae et Latinae linguae peritia impendio rara esset et insolens, expediebat eo acriori studio et magis assiduis exercitationibus ad eas eniti et aspirare; nos autem quandoquidem [p. 123] superioribus nostris peius sumus morati, melius eruditi, oportebit relictis quae haud multam habent difficultatem ad ea studia accedere ad quae et illi contulissent se si per otium licuisset; nec vos praeteriit primos quosque legum latores duriora paulo scita, et severiora quam ut ferri possint, semper edere solere, ut deflectentes et paululum relapsi homines in ipsum rectum incidant. Denique mutata nunc omnino rerum facie necesse est multas leges multasque consuetudines si non antiquari et obsolescere, coangustari saltem nec per omnia servari.[62] "Verum[63] si leves istiusmodi nugae palam defensitatae fuerint et approbatae publicamque demeruerint laudem"—sic enim arduis superciliis solent dicere—"nemo non averso ab sana et solida eruditione animo eum ad ludicra statim et histrionalem prope levitatem adiunget, adeo ut ipsa philosophorum spatia pro doctis et cordatis nugatores emissura sint vel mimis[64] et scurris proterviores."

18. At vero ego existimo eum qui iocis insubidis sic solet capi ut prae iis seria et magis utilia plane negligat, eum inquam nec in hac parte nec in illa posse admodum proficere: non quidem in seriis, quia si fuisset ad res serias tractandas natura comparatus factusque, credo non tam facile pateretur se ab iis abduci; nec in nugatoriis, quia vix queat ullus belle et lepide[65] iocari nisi et serio agere prius addidicerit.[66] [p. 124]

---

[62] This may be a precarious or forensic line to take. But it is also a developmental one, and uses humour to measure a culture's maturity, a strong and sensible line to take. Milton has earlier adverted to the fact that saltings were a sanctioned *dies fastus*, instituted by the founding fathers in their wisdom.

[63] The objecting "Magistri" add a further consideration, from "Verum" to "proterviores," as indicated in the text by speech-marks.

[64] mimis] Tillyard's reading makes better sense than *1674*'s nimis: "worse than mimers and buffoons." ("nimis" is needless with the comparative following.)

[65] lepide] *1674* lep-de

[66] A subtle, serious line of reasoning now.

17. But I have the answer to these people ready to my hand. Let them know, if they do not already know, that when the laws of our commonwealth of letters[34] were first laid down, learning had barely arrived in the islands from overseas. For that reason, because the mastery of Greek and Latin was extremely rare and unusual, it was needful to strive and strain after them with keener desire and more continuous exertion. But we, since we have more learning yet worse manners than our predecessors, ought to relinquish those studies which pose small difficulty, and to pass forward to those which they *would* have tackled if they had had the leisure.[35] Nor has it escaped your notice that all the earliest lawgivers made decrees harsher and more severe than could be borne, so that as people swerved and lapsed from them they might thus fall upon the right mean.[36] Finally, now conditions are totally different many laws and customs must be allowed, if not to decay and become obsolete, at least to become limited and not heeded at every single point. "But," say the same objectors with eyebrows raised high, "If such frivolous triflings are to be openly defended and approved, and if they have won public praise, then every student will turn away from sound and solid learning and attach himself instead to shows and histrionic superficiality; and so the very walkways of philosophers[37] would send out triflers, more shameless than actors and buffoons, not the learned and judicious alumni who are needed."

18. But in my own view, anyone who is so captivated by stupid jokes that he neglects in their favour the serious and more useful things of life, he, I say, is making good use of *neither* sphere—certainly not in serious matters, because if he were naturally adapted to handling them I am sure he would not let himself be so easily led aside from them; and not in lighter matters either, because few can jest well and wittily unless first they have learnt how to behave seriously.

---

[34] Noting that Respub. and Litterariae are both given uppercase initial letters, that England is not usually named as "Respublica Nostra," and that Milton does elsewhere invent a republic of fools (res summa stultorum), I side with Tillyard against Columbia, to take the four words as "the laws of our commonwealth of letters" not "the literary laws of our commonwealth."

[35] A curious, serious line of answer; not a scoffing rebuttal, but a platonic mythos of change in our island society.

[36] Not such a strange idea if we think of "aiming off" a target to allow for wind or distance; so I have kept "incidant" literal, to "fall upon" the mean.

[37] 'spatia' may glance at the walking or peripatetic philosophers, named after Aristotle who liked to walk about (*peripatein* in Greek) when lecturing.

19. Sed vereor, Academici, ne longius aequo deduxerim orationis filum; nolo excusare quod potui, ne inter excusandum ingravescat culpa. Iam oratoriis soluti legibus prosiliemus in comicam licentiam. In qua si forte morem meum, si rigidas verecundiae leges transversum (quod aiunt) digitum egressus fuero, sciatis, Academici, me in vestram gratiam exuisse antiquum meum et parumper deposuisse: aut si quid solute, si quid luxurianter dictum erit, id quidem non mentem et indolem meam sed temporis rationem et loci genium[67] mihi suggessisse[68] putetis. Itaque quod simile solent exuentes implorare comoedi, id ego inceptans flagito: "Plaudite, et ridete."

The sentence closes the first portion of the salting. He compares his following Prolusio to a comedy, by beginning with the plea of comic actors (Comoedi), that the audience clap and laugh (Plaudite, & ridete.).

---

[67] An interesting collocation, of the system or procedure of the salting occasion with the *genius loci*, spirit of place, where the "place" is not geographical but social or communal ("liminal space"). Time and place together sanction.

[68] suggessisse] *1674 suggesisse*

19. But I fear, O members of the University, I fear I have spun out my thread too long. I will not excuse myself for this as I might, lest the length of my excusing compound my offence. No! In a moment, freed from the laws of oratory[38] we shall leap forward into comic licence. If in doing so I go beyond my usual way and exceed the strict laws of modesty, even by a finger's breadth as the saying goes, then be it known to you, my fellow students, that I strip off and for a while lay aside my usual habit for the sake of pleasing *you*. If anything loose or licentious is said, you are to suppose it is not my mind and nature but the rules governing the time and the spirit of place prompting it. So then: what the comic actors entreat when they end their performance, I demand as mine begins—APPLAUD, and LAUGH!

---

[38] He signals the generic transition as it occurs, from the laws of Oratio to the licence of Comedy.

Prolusio. [p. 125]

> (125)
>
> ## Prolusio.
>
> Laboranti, ut videtur, & pene corruenti stultorum re summâ, equidem nescio quo merito meo Dictator sum creatus. At quor-

This 'Prolusio' is the second portion of the whole salting text. Its title signifies something more playful (-*lusio*) than the Oratio preceding it. It says, "The ship of state must be sinking, for *me* to be made its emergency ruler," and goes on to ask how he qualified for the job.

Prolusio.

1. Laboranti, ut videtur, et paene corruenti stultorum rei summae,[1] equidem nescio quo merito meo Dictator sum creatus. At quorsum ego? cum dux ille et antesignanus omnium sophistarum et sedulo ambiverit hoc munus et fortissime potuerit[2] administrare; ille enim induratus miles ad quinquaginta pridem sophistas sudibus breviculis armatos per agros Barnwellianos[3] strenue duxit, et obsessurus oppidum[4] satis militariter aquaeductum disiecit, ut per sitim posset oppidanos ad deditionem cogere; at vero abiisse nuper hominem valde doleo, siquidem eius discessu nos omnes sophistas non solum ἀκεφάλους reliquit, sed et de collatos.

2. Et iam fingite, Auditores, quamvis non sint Aprilis Calendae, festa adesse Hilaria (Matri Deum dicata) vel deo Risui rem divinam fieri. Ridete itaque et petulanti splene sustollite cachinnum, exporrigite frontem, et uncis indulgete naribus, sed naso adunco ne suspendite; profusissimo risu circumsonent omnia, et solutior cachinnus hilares excutiat lacrimas, ut iis risu exhaustis [p. 126] ne guttulam quidem habeat Dolor qua triumphum exornet suum.

---

[1] rei summae] *1674* re summâ *Errata* p. 119. *l.* 2 leg. *rei summa*e probably refers to this crux on p. 125. Has the corrector missed out some other correction, which truly was on p. 119?

[2] potuerit] *1674* potuit *Errata* potuerit

[3] *Barnwellianos*] *1674* Barwellianos. Bar<u>n</u>well is the name of the suburb or then separate township on the Newmarket side of Cambridge.

[4] oppidum] *1674* opipdum

Prolusio.

1. The republic of fools[1] is in crisis, it seems, and almost collapsing; and I have been made its emergency leader to save it—though goodness knows how I earned the distinction. Why me? Why indeed, when that famous leader and commander of the Sophisters[2] has been eagerly touting for the job, and would have carried out its duties bravely! After all, it's not long since this hardened warrior resolutely led a force of up to fifty Sophisters, armed with short staves, across Barnwell Field.[3] He was all set to besiege the town in best military fashion, and wrecked their aqueduct, in order to force the townsfolk to surrender from thirst.[4] I feel utmost grief at the man's recent departure from Cambridge: it leaves us, one and all, not only unheaded but beheaded.[5]

2. And now, my listeners, though this is not April Fools' Day, pretend we are at the feast of the Hilaria, honouring the mother of the gods; or some holy rite is being rendered to the god Laughter![6] So laugh, and raise a guffaw from your saucy spleen, smooth out your furrowed brow; let your nose curve with laughing, but don't turn it up in disdain.[7] Let the whole place re-echo laughter; let mirth make us laugh till we cry, so that our tears are used up in laughing and Grief has not even a droplet to grace its triumph.

---

[1] The phrase at once links the proceedings with traditions of licenced, seasonal fooling.
[2] Students in final year of B. A.
[3] One of two pieces of common arable land in Cambridge.
[4] i.e., some piece of organized student vandalism, or Gown against Town.
[5] One of many puns: *akephalous* = leaderless, *decollatos* = decapitated (with a glance at *capitis minutio*, loss of civil rights).
[6] Milton places his performance in a context of the festive tradition, naming one English and two Roman exemplars.
[7] Translation based on the Tillyards' (94). The speaker exaggeratedly mimes the facial expressions he wants or is banning.

3. Ego profecto si quem nimis parce diducto rictu ridentem conspexero, dicam eum scabros et cariosos dentes rubigine obductos aut indecoro ordine prominentes abscondere, aut inter prandendum hodie sic opplevisse abdomen ut non audeat ilia ulterius distendere ad risum, ne praecinenti ori succinat, et aenigmata quaedam nolens effutiat sua non Sphinx sed Sphincter anus, quae medicis interpretanda non Oedipo relinquo; nolim enim hilari vocis sono obstrepat in hoc coetu posticus gemitus: solvant ista medici qui alvum solvunt. Si quis strenuum et clarum non ediderit murmur eum ego asseverabo tam gravem et mortiferum faucibus exhalare spiritum, ut vel Aetna vel Avernus nihil spiret taetrius; aut certe allium aut porrum comedisse dudum, adeo ut non audeat aperire os, ne vicinos quosque foetido halitu enecet.

4. At vero absit porro ab hoc coetu horrendus et tartareus ille sibili sonus, nam si hic audiatur hodie, credam ego Furias et Eumenides[5] inter vos occulte latitare, et angues suos colubrosque pectoribus vestris immisisse,[6] et proinde Athamantaeos Furores vobis inspiravisse.

5. At enimvero, Academici, vestram ego in me benevolentiam demiror atque exosculor, qui me audituri per flammas et ignes irrupistis in hunc locum. Hinc enim in ipso limine scin-[p. 127] tillans ille noster Cerberus astat, et fumido latratu horribilis, flammeoque coruscans baculo favillas pleno ore egerit; illinc ardens et voracissimus Fornax noster luridos eructat ignes, et tortuosos fumi globos[7] evolvit, adeo ut non sit difficilius iter ad inferos vel invito Plutone; et certe nec ipse Iason maiori[8] cum periculo boves illos Martis πυριπνέοντας aggressus est.

---

[5] Eumenides] *1674* Euminides
[6] immisisse] *1674* immississe
[7] fumi globos] *1674* fumiglobos
[8] majori] *1674* minori Tillyard (140) corrected *minori* to *maiori* as more logical *qua* emphasizing the danger to students approaching "Fornax." Maximizing their danger is the point, not minimizing Jason's.

3. As for me, if I catch sight of anyone laughing only half-heartedly, I shall say it's because he is trying to hide his teeth, which are rotten and scabby and covered with disgusting gunk,[8] or sticking out in all directions; or else he is afraid to stretch his belly any further in laughing because he has stuffed it so full at the feast already that he might give us a duet from two orifices! He might express some gastric riddles to us, not from his Sphinx but from his sphincter; his Posterior Anal-ytics. Such riddles I leave for the medical people to interpret, not Oedipus: I don't want any groaning posteriors to obstruct the sound of merry voices here. Let the medics give the enigma an enema.[9] If anybody fails to laugh good and loud, I shall swear his breath must be so offensive and lethal that Mount Etna or Avernus could not send out fouler fumes; or at any rate swear he has eaten onions or leeks recently, so that he daren't open his mouth for fear of killing his neighbours with his stinking breath.

4. Next, there must be absent from this assembly that dreadful, hellish sound of hissing. If it were to be heard here today,[10] I would think that the Furies and Eumenides were hiding amongst you, letting loose their snakes and serpents into your hearts; and that the madness of Athamas had got into you.

5. To be sure, fellow Academicians, I feel wonder and awe at your goodwill towards me, for you have forced your way through flames and fires into this place to hear me speak. On one side, at the very threshold stands our spark-flashing Cerberus:[11] he barks out smoke to frighten us, he brandishes his flaming staff, he sends out sparks from his full mouth. On the other side, our burning voracious Furnace is belching out lurid flames; he pours out twisting globes of smoke, so that it would be as easy to penetrate hell as to get past him! The hero Jason, for sure, underwent no greater danger when he tackled those fire-breathing oxen of Mars.

---

[8] The sequence of unpleasant epithets shows he *intends* to be revolting.

[9] Let doctors who know how to loosen (*solvere*) blocked bowels "loosen" the riddle too.

[10] *audiatur*, subjunctive: he hopes his performance will *not* be hissed.

[11] A string of personal references or puns on college names follows, be they servants or undergraduates. Thus "Cerberus" could mean the gate-keeper (porter) "Sparks" (Tillyards, 140), while "Furnace" (Fornax) could be the very recent freshman Furnice, admitted on 29 May 1628. Or there may be jokes against heavy smokers.

6. Iamque, Auditores, credite vos in caelum receptos, posteaquam evasistis purgatorium,[9] et nescio quo novo miraculo ex fornace calida salvi prodiistis, neque sane mihi in mentem venit ullius herois cuius fortitudinem commode possim vestrae aequiparare, neque enim Bellerophontes ille ignivomam Chimaeram animosius debellavit, nec validissimi illi regis Arthuri pugiles, igniti et[10] flammigantis castelli incantamenta vicerunt facilius, et dissiparunt; atque hinc subit ut puros mihi auditores et lectissimos pollicear, si quid enim faecis huc advenerit post explorationem camini, ego statim dixero ignes nostros ianitores esse fatuos.

7. At felices nos et incolumes perpetuo futuros! Romae enim ad diuturnitatem imperii sempiternos ignes sollicite et religiose servabant, nos vigilibus et vivis ignibus custodimur—Quid dixi "vivis et vigilibus"? Id sane improviso lapsu praetervolavit, quippe nunc melius commemini, eos primo crepusculo exstinguere sese, et non nisi claro sudo sese re-[p. 128] suscitare. Attamen spes est tandem iterum domum nostram posse inclarescere, cum nemo infitias iverit duo maxima Academiae luminaria nostro collegio praesidere; quamvis illi nusquam maiori forent in honore quam Romae, ibi enim vel Virgines Vestales inexstinctos eos et insomnes totas noctes servarent (vel forte ordini Seraphico initiarentur flammei fratres). In hos denique optime quadrat hemistichion illud Virgilianum, "Igneus est ollis vigor": immo paene inductus sum ut credam Horatium horum nostrorum ignium mentionem fecisse; maior enim horum, dum stat inter coniugem et liberos, "micat inter omnes . . . velut inter ignes luna minores." Non possum autem praeterire foedum Ovidii errorem, qui sic cecinit, "Nataque de flamma corpora nulla vides." Videmus enim passim oberrantes igniculos hoc nostro igne genitos—hoc si negaverit Ovidius, necessum habebit uxoris pudicitiam vocare in dubium.

---

[9] The jokes bring in all three traditional (Catholic) afterworlds, and a miracle: liminal allusions, though the touch is light. The Protestant allegiance is in abeyance.

[10] The printer puts the /&/ upside down, as not infrequently happens with other letters. There are other signs of haste in the printing, and of incompleteness in the proofreading notwithstanding the Errata.

6 And now, my listeners, believe you have escaped purgatory and come forth safely out of the burning fiery furnace, by some new miracle; and have been received into heaven. I can think of no hero fit to compare with you for valour; for that renowned Bellerophon overcame the fire-vomiting Chimaera with no greater courage than yours, nor did the strong champions of King Arthur more easily conquer and scatter the enchantments of the flaming castle of fire. From all which, I know I can promise myself a pure and choice audience: if any rubbish has passed through the testing of the chimney I must say our gatekeepers are will-o'-the-wisps.[12]

7. But how lucky and safe we shall be for ever! For at Rome they guarded the eternal fire with religious care to preserve the empire to long life; but *we* are guarded by vigilant living fires. Why did I say "living" and "vigilance"? The words slipped out unexpectedly, because now I remember aright, these lamps go out at the first approach of dusk, and only rekindle in bright conditions.[13] But I do have hopes that this house can be brightly lit again, since no one can deny that two of the University's brightest lights preside over it. They would be nowhere more honoured than at Rome, mind you, because there either the Vestal Virgins would keep them blazing and wide awake all night or else these fiery brethren would be initiated into the order of the Seraphim.[14] And finally, that half-line of Virgil applies to them exactly: "They have the force of fire."[15] Yes, I am inclined to think that Horace had our Bright Lights in mind, because the elder one—standing among his wife and children—"shines amongst all, the moon amongst the lesser lights."[16] But I must mention that crashing blunder of Ovid, when he wrote that "You see no bodies born from flame."[17] We can see for ourselves, all round us, the little Sparks born from our big Spark. And if Ovid denies this, he must be impugning the wife's good name.

---

[12] Joke obscure. "elusive, shifty?"

[13] This may be a hit at the college porters, who (like policemen in the saying) are never to be found except when you don't need them; cf. the remark about will-o'-the-wisps above.

[14] The "burning" or "fiery" ones.
[15] *Aeneid* 6. 730.
[16] *Epodes* 15. 1–2.
[17] *Fasti* 6. 292.

8. Ad vos redeo, Auditores: Ne vos paeniteat tam molesti et formidolosi itineris; ecce convivium vobis apparatum! Eccas mensas ad luxum Persicum exstructas, et cibis conquisitissimis onustas, qui vel[11] Apicianam gulam oblectent et deliniant! Ferunt enim Antonio et Cleopatrae octo integros apros in epulis appositos, vobis autem primo ferculo (hem!) quinquaginta saginatos apros cervisia conditanea per triennium maceratos, et tamen adhuc adeo [p. 129] callosos, ut vel caninos dentes delassare valeant. Dein totidem opimos boves insigniter caudatos famulari nostro igni prae foribus recens assos; sed vereor ne omnem sucum in patinam exsudaverint. Ab his tot etiam en vitulina capita, sane crassa et carnosa, sed adeo pertenui cerebro ut non sufficiat ad condimentum.[12] Tum quidem et haedos plus minus centum, sed puto crebriori Veneris usu nimium macros: arietes aliquot exspectavimus speciosis et patulis cornubus, sed eos coqui nostri nondum secum attulerunt ex oppido.[13]

9. Si quis aves mavult, habemus innumeras, turundis, et offis, et scobinato caseo diu altiles: imprimis, nescio quod genus avium tam ingenio quam pluma viride, unde eas e regione psittacorum suspicor asportatas; quae quia gregatim semper volitant et eodem fere loco nidulantur, eodem etiam disco apponentur; iis vero parce velim vescamini, quia praeterquam quod admodum crudi sint et nihil in se habeant solidi nutrimenti, scabiem etiam comedentibus protrudunt (modo vera tradit comestor).

---

[11] vel] *1674* vel vel
[12] condimentum] *1674* condimen um
[13] Paragraph-division here because Milton turns from mammals to birds, which become his dominant metaphor till his cataloguing ends in eggs.

Prolusio

8. I return to you, my listeners.[18] Don't regret taking this troublesome, perilous journey: just look at the feast prepared for you! Just look at the tables, heaped up to the standard of Persian[19] luxury and laden with the choicest foods. They would delight and caress the throat of Apicius himself. They do say, eight whole boars were set before Antony and Cleopatra at a banquet; but lo and behold, for you in your first course alone see *fifty* fatted boars![20]—pickled in beer for three years, and still so tough that they can tire out even dogs' teeth. Next, the same number of prime oxen with magnificent tails, just roasted before the door by our servant Mr Fire; but I am afraid that all the meat-juice has gone into the dripping-pan. Here are another fifty calves' heads, quite fat and meaty, but so short of brain that there is not enough for seasoning.[21] Then young goats, a hundred of them (give or take): they are much too thin, I think it must be from too much rutting. We expected some rams, with fine spreading horns, but our cooks have not yet brought them in from town.[22]

9. If anyone prefers to eat birds,[23] we have any number of them, all fattened up a long time with dough and flour and powdered cheese, as follows.[24] **ITEM ONE:** A genus of bird unknown to science, as green in its nature as its plumage; so I suspect it has been imported from the home region of the parrot. Since they always fly around in a flock, and tend to nest in the same place, they will be served up on the same dish to you. But here's a health warning: dine sparingly on this dish, because besides being underdone and lacking in solid nutritional value, they produce a rash in those who eat them—if the consumer reports truly.

---

[18] Milton begins a new set of jokes, a new piece of his comic routine. The stop-and-start is typical of comedians in action, and of saltings and praevarications.

[19] Byword for conspicuous consumption in Roman poets, e.g. Horace (as *Odes* 1. 38).

[20] Milton enumerates the groups of the resident students (the Christsmen). Senior B. A. students have been "pickled in beer" for their three years at Cambridge.

[21] Third-years who will not complete the B.A.? Obvious jokes of back-handed compliment abound hereabouts.

[22] The Fellows of Christ's, who seem to have gone into town for dinner while the undergrduates fooled around at the salting?

[23] Having lampooned everybody in their groups as kinds of red meat, Milton changes his metaphor slightly and lampoons individuals as improbable forms of white meat.

[24] An elaborate ridiculous list of bird-dishes follows, like the inflated descriptions which feature on menus in pretentious restaurants.

10. Iam vero libere et genialiter epulamini; hic enim praesto est missus quem vobis prae omnibus commendo, praegrandis scilicet gallinago, per triennalem[14] saginam adeo unguinosae pinguedinis ut illi vix satis largum sit unum ferculum amplissimum, rostro eoüsque praelongo et eduro ut impune possit cum elephante aut rhinocerote certa-[p. 130]men ingredi; eam autem in hunc diem commode obtruncavimus, propterea quod praegrandium simiorum more incepit puellis insidiari et vim inferre mulieribus.

11 Hunc subsequuntur aves quaedam Hibernicae, nescio quo nomine; sed incessu et corporis filo gruibus persimiles, quamvis utplurimum soleant in postremam mensam asservari; hic quidem est novus et rarus magis quam salutaris cibus: his itaque abstineatis moneo, sunt enim efficacissimi (modo vera tradit comestor) ad generandos pediculos inguinales: has igitur arbitror ego agasonibus utiliores futuras; nam cum sint naturae vividae, vegetae, et saltaturientes,[15] si equis strigosis per podicem ingerantur, reddent eos protinus vivaciores et velociores quam si decem vivas anguillas in ventre haberent.

12. Anseres etiam complures aspicite, et huius anni et superiorum argutos valde, et ranis Aristophanicis vocaliores; quos quidem facile dignoscetis; mirum enim est ni se iam prodiderint sibilando, statim fortasse audietis.

13. Ova insuper aliquot habemus, sed ea κακοῦ κόρακος.[16] Frugum vero nihil praeterquam mala et mespila, eaque infelicis arboris, nec satis matura; praestabit itaque iterum ad Solem suspendi.

---

[14] per triennalem] *1674* pertriennalem
[15] possible resumption of salt-puns here, within the flashy coinage (*saltare* / *sal*, leaping / wit).
[16] See Tillyard, 136: the Greek saying in full means "a bad crow lays a bad egg" κακοῦ κόρακος κακὸν ᾠόν.

10. ITEM TWO: But tuck in freely to our next item, because here comes a dish which has my five-star rating; a colossal turkey, of such oily fatness from three years' fattening that one vast dish can barely fit it. It has such a long hard beak that it could enter a contest with an elephant or rhinoceros.[25] But for convenience we have cut off its beak today because like the large apes it was ambushing girls and attacking women.

11. ITEM THREE: Next, some Irish birds; name unknown to me, but in gait and lanky looks resembling cranes. As a rule, they are kept till the last course. Now these are a new dish, rare rather than wholesome in fact. Take my advice, abstain: if our food-taster has got it right, these are the best food for giving you lice, in the balls. They'll be more use to ostlers accordingly, because they are by nature lively and brisk and prancing creatures, and if they are given as a suppository to skinny horses will make the horses livelier and quicker than if they had ten live eels in their bellies.[26]

12. ITEM FOUR: And now look at a lot of geese, some hatched this year and some older. They are a noisy bunch, more vocal than those Frogs of Aristophanes.[27] You will easily recognise them; indeed it's a wonder they have not already betrayed themselves by hissing. Perhaps you will hear them now.[28]

13. ITEM FIVE: on the menu is eggs. We do have a few, but they are bad eggs.[29] **ITEM SIX**, fruit. Nothing for you but apples and medlars, which come from an unlucky tree,[30] and they're not ripe, so we'll hang them up again to ripen in the sun.

---

[25] Joking about noses now, and pun on *certamen* (fight, or contest-for-largest-nose).

[26] The comparisons are becoming wilder, almost surreal or magical.

[27] Who chant hilarious croaking choruses; an image of loud voices all talking at once.

[28] Pause and cue for "geese" present to boo Milton, others to counter-cheer.

[29] English slang for "rogues" or "sleaze-balls," to keep something of the Greek proverb quoted, "A bad crow lays bad eggs" (Tillyards, 97, 136).

[30] The gallows "tree."

14. Videtis apparatus nostros: quaeso vos, quibus palato sunt, comissamini. Verum hariolor dicturos vos, epulas hasce (veluti nocturnae illae dapes quae a Daemone ve-[p. 131]neficis apparantur) nullo condiri sale,[16] vereorque ne discedatis ieiuniores quam venistis.[17]

15. Verum ad ea pergo quae *me* propius attinent. Romani sua habuere[18] Floralia, rustici sua Palilia,[19] pistores sua Fornacalia, nos quoque potissimum hoc tempore rerum et negotiorum vacui Socratico more ludere solemus. Itaque hospitia Leguleiorum suos habent quos vocant[20] Dominos, vel hinc indicantes quam sint honoris ambitiosi. Nos autem, Academici, ad paternitatem[21] quam proxime accedere cupientes id ficto nomine usurpare gestimus, quod vero non audemus saltem non nisi in occulto; quemadmodum puellae nuptias lusorias et puerperia sollemniter fingunt, earum rerum quas anhelant et cupiunt umbras captantes et amplectentes.

16. Quorsum autem eo qui proxime se circumegit anno intermissa fuerit haec sollennitas, ego sane haud possum divinare—nisi quod ii qui Patres[22] futuri erant, adeo strenue se gesserint[23] in oppido ut is cui id negotii dabatur tantorum misertus laborum ultro iusserit eos ab hac cura otiosos esse.

---

[16] Salt-reference here, after salt-pun earlier.

[17] Important break here, of larger than paragraph magnitude. After the ludicrous cataloguing, Milton now reminds his audience of the thesis argued in the Oratio, aligns the salting itself with ancient festivals, and under this doubly sanctioning aegis forshadows a personal statement, of importance to himself.

[18] Circumflex is a mistake on *1674's* /a/ here: missorted types, uncorrected later.

[19] Palilia (or Parilia)] *1674* Patilia

[20] vocant] *1674* vo-ant

[21] To salt-references Milton now adds those of graduation, at which each undergraduate performer was termed the "son" of his tutor or other senior as "father," in a standard parody of baptism or confirmation.

[22] Either the salting was to have more than one Father, as could happen, or the riot eliminated more than one candidate for salting-Father. Either way, this is not quite what ¶ 1 led us to expect.

[23] se gesserint] *1674* regesserint, corrected in *Errata*

14. That's it, then. You see what we've provided for you, and I beg you to eat up whatever you fancy. But I predict that you will say these dishes are like the ones served up by the devil to witches—unseasoned with *salt*.[31] I am afraid you may go away hungrier than you came.

15. But now I turn to something which more concerns *myself*.[32] The Romans had their Floralia; rustics had their Palilia; bakers had their Fornacalia: we too keep up the custom of making holiday as Socrates advised, and especially at this time of year when we are free of business. So the Inns of Court have their "Lords" as they call them, "Lords of Misrule," showing even in this their ambition for status. And we Academicians likewise, in our desire to get as close as we can to paternity, desire to take on as a pseudonym the role we do not risk, except in secret—just as little girls have the custom of playing at weddings and births, striving to catch and cuddle the shadows of the things which they yearn for.

16. Now as to why this solemn custom was omitted last year, I cannot possibly tell, unless it was that those who were going to be its Fathers behaved so forcefully in the town that the authority who had the job of assigning Fatherhoods took pity on their great exertions and voluntarily decreed to exempt them from such nervous stress.[33]

---

[31] First of a new chain of puns, on salt / salting; reaches its crescendo later on.

[32] Licence was given to the MC at a salting, to make a personal plea or defence or statement. Milton uses the licence to scotch or defuse his nickname, "the Lady" (*Domina*).

[33] Undergraduate rioting sometimes led to cancellation of saltings, as well as to ringleaders being suspended from university. A similar set of events and resulting circumspection surrounds the salting text of Thomas Randolph, across at Trinity.

17. At vero unde est quod ego tam subito factus sum Pater? Dii vestram fidem! Quid hoc est prodigii Pliniana exsuperantis portenta! Numnam ego percusso angue Tiresiae fatum expertus sum? Ecqua me Thessala saga magico perfudit unguento? An denique ego a deo aliquo vitiatus,[24] ut olim Caeneus,[25] virilitatem pactus sum stupri pretium, ut sic repente ἐκ θηλείας εἰς ἄρρενα [p. 132] ἀλλαχθείην ἄν[26]?

18. A quibusdam, audivi nuper "Domina."[27] At cur videor illis parum masculus? Ecquis Prisciani pudor? Itane propria quae maribus femineo generi tribuunt insulsi[28] grammaticastri? Scilicet quia scyphos capacissimos nunquam valui pancratice haurire, aut quia manus tenenda stiva non occaluit, aut quia nunquam ad meridianum solem supinus iacui septennis bubulcus; fortasse demum quod nunquam me virum praestiti eo modo quo illi ganeones. Verum utinam illi possint tam facile exuere asinos quam ego quicquid est feminae. At videte quam insubide, quam incogitate mihi obiecerint id quod ego iure optimo mihi vertam gloriae. Namque et ipse Demosthenes ab aemulis adversariisque parum vir dictus est. Q. itidem Hortensius omnium Oratorum post M. Tullium clarissimus, "Dionysia Psaltria" appellatus est a L. Torquato. Cui ille, "Dionysia," inquit, "malo equidem esse quam quod tu, Torquate—ἄμουσος ἀγροδίαιτος, ἀπρόσιτος."[29]

---

[24] saga . . . vitiatus] *1674* reads only *saga cui vitiatus*: . . . aliquo: Errata corrects, saying "p. 131 l. 28 post *saga*, dele *cui*, & sic lege *magico perfudit unguento? an denique ego a Deo aliquo vitiatus*, &c.

[25] Caeneus] *1674* Cnoeeus

[26] ἀλλαχθείην] *1674* ἄλλα χθείην (miscorrected in Columbia)

[27] Masson, *Life*, 1: 260, points out that the words could mean either "I used lately to be nicknamed 'The Lady'" or "I heard some of you lately call out 'Lady.'" He opts for the first, but (a) "used to be" is not accurate for "audivi" and (b) it would be interesting if the second were the case, for it would mean that Milton has just been heckled, and speaks the following words extempore, for that would mean we are reading a text not only scripted before performance but incorporating unscripted words from the performance itself. Columbia (Masson again) and Tillyard both take it the first way, rendering "audivi" as preterite ("Some of late called me") or perfect ("I have lately heard"). Reluctantly, I must side with them: a heckler would be cited most naturally in the present tense.

[28] insulsi: more salt-punning.

[29] ἀπρόσιτος] = "unapproachable," as *1674*'s "ἀπρόσυτος" is not recorded. The triad is based on Aulus Gellius, *Noctes Atticae*, 1. 5, "amousos, anaphroditos, aprosdionusos," (having nothing of the Muses, nothing of Venus, nothing of Dionysus).

17. But how come I am so quickly become a Father?[34] Ye gods! What a prodigy, surpassing the ones in Pliny! Have I killed a snake and suffered the fate of Tiresias? Has some Thessalian witch smeared me with magic ointment? Or have I been violated by some god, as Caeneus was of old, and won my masculine gender as payment for the deed, to be suddenly altered from female into male?

18. For some have recently called me "Lady." But why do I seem unmanly to them? Have they no respect for Priscian?[35] Do these witless grammar-bunglers attribute to the feminine what is properly masculine? I suppose they do it because I have never had strength to go in for drinking-competitions, or because my hand has not grown calloused holding a plough-handle, or because I was not an oxherd by the age of seven and so did not lie on my back in the midday sun; or lastly perhaps because I have not proved my manhood in the way these debauchees do. I wish they could as easily stop being asses as I could stop being a woman! And look how foolishly and witlessly they object to what is rightly a matter of honour to me. For Demosthenes himself was called "too little of a man" by his rivals and opponents. Hortensius, too, second only to Cicero among Roman orators, was called "Dionysia, a singing woman," by L. Torquatus. Hortensius replied: "I would rather be this 'Dionysia' than what you are, Torquatus—tasteless, boorish, and crass."

---

[34] From the preamble about paternity, in the two senses of literal fathering and the Cambridge jargon of "Fathers" presenting "Sons" at university exercises, Milton moves to asking the audience to think how it feels (a) to be so suddenly made a "Father" and (b) to have been saddled with the undesirable gendered nickname "Lady"; (a) belies (b).

[35] "Priscian," the grammarian. Milton echoes a tag from Lyly's *Grammar* ("propria quae maribus" etc.), to the effect that grammar would collapse if gender were so fluid.

19. Ego vero quicquid hoc "Domini" aut "Dominae" est a me longe amolior atque reiicio: nisi in rostris atque subselliis vestris, Academici, dominari[30] non cupio. Quis iam prohibebit me quin laetar tam auspicato et felici omine, exultemque gaudio me tantis viris eiusdem opprobrii societate coniunctum! Interea ut bonos omnes et praestantes supra invidiam positos arbitror, ita hos lividos adeo [p. 133] omnium infimos puto ut ne[31] digni sint qui maledicantur.[32]

20.[33] Ad filios itaque pater me converto, quorum cerno speciosum numerum, et video etiam lepidulos nebulones occulto nutu me patrem fateri.

21. De nominibus quaeritis? Nolo sub nominibus ferculorum filios meos epulandos vobis tradere; id enim Tantali et Lycaonis feritati nimium esset affine. Nec membrorum insignibo nominibus, ne putetis me pro integris hominibus tot frusta hominum genuisse. Nec ad vinorum genera eos nuncupare volupe est, ne quicquid dixero sit ἀπροσδιόνυσον, et nihil ad Bacchum. Volo ad praedicamentorum numerum nominatos, ut sic et ingenuos natales et liberalem vitae rationem exprimam; et eadem opera curabo uti omnes ad aliquem gradum ante meum obitum provecti sint.[34]

---

[30] He exults to be "lord" over this feast, or also (as Tillyard, 141) to be lord of the exercises in general? As "Dominus" was the Inns of Court equivalent name for Cambridge's "Pater," I think Tillyard extends the term unduly beyond the salting-lordship.

[31] ne] I would expect the syntax to be either "non digni" or "ne digni quidem." This, like the end of ¶17, may be a damaged or obscure page of the MS.

[32] maledicantur] *1674* maledicant Tillyard in *YPW*, 1: 284, proposes maledicantum, presumably a misprint for maledicantur.

[33] Another major break here, as Milton turns from his personal statement to explicit address to his appointed task as Father of the salting Sons.

[34] The three dismissed naming-principles and the one he does choose are punctuated heavily here. It is essential for the reader to pause, think of the performance-situation, and register points where Milton could have collected a laugh.

19. Indeed I utterly repudiate whatever relates to "Lord" or "Lady." I do not wish to be any sort of overlord except in *your* forums and tribunals, O my fellow-students. And who will now stop me rejoicing in so favourable and happy an omen, and exulting that I am united by the reproach of the nickname with such great names? Anyhow, I consider all good and excellent men to be above envy; and by the same token I rank these spiteful people so low that they are not worth the retaliation of namecalling.

20. And so in my role as "Father" I turn to my sons, and I look at the glorious number of them; I can see the fine rascals acknowledge me as their father by a sly nod.

21. Do you ask about their names?[36] I refuse to name my sons after dishes: this would be handing them over to you to be eaten, like barbarous Tantalus and Lycaon serving up their sons for dinner! And I refuse to name them after parts of the body,[37] in case you should think I have been fathering mere limbs or fragments. Nor do I enjoy naming them after vintages: you will say I can drink, not think.[38] No: my categorical imperative is to name them after the ten Aristotelian Categories; their noble birth, and liberal habits, will surely bring home the Bacon. I shall make sure that they all advance to some degree before I die.

---

[36] This was a set feature of saltings.

[37] As is recorded of one St John's College salting; was it becoming a cliché of the genre?

[38] Miscellaneous puns follow thicker and faster than ever in this paragraph, changing to specifically "salt / salting" puns in the next.

22. Quod ad sales[35] meos, nolo ego edentulos (sic enim tritos) et veteres dicatis, et aniculam aliquam tussientem eos exspuisse: proinde credo neminem sales meos dentatos inculpaturum, nisi qui ipse nullos habet dentes, ideoque reprehensurum quia non sunt ipsius similes. Et certe in praesens ego exoptarem obtigisse mihi Horatii sortem, nempe ut essem salsamentarii filius; tunc enim sales mihi essent ad unguem; vos etiam sale ita pulchre defricatos dimitterem, ut nostros milites qui nuper ab Insula Reana capessere fugam non magis paeniteret salis petiti.

23. Non libet mihi [p. 134] in consilio vobis exhibendo, mei gnati, gnaviter esssse operoso, ne plus operae vobis erudiendis quam gignendis insumpsisse videar. Tantum caveat quisque ne ex filio fiat nepos; liberique mei ne colant Liberum, si me velint patrem.

24. Si qua ego alia praecepta dedero, ea lingua vernacula proferenda sentio; conaborque pro viribus ut omnia intelligatis.

25. Ceterum exorandi sunt mihi Neptunus, Apollo, Vulcanus, et omnes dii Fabri, uti latera mei vel tabulatis corroborare vel ferreis laminis circumligare velint. Quin etiam et[36] supplicanda mihi est dea Ceres, ut quae humerum eburneum Pelopi dederit, mihi pariter latera paene absumpta reparare dignetur. Neque enim est cur miretur quislibet si post tantum clamorem et tot filiorum genituram paulo infirmiora sint.

26. In his itaque sensu Neroniano ultra quam satis est moratus sum: nunc Leges Academicas veluti Romuli muros transiliens e Latinis ad Anglicana transcurro.[37] Vos quibus istaec arrident, aures atque animos nunc mihi attentos date.

---

[35] Now the puns become a throng of salt-jokes.

[36] et] *1674*, at Corrected in Errata

[37] Since other saltings moved out of Latin into English, it is unclear what regulation Milton says he is "leaping over." Even if his *college* liked it all to be in Latin, he would still not be breaking any Lex *Academica*.

22. As to the salt of my wit, I don't want you to call it toothless and ancient, the sort of thing some coughing crone would spit up. I don't think anyone will find fault with my wit as having been too biting either—and I don't care if some toothless nitwit complains of my teeth because they are not like his own.[39] For sure, I wish I had Horace's luck, born the son of a fishwife, for then I would have salt wit to perfection; yes, and I should send you off so well seasoned that you would regret asking for salt—like our army who got salt put on their tails as they fled from the Salt Islands.

23. My sons, your father has no wish to press heavy advice on you. After all, why should I spend more effort in educating you than I spent in fathering you? But take care to be my sons, not the Prodigal Son. Let not my sons worship at the bar, or I shall debar them.[40]

24. I shall give you my other advice vernacularly, and try to make everything Absolutely Totally Clear.[41]

25. It only remains to pray to Neptune, Apollo and Vulcan, and to all the gods called Smith, to support my body with trusses or make me a metal surgical support. And I pray to Ceres, too, who gave Pelops his ivory shoulder-blade, to repair my own ruined body parts; they are worn out after so much shouting, and the procreating of so many sons.

26. But enough of fooling around![42] And enough of these dreadful puns![43] Now I shall hop over the University Regulations, as if they were Romulus' wall.[44] I am running away from Latin into English. You like that better: so give me your ears and minds!

---

[39] "Let me be different, let me by myself," — the plea is in tune with festival-axioms.

[40] The jingle "bar / debar" tries to catch the pun on *liberi* / *Liberum*.

[41] That is, the rest of the performance is in English, which should help some of the sons to understand; but there are lost jokes lurking hereabouts too.

[42] "moratus" = (1) delaying, (2) playing the fool.

[43] Literally, "neronianisms"; Nero liked making tasteless, cruel puns.

[44] Romulus' brother Remus mocked his brother's attempt at building city walls as futile, and to emphasize the point he hopped over the incipient wall.

> ra sint, In his itaque sensu *Neroniano* ultra quam satis est, moratus sum: nunc Leges Academicas veluti *Romuli* muros transiliens à Latinis ad Anglicana transcurro. Vos quibus istæc arrident, aures atque animos nunc mihi attentos date.

The sentence declares "enough of these tasteless puns (worthy of Nero): let us pass from Latin things to English ones, while you who like that sort of thing pay me close attention." Milton seems to be assuring listeners who could not follow all the Latin wit that his English wit will suit them better—possibly an edged remark.

> (64)
>
> Anno Ætatis 19. *At a Vacation Exercise in the Colledge, part* Latin, *part* English. *The Latin speeches ended, the* English *thus began.*
>
> Hail native Language, that by sinews weak
> Didst move my first endeavouring tongue to speak,

The English verses comprise portion three of the bilingual salting, though they were separated from the rest in order to be added to the English poems of *Poems 1673*.

ERRATA.[38]

p. 113. *l.* 8. leg. *Philosophiae.*
p. 118. *l.* 9. leg. *libentias.*
p. 119. *l.* 2. leg. *rei summae.*
l. 6. leg. *potuerit.*

---

[38] The *1674* Errata for the two Latin portions of Prolusion VI are here given a line each, though in *1674* they are run on. The page numbers refer to *1674* pagination.

p. 131. *l.* 23. pro *regesserint*, leg. *se gesserint.*
p. 131. *l.* 28. post *saga*, dele *cui*, & sic lege *magico perfudit unguento? an denique ego a Deo aliquo vitiatus*, &c.
p. 134. *l.* 12. pro *at*, leg. &.

[p. 64]

Anno *Aetatis* 19. At a Vacation Exercise in the Colledge, *part* Latin, *part* English. *The* Latin *speeches ended, the* English *thus began.*

HAil native Language, that by sinews weak
Didst move my first endeavouring tongue to speak,
And mad'st imperfect words with childish tripps,[39]
Half unpronounc't, slide through my infant-lipps,
Driving dum silence from the portal dore,   5
Where he had mutely sate two years before:[40]
Here I salute thee and thy pardon ask,
That now I use thee in my latter task:
Small loss it is that thence can come unto thee,
I know my tongue but little Grace can do thee.[41]   10
Thou needst not be ambitious to be first,
Believe me I have thither[42] packed the worst:
And, if it happen as I did forecast,
The daintiest dishes shall be serv'd up last.
I pray thee then deny me not thy aide   15
For this same small neglect that I have made:
But haste thee strait to do me once a Pleasure,
And from thy wardrope bring thy chiefest treasure;
Not those new fangled toys, and trimming flight
Which takes our late fantasticks with delight, [p. 65]   20
But cull those richest Robes, and gay'st attire
Which deepest Spirits, and choicest Wits desire:
I have some naked thoughts that rove about
And loudly knock to have their passage out;
And wearie of their place do only stay   25

---

[39] tripps] tripp s in *1673.*
[40] If pressed, this would assert Milton learnt to speak at two years old.
[41] thee.] thee in *1673.*
[42] i.e., to the former task, the Latin.

Till thou hast deck't them in thy best aray[43];
That so they may without suspect or fears
Fly swiftly to this fair Assembly's ears;
Yet I had rather, if I were to chuse,
Thy service in some graver subiect use, 30
Such as may make thee search thy coffers[44] round,
Before thou cloath my fancy in fit sound:
Such where the deep transported mind may soare
Above the wheeling poles, and at Heav'ns dore
Look in, and see each blissful Deitie 35
How he before the thunderous throne doth lie,
Listening to what unshorn *Apollo* sings
To th'touch of golden wires, while *Hebe* brings
Immortal Nectar to her kingly Sire:
Than passing through the Spherse[45] of watchful fire, 40
And mistie Regions of wide air next under,
And hills of Snow and lofts[46] of piled Thunder,
May tell at length how green-ey'd *Neptune* raves,
In Heav'ns defiance mustering all his waves; [p. 66]
Then sing of secret things that came to pass 45
When Beldam Nature in her cradle was;
And last of Kings and Queens and *Hero's* old,
Such as the wise *Demodocus* once told
In solemn Songs at King *Alcinous* feast,
While sad Ulisses soul and all the rest 50
Are held with his melodious harmonie
In willing chains and sweet captivitie.
But fie my wandring Muse how thou dost stray!
Expectance calls thee now another way,
Thou know'st it must be now thy only bent 55
To keep in compass of thy Predicament:[47]

---

[43] Until you, English, have clothed my naked thoughts with your best available clothes (highest style?) After a clear apology for some low (buffoonish) Latin preceding, we are to expect a high style in the ensuing pageant, after this invocation ends at line 58. This is despite the wish (29-30) he were using English for "some graver subject" than a salting pageant; in other words, the register after 58 is hardly less ambitious.

[44] chests for "clothes," i.e., words. English is still a costumier or wardrobe-mistress.

[45] Spherse] sic, for "Spheres."

[46] Like attics, storing Jove's thunderbolts.

[47] Technical language at last enters the English, which hitherto has kept remarkably if not designedly to Anglo-Saxon-derived diction. The rougher rhythm of this line ("comp'ss") perhaps heralds the change.

Then quick about thy purpos'd business come,
That to the next I may resign my Roome.[48]

Then Ens *is represented as father of the Predicaments his ten Sons, whereof the Eldest stood for* Substance *with his Canons,*[49] *which*[50] *Ens thus speaking, explains.*

GOod luck befriend thee Son; for at thy birth
The Faery Ladies daunc't upon the hearth; 60
Thy drowsie Nurse hath sworn she did them spie
Come tripping to the Room where thou didst lie; [p. 67]
And sweetly singing round about thy Bed
Strew all their blessings on thy sleeping Head.
She heard them give thee this, that thou should'st still 65
From eyes of mortals walk invisible,
Yet there is something that doth force my fear,
For once it was my dismal[51] hap to hear
A *Sybil* old, bow-bent with crooked age,
That far events full wisely could presage, 70
And in times long and dark Prospective Glass
Fore-saw what future dayes should bring to pass,
Your Son, said she (nor can you it prevent)
Shall subiect be to many an Accident.[52]
O're all his Brethren he shall Reign as King, 75
Yet every one shall make him underling,
And those that cannot live from him asunder
Ungratefully shall strive to keep him under,
In worth and excellence he shall out-go them

---

[48] Who is this "next," and who has been the speaker till now? The next is "Ens," and "I" is Milton, who now steps down and into the robes of Ens, whatever those were. This implies a pause and re-grouping on stage: the stage direction implies that the ten costumed sons come on stage together, Milton as their father Ens being their spokesman, till line 90 and again from 91-100. Eight of the sons speak their own lines, in prose.

[49] Rules, laws, principles; but does the impersonator hold up some emblems of Aristotelean teaching about Substance? This might be amusing (a giant tee-square or protractor). Since it transpires that he is invisible (66) yet must be visible on stage, the joke may be that he holds up some very large objects.

[50] What is the exact antecedent, or is it not exact but the whole preceding tableau?

[51] Unlucky, foreboding: pertaining to a *dies mali*.

[52] Nice pun: ground or subjectum to the accidentia (Colour, shape and so on); also accident-prone. OED II.6 and I.1.b.

Yet being above them, he shall be below them;   80
From others he shall stand in need of nothing,[53]
Yet on his Brothers shall depend for Cloathing.[54]
To find a Foe it shall not be his hap,
And peace shall lull him in her flowry lap;
Yet shall he live in strife, and at his dore   85
Devouring war shall never cease to roare:
Yea it shall be his natural property
To harbour those that are at enmity.
What power, what force, what mighty spell, if not
Your learned hands, can loose this Gordian knot?[55]   90

The next Quantity *and* Quality, *spake in Prose,*[56] *then* Relation *was call'd by his Name.*

RIvers arise; whether thou be the Son,
Of utmost *Tweed*, or *Oose*, or gulphie *Dun*,
Or *Trent*, who like some earth-born Giant spreads
His thirty Armes along the indented Meads,
Or sullen *Mole* that runneth underneath,   95
Or *Severn* swift, guilty of Maidens death,[57]
Or rockie *Avon*, or of Sedgie *Lee*,
Or coaly *Tine*,[58] or antient hollowed *Dee*,
Or *Humber* loud that keepst the[59] *Scythians* Name,
Or *Medway* smooth, or Royal Towred *Thame*.   100

---

[53] Pronounced "no thing," for the rhyme.

[54] The piled-up paradoxes reflect the sybilline or oracular idiom of the Sybil (cf. the notorious oracles of Delphi, habitually incomprehensible and self-contradictory until hindsight revealed their meaning, always too late for evasive action.)

[55] Not / knot is a true rhyme for poets like Milton or Spenser reared on Italian verse, in which homophones may rhyme because they are far from homonyms; the *sense* is felt before the sound.

[56] We have no knowledge of whose prose it was, nor of why Milton did not script verse for these two Sons (Predicaments). They seem no more prosaic than Relation who does receive verse.

[57] Sabrina's, see Milton's *Masque*.

[58] Hence the expression, "coals to Newcastle."

[59] keepst the] keeps'the *1673.*

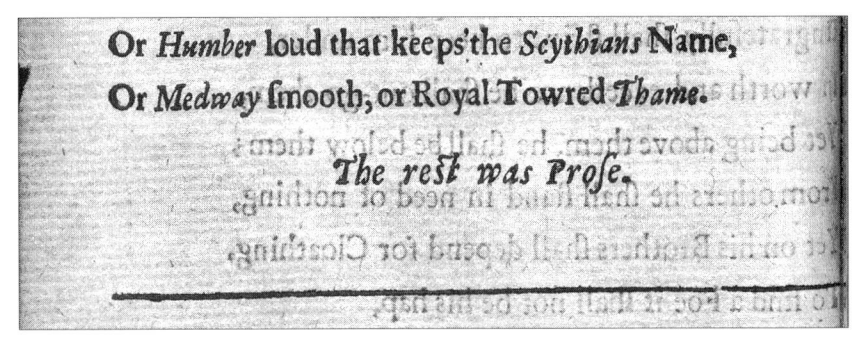

The rest was Prose

> Or *Humber* loud that keeps the *Scythians* Name,
> Or *Medway* smooth, or Royal Towred *Thame.*
>
> *The rest was Prose.*

Because "The rest was Prose" it was omitted from *Poems 1673*; but did it go missing at the printer's or back among Milton's papers?

Bibliography

PRIMARY TEXTS

Camdeni Insignia. Oxford: Oxford University Press, 1624.
Cantabrigium Dolor et Solamen. Cambridge: Cambridge University Press, 1625.
Cleveland, John. *The Works of John Cleveland*. London: O. Blagrave, 1687.
Early Lives of John Milton, ed. Helen Darbishire. London: Constable, 1932.
Fletcher, Phineas, *Locustae* (pub. 1627 but composed earlier), ed. Estelle Haan. Supplementa Humanistica Lovaniensia 9. Leuven: Leuven University Press, 1996.
Hobbes, Thomas. *Behemoth; or the Long Parliament* [1668], ed. Ferdinand Tönnies., 2nd. ed. London: Cass, 1969.
Horace, *Epodes*, ed. David Mankin. Cambridge Greek and Latin Classics. Cambridge: Cambridge University Press, 1995.
Horace, *The Odes*, ed. Kenneth Quinn. Classical Series. London: Macmillan, 1980.

Milton, John [alphabetically by name of editor]
John Milton. Complete Shorter Poems, ed. John Carey. 2nd. ed. London: Longman, 1997.
John Milton. Political Writings, ed. Martin Dzelzainis, trans. Claire Gruzelier. Cambridge Texts in the History of Political Thought. Cambridge: Cambridge University Press, 1991.
The Riverside Milton, ed. Roy Flannagan. Boston: Houghton Mifflin, 1998.
John Milton. Latin Writings. A Selection, ed. and trans. John K. Hale. Bibliotheca Latinitatis Novae. Assen: van Gorcum and Tempe: MRTS, 1998.
The Poems of John Milton, with Notes, ed. T. Keightley. 2 vols. London, 1859.
The Latin Poems of John Milton, ed. Walter MacKellar. Cornell Studies in English 15. New York: Columbia University Press, for Cornell University, 1930.
Poetical Works of John Milton, ed. David Masson. 3 vols. London: Macmillan, 1890.
The Prose Works of Milton, ed. J. Max Patrick. Garden City, NY: Doubleday Anchor, 1967.
The Works of John Milton, gen. ed. Frank Allen Patterson. The Columbia

Edition. 18 vols. New York: Columbia University Press, 1931-1938.
Complete Prose Works of John Milton. gen. ed. Don M. Wolfe. 8 vols. New Haven: Yale University Press, 1953-1982.
Nelson, Alan H., ed. *Records of English Drama. Cambridge.* 2 vols. Toronto: University of Toronto Press, 1989.
Nichols, John, ed. *The Progresses and Public Processions of Queen Elizabeth.* 3 vols. London: J. Nicholls, 1788, 1805, 1828; repr. New York: AMS Press, 1969.
Randolph, Thomas, *Poetical and Dramatic Works*, ed. W. C. Hazlitt. 2 vols. London: Reeves & Turner, 1875; repr. New York: B. Blom, 1968.
Sidney, Philip. *Miscellaneous Prose of Sir Philip Sidney*, ed. Katherine Duncan-Jones and Jan van Dorsten. Oxford: Clarendon Press, 1973.
Skinner, Cyriack. "The Anonymous Life of Milton." In *The Riverside Milton*, ed. Roy Flanagan. Boston: Houghton Mifflin, 1998, 6–12.
Winterbottom, Michael, ed. and comm. *Roman Declamation.* Bristol: Bristol Classical Press, 1980.
Wood, Anthony. *The Life and Times of Anthony Wood, Antiquary, of Oxford, 1632-1695, Described by Himself*, ed. Andrew Clark. 5 vols. Oxford: Oxford University Press, 1891-1900.

SECONDARY TEXTS

Anderson, Bernhard W. *The Living World of the Old Testament.* 3rd ed. London: Longman, 1978.
Bill, E. G. W. *Education at Christ Church Oxford 1660-1800.* Oxford: Clarendon Press, 1988.
Binns, J. W. *Intellectual Culture in Elizabethan and Jacobean England: The Latin Writings of the Age.* ARCA 24. Leeds: Francis Cairns, 1990.
Burton, K. M. "Cambridge Exercises in the Seventeenth Century." *The Eagle* [journal of St John's College] 54 (1951): 248-58.
Bush, Douglas, ed. *A Variorum Commentary on the Poems of John Milton*, vol. 1. New York: Columbia University Press, 1970.
Campbell, Gordon. *A Milton Chronology.* London: Macmillan, 1997.
Cheek, Macon P. "Milton's *In Quintum Novembris*: An Epic Foreshadowing." *Studies in Philology* 54 (1957): 172-84.
Clarke, M. L. *Rhetoric at Rome: A Historical Survey.* 3rd ed. rev. with new intro. by D. H. Berry. London: Routledge, 1996.
Costello, William T., S. J. *The Scholastic Curriculum at Early Seventeenth-Century Cambridge.* Cambridge: Harvard University Press, 1958.

Cressy, David. *Bonfires and Bells: National Memory and the Protestant Calendar in Elizabethan and Stuart England*. Berkeley: University of California Press, 1989.

Daiches, David. *Milton*. London: Hutchinson, 1957.

Eissfeldt, Otto. *The Old Testament: An Introduction*, trans. Peter Ackroyd. Oxford: Blackwell, 1965.

Emery, Robert. "Salting Freshmen: An Old Academic Tradition." *Notes and Queries* 40 (1993): 351.

Evans, J. Martin. *The Miltonic Moment*. Lexington: University of Kentucky Press, 1998.

Feingold, Mordechai. "The Humanities." Chap. 3 in *The History of the University of Oxford*: vol. 4, *Seventeenth-Century Oxford*, ed. Nicholas Tyacke, 211-357. Oxford: Clarendon Press, 1997.

Fletcher, Harris Francis. *Milton's Intellectual Development*. 2 vols. Urbana: University of Illinois Press, 1956-1961.

Ford, Philip J. *George Buchanan. Prince of Poets*. Aberdeen: Aberdeen University Press, 1982.

Fraser, Antonia. *The Gunpowder Plot: Terror and Faith in 1605*. London: Weidenfeld, 1996.

Freidberg, Elizabeth Ann Perryman. "Certain Small Entertainments: The Texts and Contexts of Thomas Randolph's Poems and College Entertainments." 2 vols. Ph.D. diss. Cambridge University, 1994.

Gardiner, Samuel R. *A History of England under the Duke of Buckingham and Charles I, 1624-1628*. 2 vols, London: Longmans, 1875.

Gardiner, Samuel R. *History of England from the Accession of James I to the Outbreak of the Civil War 1603-1642*. 10 vols. London: Longmans, 1883. Vol. 1: *1603-7*.

Geertz, Clifford. "Deep Play: Notes on the Balinese Cockfight." *The Interpretation of Cultures. Selected Essays*. London: Hutchinson, 1975.

Haan, Estelle. "Milton's *In Quintum Novembris* and the Anglo-Latin Gunpowder Epic." *Humanistica Lovaniensia* 41 (1992): 221-95; 42 (1993) 368-93.

Haan, Estelle. "Milton's *Naturam Non Pati Senium* and Hakewill." *Medievalia et Humanistica* 24 (1997): 147-67.

Haan, Estelle. "Milton and Two Italian Humanists: Some Hitherto Unnoticed Neo-Latin Echoes in *In Obitum Procancellarii Medici* and *In Obitum Praesulis Eliensis*." *Notes and Queries* 44 (1997): 176-81.

Haan, Estelle. *From* Academia *to* Amicitia: *Milton's Latin Writings and the Italian Academies*. Transactions of the American Philosophical Society 88.6. Philadelphia: American Philosophical Society, 1998.

Hale, John K. "Artistry and Originality in Milton's Latin Poems." *Milton Quarterly* 27 (1993): 138-49.

Hale, John K. *Milton's Languages: The Impact of Multilingualism on Style.* Cambridge: Cambridge University Press, 1997.

Hale, John K. "The Pre-Criticism of Milton's Latin Verse." In *Of Poetry and Politics: New Essays on Milton and His World*, ed. Paul G. Stanwood. MRTS 126. Binghamton: MRTS, 1995. 17-34.

Hale, John K. "George Herbert's Oration before King James, Cambridge 1623." In *Acta Conventus Neo-Latini Cantabrigiensis*, ed. R. Schnur et al., 253-62. MRTS 259. Tempe: MRTS, 2003.

Hartmann, Thomas R. "Milton's Prolusions." Ph.D. diss. Columbia University, 1963.

Helander, Hans. "Neo-Latin Studies: Significance and Prospects." *Symbolae Osloenses* 76 (2001): 5-44.

Henderson, Felicity. "Putting the Dons in Their Place: A Restoration Oxford *Terrae Filius* Speech." *History of Universities* 16 (2000): 32-64.

Herbert-Brown, Geraldine, *Ovid and the Fasti. A Historical Study* Oxford: Clarendon Press, 1994.

Herbert-Brown, Geraldine, Ed. *Ovid's* Fasti. *Historical Readings at Its Bimillennium*. Oxford: Oxford University Press, 2002.

Highet, Gilbert. *Juvenal.* Oxford: Clarendon Press, 1954.

IJsewijn, Jozef, with Dirk Sacré. *Companion to Neo-Latin Studies. Part Two: Literary, Linguistic, Philological, and Editorial Questions*. 2nd. ed. Supplementa Humanistica Lovaniensia 14. Leuven: Leuven University Press, 1998.

Kallendorf, Hilaire. "Exorcism and the Interstices of Language: Ruggle's *Ignoramus* and the Demonization of Renaissance English Neo-Latin." In *Acta Conventus Neo-Latini Cantabrigiensis*, ed. R. Schnur et al., 303-10. MRTS 259. Tempe: MRTS, 2003, 303–10.

Kennedy, George A. *A New History of Classical Rhetoric.* Princeton: Princeton University Press, 1994.

Ketton-Cramer, R. W. *Thomas Gray: A Biography.* Cambridge: Cambridge University Press, 1955.

Lamb, H. H. *Climate History and the Modern World.* London: Methuen, 1982.

Leedham-Green, Elisabeth. *A Concise History of the University of Cambridge.* Cambridge: Cambridge University Press, 1996.

Le Roy Ladurie, Emmanuel. *Carnival in Romans*, trans. Mary Feeney. New York: Braziller, 1979.

Lewis, C. S. "From the Latin of Milton's *De Idea Platonica*." *English*, 5 (1944-45): 195.

McConica, James, ed. *The History of the University of Oxford:* Vol. 3, *The Collegiate University.* Oxford: Clarendon Press, 1986.

McCullough, Peter. *Sermons at Court. Politics and Religion in Elizabethan and Jacobean Preaching.* Cambridge: Cambridge University Press, 1998.

McFarlane, I. D. *Buchanan.* London: Duckworth, 1981.

Masson, David. *The Life of John Milton and History of His Time.* 6 vols. Cambridge: Macmillan, 1859.

Money, D. K. *The English Horace. Anthony Alsop and the Tradition of British Latin Verse.* Oxford: Oxford University Press for the British Academy, 1998.

Moseley, C. W. R. D., *The Poetic Birth: Milton's Poems of 1645.* Aldershot: Scolar Press, 1991.

Nelson, Alan H. *Early Cambridge Theatres.* Cambridge: Cambridge University Press, 1994.

Ong, Walter J., S. J. "Latin Language Study as a Renaissance Puberty Rite." *Studies in Philology* 56 (1959): 103-24.

Parker, Rowland. *Town and Gown: The 700 Years' War in Cambridge.* Cambridge: Patrick Stephens, 1983.

Parker, William Riley. *Milton. A Biography,* rev. Gordon Campbell. 2 vols. Oxford: Clarendon Press, 1996.

Pastor: Ludwig, Freiherr von Pastor, *The History of the Popes from the Close of the Middle Ages Drawn from the Secret Archives of the Vatican and Other Original Sources,* trans. Dom Ernest Graf, OSB. 40 vols. London: Kegan Paul, 1891-1953. Vol. 25: *Leo XI and Paul V, 1605-1621* (1937).

Pollard, A. H. "The Bibliography of Milton." *The Library* n.s. 37. 10 (1909): 1.

Rabbie, Erwin. "Editing Neo-Latin Texts." *Editio* 10 (1996): 25-48.

Radzinowicz, Mary Ann. "'To Play in the Socratic Manner': Oxymoron in Milton's *At a Vacation Exercise in the College,*" *University of Hartford Studies in Literature* 17 (1985): 1-11.

Rashdall, Hastings. *The Universities of Europe in the Middle Ages,* ed. F. M. Powicke and A. B. Emden. 3 vols. Oxford: Oxford University Press, 1895, repr. and rev. 1936 .

Raven, D. S., *Latin Metre: An Introduction* (London: Faber, 1965).

Revard, Stella. *Milton and the Tangles of Neaera's Hair: The Making of the 1645 Poems.* Columbia, MO, and London: University of Missouri Press, 1997.

Revard, Stella. "Milton and Cambridge." In *Acta Conventus Neo-Latini Cantabrigiensis,* ed. R. Schnur et al., 259. Tempe: MRTS, 2003. 455–62.

Richek, Roslyn. "Thomas Randolph's Salting (1627), its Text, and John Milton's Sixth Prolusion as Another Salting." *English Literary Renaissance* 12 (1982): 102-31.

Rigg, A. G. "Latin Meter: Rhyming Dactylic Verses." In *Dictionary of the Middle Ages*, ed. J. R. Strayer et al., 12 vols. (New York: Scribner, 1982), 7: 372-73.

Ross, W. D. *Aristotle*. London: Methuen, 1923.

Russell, Donald A. *Greek Declamation*. Cambridge: Cambridge University Press, 1983.

Stray, Christopher. *Classics Transformed: Schools, Universities, and Society in England 1830-1960*. Oxford: Clarendon Press, 1998.

Syme, Ronald. *History in Ovid*. Oxford: Clarendon Press, 1978.

Tung, Mason. "Milton's Adaptation in *In Quintum Novembris* of Virgil's *Fama*." *Milton Quarterly* 12 (1975): 90-95.

Turner, Victor. *The Ritual Process: Structure and Anti-Structure*. London: Routledge, 1969.

Tyacke, Nicholas, ed. *The History of the University of Oxford*: vol. 4, *Seventeenth-Century Oxford*. Oxford: Clarendon Press, 1997.

Williams, F. "A Textual Problem in One of Milton's Latin Poems." *Notes & Queries* 49 (2002): 334-36.

Woodcock, E. C. *A New Latin Syntax*. London: Methuen, 1959.

Wordsworth, Christopher. *Scholae Academicae*. London: Cass, 1877, also Cambridge: Cambridge University Press, 1877, repr. 1910; repr. New York: Kelley, 1969.

Index

A
act verses, 5, Ch. 2 passim
afterlife, Chs. 6 & 7
alcaics, 131–33, 137, Ch. 7 passim
Alsop, Anthony, 132 n.
Anonymous Biographer of Milton, 2, 123
Anon., "Non datur motus," 37–38
Anon., "Omnes homines naturaliter,' 39–40
anthologies, 6, Ch. 7
Archilochus, 59
arete, 145
Aristotle, 15, 16, 23, 28 & n., 57–58, 70, 82, 84 & nn., 85, 86, 90, 93, 95, 263 & nn.
As-if, 17, 80–81
Auditoria and audiences, 6 & n., 91–92, 161, 165–66, 214, 226–27, 245 n., 246 n., 251 n., 253 & nn., 254–55

B
Baker, Janet, 75–76
Baroni, Leonora, 75
beer, bells, bonfires, 171 n., 172 n.
Bible, 46 n., 92, 95, 116–17, 120 n., 137, 142 n., Ch. 8 passim, 193 n., 203 n., 222
Bolde, Alexander, 22–23, 40–44
bomolochos, 227, 229
Buchanan, George, Ch. 8 passim
Buckingham, Duke of, George Villiers, Ch. 8 passim, 185 n., 204
Bush, Douglas, 51–52

C
Cambridge University, 89, 99, 123, Ch. 6, 171 n., 186–87
  Christ's College, 6, 35, 36, 91–92, 126 & n., 149, 165, 183 & n., 211–12; Part Four esp. 246 n.
  Exercises xi, Introduction passim, 123, 227
  King's College, 149
  miscellanies, 150
  saltings, 197–98, 199–207
  St John's College, 212 n., 285 n.
  Trinity College, 200 n., 201
  worthies, Chs. 6 & 7
Camden, William, Ch. 7 passim
Campion, Thomas, 177 n.
Carey, John, 51–55
carnival, 199 & n.
Catholics, Ch. 8 passim
Charles I, 72–75, Ch. 7 passim, 172–73
Cicero, 70 & n., 71, 74, 86, 103, 109, 115
Clarendon, Earl of, Edward Hyde, 16
Cleveland, John, 76 n.
Coleridge, 51–55
communitas, 231–35
controversiae, 68, 69, 70
Costello, William, 18 &n., Ch. 1 passim, 71, 110, 112

D

declamations, 5, 10, Chs.3 & 4, Ch. 5 passim, 248–49
Democritus, 246
Demosthenes, 106
dies fastus, 180
Diggle, James, 72, 75–76, 79–80
Diodati, Charles, 130, Ch. 7 passim, 224
disputations, 3–4 and Introduction, passim, 15, Ch. 1
Dolor et Solamen (1625), 158–61

E

Editio princeps of Salting-Text, Part Four
egghead, 235
eironeia, 194, 216, 229
elegiac couplets, 37 & n., 39, 40–41, 43–44, 131–33, 137, 143
Elizabeth I, 127
Epicurus, 104
epigram, 164
Erasmus, Part Four passim, esp. 260–61 & n.
ethos, 93, 104
Evans, J. Martin, 168 n.
exercitationes ludicras, 244

F

Fathers, Sons, Brothers, 3–4, 192, Ch. 9 passim, 232, 235, 280–81 and *Prolusio* passim
Feingold, Mordechai, 16
festivals, Roman, 270–71, 280–81
Fletcher, H. F., 52
Fletcher, Phineas, 167 nn., 172 & n.

folly, traditions and praise of, Part Four esp. 246, 258 n.
Freidberg, Elizabeth, 196 n., 200–02 & nn., 204 n., 208

G

Geertz, Clifford, 235
Gil, Alexander, Jr., 35, 46–47
Goodman, Godfrey, 46 n.

H

Haan, Estelle, 46 n., 152, 167 & nn., 168 n., 170 n., 196 n.
Hakewill, George, 46 & n.
Hartmann, Thomas R., 23–26, 77
Herbert, George, 5, 72–75
hexameters, 37 & n., 38 & n., 40, 43–44, 45, 189 & n., 190 & n., 224 & n.
Hobbes, Thomas, Ch. 5 passim
Homer, 261 & n.
Horace, 51, 58–60, 131–33, 138–42, Ch. 7 passim, 213, 286

I

iambics, 58–60, 132–33, 137, 138–42
Ignoramus, 191 & n.
Inns of Court (Leguleii), 280–81

J

James, VI and I, King, 1, 72–75, Chs. 7 & 8 passim
Javellus, 291
Juvenal, 68, 69 n.

K

Keightley, Thomas, 59–60, 62

L

lacrimae, 143
"Lady of Christ's" (Domina), 280–85 & nn.
Latin, macaronic, 189–90, 233 n.
Latin, medieval, 188–89, 233 n.
Latin, Neo-Latin, 10–11, 47–49, 167–68
Latin, rhyming, 203, 233 n.
Lawrence, D. H., 124 n.
Lennox, Duke of, James Stuart, 158–60
Lewis, C. S., 52–53
limen, liminality, 234
litotes, 102 & n.
logos, 93, 104
Longinus, 82
Lord of Misrule, 206, 280–81, 284 & n., 286–87 & nn.
Love, Harold, 151
Lucretius, 38, 45, 50

M

macaronic: see Latin
Masson, David, 51, 77 n., 165, 224 n.
matriculation, 3 n
medieval: see Latin
metaphorizing at saltings: 284–85
   dishes of a meal. 276–81 & nn.
   fire, castles, afterworlds, 272–75 & nn.
   gallows, 279
   limbs, 284–85
   noses and beaks, 279 & nn.
   Praedicaments (Categories) of Aristotle, 284–93
   rivers, 292–93
   salt and seasoning, *see* salt-puns
   wines, 284–85

Milton, John,
   A Masque, 97, 292 n.
   Ad Salsillum, 59
   Areopagitica, 179 & n.
   At a Vacation Exercise, Ch. 9 passim, Part Four
   De Idea Platonica, Ch. 2, 228
   Defences, 31, 92, Ch. 5
   Defensio Prima, Ch. 5
   Elegia I, 126, 134 & n., 135
   Elegia II, 130–31
   Elegia III, 49 n., Ch. 6 passim
   Elegia IV, 222
   Elegia V, 222–23, 224
   Epistulae, 35, 46
   Epitaphium Damonis, 130 & n., 224, 225
   Funerary poems, 1626, Ch. 6
   Gunpowder epigrams, 161–62, Ch. 8 passim
   Hobson poems, 150
   Il Penseroso, 5, 70, 138
   In Obitum Praesulis, 59, Ch. 6 passim, 224
   In Obitum Procancellarii, 130–31, 135–36, Ch. 7
   In Quintum Novembris, 10, 124, Ch. 8
   L'Allegro, 5, 70, 138
   Lycidas, 130 & n., 135, 150, 155 n., 225
   Naturam Non Pati Senium, Ch. 2
   Ode: Ad Joannem Roüsium, 155 n.
   Paradise Lost, 118, 124 n., 166 & n., 179, 195, 223
   Poems...1645, 163–64, 221
   Prolusion I, 77–82
   Prolusion II, 82–86

Prolusion III, 86–90
Prolusion IV, 21–27
Prolusion V, 27–31, 33
Prolusion VI (*see also* saltings *and* Salting-Text), 67
Prolusion VII, 31 n., 39, Ch. 4
Prolusiones, 19–21, 31, 209
Sonnets, 138, 195 n., 231
Text and Translation of Salting, 230–42
music, 75–76, 79–80

N
Nelson, Alan H., 196 n., 200 n.
November 5 rituals, 7, 124, Ch. 8

O
odes, Ch. 7 passim
Ovid, 37 n., 38, 40, 49 & n., 50, 68, 131–33, 137, 168, Ch. 8, passim, 232, 274–75
Oxford University, 173 n.
   anthologies, Ch. 7 passim
   Exercises, 2, 14, 15–17
   Terrae Filius, 232
   verse performances, 165 & n.
oxymoron, 215–216

P
pathos (*see also ethos, logos*) 93
philistine, 235
Plato, 45, 51–64, 81, 82, 86, 89, 97
Pope and Papacy, Ch. 8 passim
Praevaricator (Varier), 4, 31 n., 192–93, 203 n.
prolusio, 203 n., 204 n., 209
punctuation, 95 n., 156 n., 244 n.
Pythagoras, 82, 83–84, 86

Q
Quintilian, 71
Quirinus, 181

R
Radzinowicz, Mary Ann, 214 n. 215, 229
Randolph, Thomas, 4, 31 n., Part Three passim
republic of fools topos, 206, 230, 265 n., 269–71
republic of letters, 265 & n.
Revard, Stella, 47 n., 167–68
Rhé, Isle de, 204, 213, 286–87
Richek, Roslyn, 196 n., 197 n., 208 n.
rites de passage, 7, 9, 124–25, 186–87, 198–99, 226–35

S
Salmasius, 95, Ch. 5 passim
saltings, 7, 184, Ch. 9 & Part Four
Salting-Text, 239–41; Translation 241–42, Errata 288–89, the final English prose 293
salt-puns, 256 n., 258 n., 260–61 &c, 262 & n., and *Prolusio* passim
Satan, Ch. 8 passim
satire, 60–61
Scholasticism, 17, 86–90
sententiae, 69
serio ludere, 218
Shakespeare, 48 n., 60, 69, 138, 143, 150
ship of fools topos, 206, 230, 246–47
Sidney, 65 & n.
Sitz im Leben, 7–8, 235
Socrates, 192–94, 214 n., 215–216, 260–61, 280–81

Spenser, 157
St Paul's School, 152
Suarez, 23–26
suasoriae, 68, 70
Syme, Ronald, 181

T

Tacitus, 74
Terrae Filius, 232
Tillyard, E. M. W. and Phyllis, 20–21
togas, *togati*, 94, 135, 144, 187
Topham, Antony, 160–61
tribe, 157, 199, 228, 231–35
truth lost (topos), 31 n.
Turner, Alberta, 150–51
Turner, Victor, 231–35

U

underworld and afterlife, Chs. 6 & 7

V

vandalism, 271, 281 & n.
versification–machine, 38 n.
Virgil, 49, 74, 103, 144, 170 n., 173 n., 177, 274–75

W

Winterton, Ralph, 149
Wood, Anthony à, 196 n., 197, 218 n.

Y

Young, Thomas, 222